REVERBERATING ECHOES

ECHOES

PARASURAMA'S LEGACY UNVEILED

AMRESH VASHISHT

My MOTHER

SWARAJ SHARMA

(10.03.1936 – 19.06.2017)

AND

TO MY DEVOTED WIFE ANUPMA

Dr. Amisha, Dr. Shree, Kevin

Animesh & Priya

Contents

Contents

Preface

अग्रतः चतुरोवेदाः पृष्ठतः सशरंधनुः ।
इदंब्राह्ममइदंक्षात्रंशापादपिशिरादपि ॥

उसके सामने चार वेद हैं, और उसके पीछे एक तीर वाला धनुष है।
यह ब्राह्मण है और यह श्राप या बाण से क्षत्रिय है।

Parshuram who is well-versed with the four Vedas and sports the bow and arrow upon His back (that is the one who has the radiance of both the *Brahman* and the *Kshatriya*) will destroy evildoers either with a curse or with an arrow.

In the vast tapestry of Indian mythology and legends, there exists a figure that stands out as a beacon of valor, resilience, and unwavering determination. His name is Parashurama, the sixth avatar of Lord Vishnu, and his story has captured the imaginations of countless generations. From ancient scriptures to folklore passed down through oral traditions, the tales of Parashurama have woven themselves into the very fabric of Indian culture.

This book is an exploration of the life and legacy of Parashurama, an extraordinary character who embodies the complexities of human nature and the triumph of righteousness. It delves deep into the rich mythology and historical narratives surrounding this legendary warrior sage, seeking to unravel the truth and meaning behind his divine existence. It was hard to write on such a personality which was almost forgotten by the Hindu religious scripts. He was mentioned here and there rarely. The reason, I noticed about his non recognition was his militancy. A Brahmin with the Kshatriya tejas was not carried well with the Hindu literature though he deserved the most.

The facts of Parashurama begin in a time when darkness enveloped the world, and evil reigned supreme. Born as the son of sage Jamadagni and the Renuka, Parashurama emerged as a prodigious warrior, armed with his signature weapon, the divine axe known as Parashu. With unparalleled strength and a fierce determination to rid the world of wickedness, he embarked on a journey that would shape the destiny of nations.

As we traverse the pages of this book, we will witness the mighty feats of Parashurama as he single-handedly vanquishes a multitude of demons and tyrannical rulers. His unwavering dedication to justice and his unwavering adherence to his duty as a warrior and protector of the innocent make him a formidable force to be reckoned with.

However, Parashurama's story is not merely one of battles and conquests. It is a tale of self-discovery and redemption, as he grapples with the consequences of his actions and seeks to find solace in the path of righteousness. We will delve into the transformative moments of his life, exploring the lessons he learns, the sacrifices he makes, and the profound impact he has on the world around him.

Throughout this book, we will also explore the cultural significance of Parashurama and his enduring influence on various aspects of Indian society. From the sacred temples dedicated to his worship to the traditions and rituals that bear his name, his presence echoes through the annals of time, inspiring generations to strive for excellence and uphold the values of integrity and justice.

By delving into the world of Parashurama, we embark on a journey that transcends the boundaries of time and space. It is a journey that takes us to the very core of our own humanity, forcing us to confront our weaknesses, seek our purpose, and find the strength to overcome the adversities that life presents.

May this exploration of Parashurama's life serve as a source of inspiration and enlightenment, guiding us towards a deeper understanding of ourselves and the world in which we live? Let us embark on this captivating odyssey together, as we unravel the enigmatic tapestry of Parashurama's existence and discover the profound wisdom hidden within his legend.

I have, therefore, written rather represented the facts in this book in a way which, I hope, would clarify many questions that have not been attempted so far. This is not intended to be a scholarly work. I am sure, there are many who can do it far better than I, but it is meant for the general readers who want to enlarge their knowledge about the ever living warrior.

In the course of writing this book, I have consulted several books, Puranas, Vedas, archive sites and articles written by many scholars on Parashurama. I acknowledge with gratitude that I have liberally used their material with the idea that knowledge is for propagation. I have tried my best to give their due references. If I have failed to mention the references,

I seek an apology with folded hands.

In the last but not the least, to my beloved son, Animesh Vashisht, whose unwavering support and inspiration guided every word written on these pages. This book would not have come to life without his invaluable contributions. Thank you for being the driving force behind my journey as an author."

CA. AMRESH VASHISHT
MEERUT, UP
19.06.2023

CHAPTER ONE

WARRIOR WITH AXE

"Parashurama, the Brahmin, is the sixth avatar of Vishnu. Lord Vishnu incarnates himself in this world to avenge arrogant Kshatriyas who were suppressing the Brahmins. The word Parashurama is derived from two words: Parasu, meaning 'axe,' and Lord Rama. So, Parashurama means 'Rama with an axe.' Parashurama was an ardent disciple of Shiva and learned martial arts from him. He acquired the Bhargavastra, an axe, and Vijaya as his personal bow, as a gift from Mahadev Shiva.

He is the son of Renuka and one of the Saptarishees, Sage Jamadagni. He lived during the last Dvapara Yuga and is one of the seven immortals or Chiranjeevi in Hinduism. He received an axe after undertaking terrible penance to please Lord Shiva, who, in turn, taught him martial arts.

Jamadagni Rishi was a sage who was the son of Bhriguvanshi Rucheeka and is counted among the Saptarishees. In Puranas, his wife was Renuka, and his ashram was on the banks of the Saraswati. On Vaishakh Shukla Tritiya, a son was born to him, known as Parashurama.

Parashurama is most known for ridding the world of Kshatriyas twenty-one times after the mighty king Kartavirya killed his father. He played important roles in the Mahabharata and Ramayana, serving as a mentor to Bhisma, Karna, and Drona. Parashurama also fought back the advancing seas to save the lands of Konkan and Kerala.

Parashurama was known for his love for righteousness. He was a great warrior and he was known to be the Guru to Bhisma, Dronacharya, and Karna. However, in advance, Parashurama knew that Karna would do injustice in favour of his friend Duryodhana in the Kurukshetra war. So, as the duty of a good guru, he decides to teach him the Brahmashastra, but he also cursed Karna that the knowledge would not be of any use to him.

Parasurama rebelled against unjust rulers of his time like Kartaviryarjuna, who unjustly slaughtered unarmed Jamadagni and stole their cow.

That does not mean he hated the Kshatriyas. Many prominent Kshatriyas like Bhisma were trained in arms and warfare under him.

When grave injustice was done to the Kshatriya princess Amba and nobody could oppose the might of Kuru's, who came to the rescue of Amba and ensured her justice?

Yes, it was none other than Parasurama!

He helped everybody who came to him.

He conquered every region.

Yet, he desired nothing.

He donated everything to Rishi Kashyapa and retired to live the life of an ascetic in Mahendragiri hills.

A fearless warrior himself, Parashurama never backed down from any challenge. Many consider him to be a masculine icon to be worshiped and admired by the Hindus. His progenitor Jamadagni was a skilled archer and was skilled in the art of weapons.

Parashurama is also known as an immortal, which fought back the advancing ocean, which was going to hit the lands of Kokan and Malabar. The area between Maharashtra and Karnataka is known as Parashurama Kshetra.

According to another legend, Parashurama once went to meet Lord Shiva. As he reached the door, Lord Ganesha confronted Parashurama and stopped him from meeting with Lord Shiva. Angry and furious, Parashurama threw the axe given by Lord Shiva at Ganesha. Knowing that the axe was given by Lord Shiva, Ganesha allowed the axe to cut away one of his tusks.

While Krishna belonged to the warrior class and yet decided against interfering in the matters of mortals during the Mahabharata, acting only as a Parthasarathy, the charioteer of Arjuna, Parashurama took an active interest in restoring balance to the Earth.

He traveled to central India at the northern end of the Eastern Ghats and western Orissa and ascended the Mahendra Mountains. Before he left, Parashurama distributed the territories he conquered among a clan of Brahmins called the Bhumihar, who ruled for many centuries. The kingdoms included the Cheras, Pandyas, Dravida, Mushika, Karnata, and Konkani.

Unlike other incarnations of Vishnu, Parashurama is a Chiranjeevi and is said to still be doing penance today in Mahendragiri.

He neither had his army nor his own kingdom, yet he never gave up and always accepted the challenges of his opponents in the battlefield. Parashurama knew that war isn't won by those who follow the rules but by those who make their own rules and impose them upon their enemies.

Parashurama's adventures have proved to be highly motivational and have always inspired the Brahmans to be righteous and to stand by the gods.

Parashurama's story is proof that one man can make a big difference and that a determined soul can even force the gods to interfere in the affairs of men.

Parashurama wasn't just an ordinary sage. He was a man who proved that no military power in the world can defeat the power of 'will.' A man is only as strong as his will.

By the end of the Vedic period, Parashurama had grown weary of bloodshed and became a sanyasi, giving up his possessions to practice penance. The first book of the Mahabharata writes: 'The son of Jamadagni, after twenty-one times making the Earth bereft of Kshatriyas went to that

best of mountains, Mahendra, and there began his ascetic penance.'
—**Mahabharata 1:14"**

• 4 •

CHAPTER TWO

MAHAVISHNU

As per Hindu mythology, the origin of life starts with origination of Brahma. Brahma originated from the navel of Mahavishnu. Brahma started creation after obtaining permission from Lord Vishnu. In the beginning Brahma created Marici, Angiras, Atri, Vashisht, Pulaha, Kratu, and Pulastya from the mind. They are therefore called the Manasaputras of Brahma. (Manas = mind, Putra, =son). From his wrath came Rudra, from his lap came Narada, from his right thumb Daksa, from his mind Sanaka and others and from his left thumb Virani.

Descending in order from Mahavishnu -Brahma - Bhrigu-Chyavana - Aurva - Rucheeka - Jamadagni-Parasurama.

MAHAVISHNU

It is mentioned in **Devi Purana,Skandha** 1, In the beginning Mahavishnu lay on a banana leaf in the shape of a baby and began to think, "Who am I?

Who created me? What for? What is my work? Where to work?" and so on. At that time an ethereal voice said:

सर्वरहखलवदिामेव: अर्हण्यअदस्तसिनातनम्
"Sarva rhkhalvida mevah arhnany adasti sanatanam".
All these are myself. Except me there is nothing eternal.

Mahavishnu listened attentively to the ethereal voice and was struck with wonder. He realized that the oracle belonged to Mahadevi, who appeared before him in a divine form. Mahadevi had four hands and wielded sacred weapons such as the conch (Sankha), wheel (Cakra), club (Gada), and lotus (Padma). She was adorned with glorious clothes and ornaments, accompanied by her powers (Saktis) named Rati, Bhiiti, Buddhi, Mati, Kirti, Dhrti, Smrti, Sraddha, Medha, Svadha, Svaha, Ksudha, Nidra, Daya, Gati, Tusti, Pusti, Ksama, Lajja, Jrrhbha, and Tandra.

Addressing Mahavishnu, Mahadevi spoke, "Oh, Vishnu, there is no need for wonder. Whenever the universe undergoes the cycles of creation, preservation, and destruction, you are born as a result of the immense power of the supreme spirit. It appears that you have forgotten these matters. Understand that the supreme power transcends all qualities, while we, including myself, possess qualities. Your primary quality is Sattva, characterized by purity, harmony, and balance."

Mahadevi continued, "From your navel, Brahma, the creator, will be born. His attribute is Rajoguna, representing activity, passion, or motion. From the space between his eyebrows, Rudra, the destroyer, will be born, and his attribute will be Tamasaguna, symbolizing darkness or inertia. Brahma, through his penance, will acquire the ability to create, and with his attribute of Rajoguna, he will fashion the world in the color of blood. You, Vishnu, will be the preserver of that world. Eventually, Rudra will bring about the destruction of that world at the end of the Kalpa, the age of the universe."

Mahavishnu listened carefully, acknowledging the cosmic order and the roles assigned to each deity in the grand cycle of creation, preservation, and destruction.

Lord Vishnu holds a prominent position among the Hindu deities and is revered as one of the principal gods. One of the distinguishing aspects of Lord Vishnu is his numerous incarnations, known as avatars.

Lord Vishnu's avatars are believed to be manifestations or embodiments of different divine figures, through which he interacts with the world. These avatars serve specific purposes and often appear in times of crisis or to restore balance and protect dharma, the righteous order of the universe.

One well-known legend associated with Lord Vishnu is the story of his three strides across the universe. It symbolizes his immense power and authority over all realms. In this legend, Lord Vishnu, in his Vamana (dwarf) avatar, takes three steps and covers the entire universe, establishing his supremacy.

Lord Vishnu's avatars are diverse and varied, ranging from the Matsya (fish) avatar, where he saves humanity from a catastrophic flood, to the Kurma (turtle) avatar, where he supports the cosmic churning of the ocean. Other notable avatars include Lord Rama, Lord Krishna, and Lord Buddha.

Lord Vishnu is often associated with the Sun and is depicted as the preserver and sustainer of the universe. His vehicle, or vahana, is Garuda, the eagle, who carries him across the celestial realms. Vaikuntha is the heavenly abode of Lord Vishnu, where he resides along with his consort, Goddess Lakshmi.

Overall, Lord Vishnu's presence in Hindu mythology and religion represents the eternal and divine aspect of existence, and his avatars serve as guides, protectors, and sources of inspiration for devotees.

गवद-गीता में, कृष्ण अर्जुन को युद्ध के मैदान में बताते हों "जब भी धर्म का ह्रास [धर्म] होता है और अधर्म का उदय होता है तब में स्वयं को आगे भेजता हूँ सज्जनों की रक्षा के लिए, दुष्टों के विनाश के लिए और धर्म की स्थापना के लिए, में युग-युग में प्रकट होता हूं संपूर्ण अवतार या कहें अवतारों का सिद्धांत इसी अवधारणा पर आधारित हों

In Bhagavad-Gita, Krishna tells Arjuna at the battleground. "Whenever there is a decline of righteousness [dharma] and rise of unrighteousness then I send forth Myself. For the protection of the good, for the destruction of the wicked, and for the establishment of righteousness, I come into being from age to age. The whole incarnation or say avatars theory based on this concept.

As per **Chapter 40 of Harivarhsa**, Parasurama is said to be incarnation of Mahavishnu. There is definite Cause for incarnation. Once God Agni went to Karta-viryarjuna and begged for food. The king allowed him to take from his vast territory as much food as he wanted from anywhere, he liked. Agni started burning forests and mountains and consuming them. Deep inside one of the forests a sage named Apava was performing penance and the fire burnt the ashrama of Apava also. Enraged at this the sage cursed thus: "Karta-viryarjuna is at the root of this havoc. The arrogance of Ksatriyas has increased beyond limits. Mahavishnu would therefore be born on earth as Parasurama to destroy this arrogance of the Ksatriyas." Accordingly, Mahavishnu was born as Parasurama in the Bhargava race. So, Parasurama was one of the incarnations of Lord Vishnu, born to destroy the Kshatriya race.

CURSE OF BHRIGU FOR INCARNATIONS

There was a feud between Shukracharya, the Guru of the Asuras, and Brihaspati, who was elected as the head priest of the Devtas by Lord Indra. This disagreement led Shukracharya to seek Lord Shiva's assistance, and he obtained the potent mantra of invincibility known as 'Mrita Sanjivani.' Shukracharya offered refuge to the Asuras at his father Maharishi Bhrigu's ashram.

In Shukracharya's absence, the Devtas, taking advantage of the situation, attacked the unarmed Asuras. However, the Asuras sought shelter from Bhrigu's wife, Kavyamata, who used her yogic powers to immobilize Indra and protect the Asuras. The Devtas, alarmed by the situation, sought refuge at the feet of Lord Vishnu.

To protect the Devtas, Vishnu entered Indra's body, and Kavyamata, furious at this turn of events, warned to incinerate everyone unless they retreated. Indra, instigated by his own anger, decided to destroy Bhrigu's wife. In response, Vishnu used his Sudarshana Chakra to save Indra and the Devtas, severing Kavyamata head in the process.

Sage Bhrigu, upon witnessing the condition of his wife, became enraged and cursed Lord Vishnu to be born on Earth multiple times, experiencing the pain of birth and death repeatedly. This legendary curse compelled Vishnu to undertake numerous avatars on Earth, enduring the sufferings of mortal existence as a consequence.

Although Bhrigu later revived his wife by sprinkling holy water from his Kamandala (water pot), his anger and vengeance towards Lord Vishnu remained. As a result of Bhrigu's curse, Vishnu had to assume various incarnations, both complete and partial. The complete incarnations are famously known as the Dasavataras, which encompass ten principal avatars of Lord Vishnu.

SIXTH AVTARA- INCARNATION AS PARASURAMA

Yes, according to the Bhagavata Purana, Lord Vishnu's sixth incarnation is known as Parasurama. In this avatar, Lord Vishnu took birth as the son of Jamadagni and Renuka. Jamadagni was a revered sage belonging to the Bhargava lineage, and Renuka was his wife.

Before the birth of Parasurama, Jamadagni and Renuka sought divine providence through meditation at Tap Ka Tiba near Renuka Lake. Lord Shiva blessed them, and at Lord Shiva's request, Lord Vishnu assured them that he would be their fifth son. Renuka and Jamadagni named their youngest son Rambhadra.

The primary purpose of Lord Parashurama's incarnation was to put an end to the dominance of the Kshatriya kings who had deviated from righteous paths and had become a burden on the earth. Parashurama's mission was to restore balance and righteousness by eliminating the corrupt and oppressive Kshatriya rulers. He wielded an axe, symbolizing his relentless pursuit of justice and the destruction of evil.

Parasurama is often referred to as an "Avesha Avatar" of Lord Vishnu, which means that Lord Vishnu empowered him with divine energy and descended into him to carry out the task at hand. Through his valiant efforts, Parasurama played a crucial role in upholding dharma and preserving the earth from unrighteousness during his time.

According to the Brahmanda Purana, there are different versions of the circumstances leading to Lord Vishnu's birth as Parasurama.

In one version, Bhumidevi, the personified goddess Earth, approached Lord Vishnu in the form of a cow and expressed her distress over the atrocities committed by wicked Kshatriya kings. Lord Vishnu promised her that he would incarnate as Parasurama to address her concerns and bring justice.

The Brahmanda Purana, Chapter 59, further elaborates that Bhumidevi approached Lord Brahma, who then took her to the Milk Ocean and shared her grievances with Lord Vishnu. In response, Lord Vishnu pledged to take birth as the son of Jamadagni and eliminate the wicked kings. Renuka, the wife of Jamadagni, gave birth to Parasurama as a result.

It is interesting to note that the texts also mention that while Parasurama was alive, he lost the essence of Vishnu, indicating that he did not possess the complete divine consciousness of Lord Vishnu. This highlights the distinct nature of Lord Vishnu's subsequent avatars, such as Lord Rama and Lord Krishna, where Vishnu appeared in his complete form.

The name "Parasurama" itself signifies Lord Rama with an axe, emphasizing the divine connection between the two avatars. It is believed that the story of Parasurama takes place in the Tretayuga, one of the four ages described in Hindu cosmology.

PEER INCARNITIONS

Mahavishnu had to undertake so many incarnations, complete as well as partial. Complete incarnations are ten in number. They are called Dasavataras. Another version is that Mahavishnu had taken the twenty-six incarnations. Dasavataras are the common.

The Dasavataras are - *First Avatar- Matsya avatar (Fish Incarnation), Second Avtara- Kurmdvatdra. (Incarnation as a tortoise)-Kurma (turtle),Third Avtara- Vardhavatara. (Incarnation as a Pig), Forth Avatar-Narasimhdvatara. (Incarnation as lion-man), Fifth Avtara- Vdmandvatdra. (Incarnation as a Dwarf, ,Sixth Avtara- Parasurdmdvatdra. (Incarnation as Parasurama), Seventh Avtara-Raghupati Rama- (Incarnation as Sri Rama), Eighth and Ninth Avtara- Balabhadrardmdvatdra and Sri Krsndvatdra (The incarnation of Balrama and Krishn)and the Tenth Avtara Kalkyavatdra (The incarnation as Kalki)*

The above are the usually recognised Avatars, but the number is sometimes extended. The Bhagavata Purana is the fifth place in the order of Puranas, but it is the most famous across the globe. Vaishnavas consider this Purana of 12 wings, 335 chapters, and 18 thousand shlokas as Mahapurana.

Bhagavata Purana enumerates twenty-two incarnations:—*(1) Purusha, the male, the progenitor (2) Varaha, the boar (3) Narada, the great sage (4) Nara and Narayana (5) Kapila, the great sage; (6) Dattatreya, a sage (7) Yajna, sacrifice (8)Dushyanta,a righteous king, father of Bharata (9.) Prathu, a king (10) Matsya, the fish; (11) Kurma, the tortoise (12) and (13) Dhanwantari, the physician of the gods (14) -Narasimha, the man-lion; (15)*

Yamana, the dwarf (16) Parasurama; (17) Yeda-Vyasa (18) Rama (19) Bala-rama; (20.) Knshraa; (21.)Buddha; (22) Kalki But after this it adds—"The incarnations of Vishnu are innumerable, like the rivulets flowing from-an inexhaustible lake, I,Manus, gods, sons of Manus,Prajapatis, are all portions of him."

Sri Mahadevi Bhagavata, Skandha 1, Chapter 3 mentioned that Mahavishnu had taken the twenty-six incarnations. The ten avatars are common, the rest of the sixteen incarnations are:

(1) Sanaka (2) Sananda (3) Sanatana (4) Sanatkumara (5) Varaha (pig) (6) Narada (7) Nara Narayanas (8)Kapila (9) Dattatreya (10) Yajna (11) Rsabha (12) Prthu (13) Matsya (fish) (14)Mohini (15)'Kurma (turtle) (16) Garuda (eagle) (17) Dhanvantari (18) Narasimha (Lion-man) (19) Vaniana (dwarf) (20) Parasurama (21) Vyasa (22) Sri Rama (23) Balabhadrarama (24) Sri Krsna (25) Buddha(26) Kalki.

The detailed versions on all the peer incarnations are given in Chapter 41.

CHAPTER THREE

BRAHMA

The God, who is the creator of this Universe. It is mentioned in the Puranas that Brahma creates, Vishnu preserves and Shiva destroys the universe. The trimurtis are Brahma, Vishnu and Mahesh (Shiva).

BRAHMA

Genealogy: Descending in order from Mahavishnu, Brahma

Accordingly from the nave of Vishnu a lotus grew up and in that lotus flower Brahma took his form. The same Brahma deva did penance before Mahavishnu and Jagadamba, who were pleased at his penance and gave him all the boons he wanted. After that Brahma began the work of creation.

As per Devi Bhagavata, Skandha 7, Brahma created with his mind the Saptarishees (seven sages) and then the Prajapatis (the lord's of emanation). From them all the movables and the immovable's in the universe came into existence.

In manusmrti, Chapter 1.9, the following stanza about the creation of Brahma occurs.

तदण्डमभवद्धैमंसहस्रांशुसमप्रभम्।
तस्मिञ्जज्ञे स्वयं ब्रह्मा सर्वलोकपितामहः ॥ ९ ॥

tadaṇḍamabhavaddhaimaṃ sahasrāṃśusamaprabham |
tasmiñjajñe svayaṃ brahmā sarvalokapitāmahaḥ || 9 ||

That became the golden egg, resplendent like the Sun; in that (egg) he (Hiraṇyagarbha) himself was born as Brahma, the 'Grand-father' of the whole world.—(9)

That egg was as radiant as the Sun, with the colour of gold. Brahma the great grandfather of everything in the world took birth by himself in it.From the supreme power; an egg fell on the water which was the first creation. That egg became a germ of goldencolour. Creating a life, which had done penance in its former births in such a way as to enable it to become Brahma, in the golden germ of the egg, the supreme power entered the life that is to become Brahma as its innerguide. That Brahma is known as the Pitamaha (Grand father of the manes) or paternal grandfather of all the worlds. Jajñe svayam Brahma—(a) 'He himself was born as Brahma', or (b) 'Brahma himself was born.'

The Vamana Purana, Chapter 43, provides insights into the creation of Brahma and the origin of the world. According to the text, before the beginning of time, when everything was submerged in the great flood, the germ of living things formed itself into a big egg. Brahma, the creator deity, was present within this egg and remained in a deep sleep for a thousand yugas (ages).

When Brahma woke up from his long slumber, he observed that the world was void. With the thought of creation arising in his mind, the attribute of Rajoguna (activity or passion) became predominant within him. Rajas, the quality of activity, is responsible for creation, while Sattva, the quality of purity, preserves the created world. During the time of destruction, Tamoguna (darkness) becomes the primary attribute.

The Supreme Spirit, known as Bhagavan, pervades over everything in all living worlds. This Eternal Being is referred to as Brahma, Vishnu, and Shiva. Understanding that the world was immersed in pure water, the Bhagavan cut open the egg, giving rise to the sacred syllable 'Om' (Omkara). From this syllable, the sounds "Bhur," "Bhuvah," and "Svah" emerged, which collectively came to be known as "Bhur Bhuvah Svah."

The radiant sun then manifested from this creation, and Brahma, the grandfather of the worlds, originated at the center of the egg. The Amarakosa, a Sanskrit lexicon, provides various names of Brahma along with their meanings.

It is important to note that different Puranas may present variations in the details of creation and the names and attributes of deities. The Vamana Purana offers its own perspective on the origin of Brahma and the world.

ब्रह्मात्मभूः सुरज्येष्ठः परमेष्ठी पतिामहः। हरिण्यगर्भो लोकेश: स्वयम्भूश्चतुरानन:॥
धाताब्जयोनर्द्रुहिणो वरिञ्चिर्चि: कमलासन:। स्रष्टा प्रजापतर्विधा वधिाता वशिवसगूर्वधि:॥
नाभजिन्माण्डज: पूर्वो नधिन: कमलोद्भव:। सदानन्दो रजोमूर्तिः सत्यको हंसवाहन:॥

"Brahmatmabhuhsurajyesthah   ParamesthIpitamahah ,Hiranyagarbholokesah Svayarhbhuscaturananah //
Dhatabjayonirdruhino Virancihkamalasanah /
Srasfaprajapatirvedha Vidhatavisvasrtvidhih //
Nabhijanmandajahpurvo
nidhanahkamalodbhavah /
Sadanandorajomurtih Sattyakohamsavahanah //

Brahma- he who increases.
Atmabhu- born of his own accord or born of the Supreme Spirit.
Surajyestha- he who came into being before all the suras (gods).
Paramesthin- he who dwells in the world of truth or Parama.
Pitamaha- grandfather of the manes such as Aryama and others.
Hiranyagarbha -having the golden egg (mundane egg) in womb.
Lokesa- the god of the worlds.
Svayarhbhu- who is born of himself.

Caturanana- who has four faces.
Dhata -who holds or bears everything.
Abjayoni -born of lotus, (abja)
Druhina -who hurts asuras.
Viranci -he who creates.
Kamalasana -who sits on lotus.
Srsja -he who creates.
Prajapati- Pad of prajas (Lord of progeny).
Vedha -he who creates.
Vidhata -he who does.
Visvasrt -who creates the world.
Vidhi -he who does or decides or judges.
Nabhijanma -born from the nave of Vishnu.
Andaja- born from the egg.
Harhsavjhana -who has swan as his conveyance.

TWELVE MAJOR WARS

There were major wars between the Devas (celestial beings) and the Asuras (demons) in Hindu mythology. These wars played significant roles in the cosmic battles of good versus evil. Here is a brief description of each war you mentioned:

1. **Narasimha War:** This war occurred during the reign of Hiranyakasipu, a powerful Asura king. Vishnu took the form of Narasimha, a half-man and half-lion avatar, to defeat Hiranyakasipu and protect his devotee Prahlada.
2. **Vamana War:** This war took place when Vali, another Asura king, was causing trouble. Vishnu appeared as Vamana, a dwarf, and sought alms from Vali. With his deceptive request, Vamana subdued Vali and restored power to the Devas.
3. **Varaha War:** Vishnu incarnated as Varaha, a boar, to rescue the earth (Bhumidevi) from the clutches of the demon Hiranyaksha. Varaha defeated Hiranyaksha and restored balance to the world.
4. **Amritamanthana War:** This war was fought between the Devas and Asuras during the churning of the ocean to obtain the nectar of immortality (amrita). It involved various mythological beings and celestial creatures and had multiple significant events and battles.

5. **Tarakamaya War:** This war took place due to the abduction of Tara, the wife of Brihaspati, by Soma (Chandra). It resulted in a conflict between the Devas and the Asuras.

6. **Ajivaka War:** This war is not widely known, and there is limited information available about it. It likely involved conflicts between the Devas and the Asuras led by Ajivaka.

7. **Tripuraghatana War:** Tripura, a powerful Asura, built three invincible cities and created havoc. Shiva destroyed the cities and defeated Tripura, ending the war.

8. **Andhaka War:** Andhaka, an Asura, had intentions to abduct Shiva's wife, Parvati. Vishnu intervened and orchestrated the downfall of Andhaka, saving Parvati.

9. **Vritrasamhara War:** Vritra, a formidable Asura, had acquired immense power and was causing chaos. Indra, aided by Vishnu, engaged in a fierce battle with Vritra and ultimately defeated him.

10. **Jita War:** This war involved Vishnu's defeat of Salva, a powerful demon, and Parashurama's eradication of evil Kshatriyas (warrior caste).

11. **Halahala War:** Asura Halahala, in the form of poison, threatened to destroy the universe. Vishnu intervened and neutralized the poison.

12. **Kolahala War:** Vishnu fought against an Asura named Kolahala, who symbolized tumult and chaos, bringing peace and harmony back to the world.

These wars depict the continuous struggle between good and evil and the divine interventions of various avatars and deities to restore balance and righteousness in the universe.

CHAPTER FOUR

BHRIGU

Genealogy. Descending in order from Vishnu, Brahma, Bhrigu

Bhrigu, the son of Brahma, is indeed considered a Manasputra or a "mind-born son" of Brahma. As Brahma embarked on the task of creation, he created various beings to assist him and populate the universe. Among them were the ten Manasputras, born directly from Brahma's mind.

The ten Manasputras are Marichi, Atri, Pulahu, Pulastya, Angiras, Kratu, Narada, Daksha, Bhrigu, and Vashishta. Each of them was born from a specific part of Brahma's body. Daksha, for instance, became a king, while the rest, including Bhrigu, chose the spiritual path.

Bhrigu, being a great sage, is renowned as the founder of the Bhargava lineage. The term "Bhargava" is used to refer to the descendants and the school of Bhrigu. The Bhargavas are known for their lineage of sages who achieved great sanctity and grandeur. Bhrigu himself was born from Brahma's skin or "tvak" according to the scriptures.

In the Bhagavad Gita, Bhrigu is mentioned in a metaphorical sense, comparing him to the Almighty. This highlights the exalted status and spiritual significance associated with Bhrigu and his lineage.

महर्षीणां भृगुरहं गिरिमस्म्येकमक्षरम्। यज्ञानां जपयज्ञोऽस्मि स्थावराणां हिमालय:॥10.25॥

Maharsinam, among the great sages, I am Bhrgu, Giram, of words, of utterances, in the form of words; I am the ekam, single; aksaram, syllable Om. Yajnanam, among rituals; I am the japa-yajnah, rituals of Japa. Sthavaranam, of the immovables, I am the Himalaya. ॥10.25॥

Vishnu Purana, Book I, Chapter 10, it is mentioned that Bhrigu soon became a famous and very powerful Rishi throughout the world. At this time, Daksha and his wife Prasuti were marrying off their twenty-four daughters. Bhrigu obtained Daksha's daughter Khyati's hand in marriage. After they were married, Bhrigu and Khyati had a daughter who became one of the most famous women in Hinduism: Lakshmi. Worshipped today as the goddess of wealth and prosperity, Lakshmi eventually married Lord Vishnu. Bhrigu and Khyati also had two sons named Dhata and Vidhata. They married Ayati and Niyati, the daughters of Meru, respectively. Dhata and Ayati had a son named Prana, whose son Dyutiman and grandson Raja van eventually led to the famed Bhrigu Vansha. Meanwhile, Vidhata and Niyati's son was Mrikandu, whose son was none other than the great Markandeya Rishi. According to the Anusasana Parva of the Mahabharata, Bhrigu and Khyati also had a third son named Kavi.

However, in **Adi Parva, 5th Chapter,** it is mentioned that Bhrigu was born from "Vahini" (fire). It shows that Bhrigu had two incarnations. The first time he was born from Brahma's skin. In course of time, the sage Bhrigu became famous. In the Daksa yaga, this sage was present as one of the Rtviks (officiating priests). On that occasion, Satldevi who was in rage and grief because her husband (Siva) was not invited to the yaga, committed suicide by jumping into the sacrificial fire. Hearing about this, Siva was enraged and the monster spirits who emerged from his matted locks caught hold of the Rtviks. Bhagavata caturtha skandha says that the Bhuta named Nandisvara, who emerged from Siva's locks, caught hold of Bhrigu and killed him. Therefore the Bhrigu who was born from Brahma's skin must be considered as having died at Daksayaga.

Bhrigu was born again in the Vaivasvata Manvantara, the current cosmic age. This second birth occurred during the famous Brahma yajna (sacrifice) conducted by Varuna, the god of water and the celestial ocean. Bhrigu was reborn from the fire as Brahma's son. In this birth, Bhrigu was raised by Varuna and his wife Carsani. Due to this association, Bhrigu is referred to as "Varunaputra" and "Carsaniputra" in some texts.

The concept of Bhrigu having multiple births and each birth giving rise to a separate family is found in certain Puranic accounts. These variations highlight the diverse narratives and regional traditions within Hindu mythology, where different lineages and genealogies are associated with Bhrigu's different incarnations.

Brahmanda Purana, Chapter 63 mentions that, once all the Bhargava rishi together once stayed in the ashrama of Aurva. Parasurama visited the ashrama one day during that time and paid respects to Bhrigu, Khyati-wife of Bhrigu, Chyavana, son of Bhrigu and Aurva, son of Chyavana and Brahmanda Purana, Chapter 64 also mentions that Atri was also among the Maharishis who had gone to witness Parashurama's tapas.

The Sampangirama family is one of the many families that contains the descendants of Parashurama . The Sampangirama family goes by many last names, the most notable being Sampangirama, Nagar, and Rao.The Sampangirama family follows the pravara (bloodline): Bhargava, Chyavana, Apnavana, Aurva, Jamadagni, Parashurama. Majority of the Sampangirama family lives in the state of Karnataka. Additionally, the family follows the Bhargava gotra, an ancient line of lineage starting from Sage Bhrigu.

As per Vishnupurana,Part I, Chapter 10, First birth: Bhrigu and his wife Khyati had a daughter Laksmi and three sons, Dhata, Vidhataand Kavi. Mahameru's daughters, Ayati and Niyati became the wives of Dhata and Vidhata, respectively.Two sons, Prana and Mrkandu were born to those two couples. Markandeya was born to Mrkandu and from Markandeya was born Veda siras. Prana had a son,Dyutiman who had a son Rajavan. From that Rajavan,Bhrigu Vansa multiplied. (Vishnupurana,Part I, Chapter 10).

The second Bhrigu Varhsa is the family which took its origin from the second birth of Bhrigu as the son of Varuna. Varuna's son, Bhrigu married the woman, Puloma. They had six children who were, Bhuta, Chyavana, Vajraslrsa, Suci, Sukra, and Savana. By his first wife Bhuta, he had his sons, "Ekadasa Rudras" (eleven Rudras) and "Rudra Parsadas" (Attendants of Rudra) and by his second wife Sarupa he had a crore of Rudras.

DAKSHA PRAJAPATI YAJNA

Maharishi (Sage) Bhrigu was one of the Prajapatis as he was the 'Brahma Manasa Putra' of Lord Sri Brahma Deva. Maharishi (Sage) Bhrigu was well-versed in all the Vedas, Shastra (Hindu Texts) and also he was a great Mantra gyata (aware of many mantras) of all times. Among the Maharishi or Brahmarishi or Rishi or Devarishi, after Devarishi Narada Muni, it is our Maharishi (Sage) Bhrigu has the highest value.

Shiva Purana, Rudra Samhita, Sati Khanda mentions about the daksha yagya.Daksha conducted a grand yagna and invited all of the devas, rishis, and other important people in the Universe. Bhrigu was one of the main priests of the yagna. However, because of Daksha and Shiva's enmity, Shiva and Sati were not invited to the yagna. Goddess Sri Sati Devi was the consort of Lord Shiva and also she was the daughter of Daksha Prajapati. Goddess Sri Sati Devi went for the Yagya without invitation by her father Daksha Prajapati. There she saw her husband Lord Shiva being insulted and in anger she fell into the Yajna Kunda (sacrificial place) and sacrificed her life in the sacrificial fire. The ganas (Shiva's soldiers) that had accompanied Sati were infuriated and started causing havoc. Some even killed themselves. Sage Bhrigu then created beings which countered the attacks of the ganas. These powerful beings created by Bhrigu's mantras defeated the ganas. The remaining ganas fled to Lord Shiva and told him what had happened.

When Lord Shiva learned about the death of his wife, he was infuriated. He created the monster spirits Virabhadra and Mahakali from his matted hair. Virabhadra and Kali ravaged the yajna and killed many of its guests. Virabhadra approached Bhrigu and threw him on the ground. Manibhadra kicked him and plucked off his moustache. . then, Virabhadra, a member of Lord Shiva's group destroyed the whole Yagya as per the instructions of Lord Shiva. Maharshi (Sage) Bhrigu was also present there. Maharishi (Sage) Bhrigu pleaded Lord Shiva for protection and Lord Shiva assured him for his safety.After the yajna was destroyed and Daksha was killed, all the gods prayed to Shiva to resuscitate Daksha. Shiva was pleased. He forgave them and revived Daksha. Shiva then said that Vashisht, Atri, Pulastya, Angiras, Pulaha, Kratu, Bhrigu, and Mariachi would be reborn in Chakshusha Manvantara.

Maharishi (Sage) Bhrigu had three consorts namely Khyati, Kavyamata and Puloma. Maharishi (Sage) Bhrigu's son Shukra (Venus) (later was called as Shukracharya) was the Guru of all the Raksasas (Demons). Daksha Prajapati arranged to do a Yagna (Yagya) and he had invited all the Devatas (Demigods) and others to this sacrifice. But, Daksha Prajapati had not invited Lord Shiva for the Yagya that he had organized.

TESTING THE TRIMURTI

Bhagavata Purana, Canto 10,Chapter 89 ,Once, a group of sages were performing a sacrifice (yagna) on the banks of the Saraswati River. A dispute arose as to who was the most superior from the Trimurti (Brahma, Vishnu, and Shiva). Some of them believed Vishnu to be the superior one, while others supported Brahma or Shiva. To settle the matter, they sent Bhrigu to go find out the truth.

Bhrigu first went to Satyaloka, Brahma's abode. There, he tested his father Brahma's humility. When he entered the court, Bhrigu did not bow down, nor did he offer any prayers. Brahma was offended by Bhrigu's lack of respect and became angry.

Bhrigu then arrived at Mount Kailash, the abode of Lord Shiva. Shiva rose to his feet to embrace his friend, but Bhrigu stepped back and said, "You are adharmic. Don't touch me." Shiva was enraged. He picked up his trident, ready to end Bhrigu's life. But fortunately, Parvati was able to pacify her husband Shiva.

Lastly, Bhrigu went to Vaikuntha and saw Vishnu sleeping on his wife Lakshmi's lap. Bhrigu kicked Vishnu in the chest. With a startle, both Vishnu and Lakshmi woke up. Bhrigu expected Vishnu to do the same as the others: feel insulted. But instead, Vishnu said, "Welcome, great Brahmin. Please forgive us for not having noticed your arrival. I am blessed to have your footprint on my chest."

Bhrigu was amazed. His eyed teared up as he bowed to Vishnu with devotion. Bhrigu then returned to other sages and told them about his findings. The sages concluded that Vishnu is the greatest of the Trimurti.

Matsya Purana, Part 1, Chapter 47, The Devas and Asuras are perennial enemies. They are always fighting. Once, in the midst of a war between the Devas and the Asuras, the Asuras had been completely routed. Shukracharya, the preceptor of the Asuras, decided to do penance to acquire powerful boons from Lord Shiva. Shukra planned to use these boons to defeat the Devas once and for all. Meanwhile, with Shukracharya away, the Asuras were even more vulnerable to attacks from the Devas. So the Asuras went to Bhrigu's ashram for refuge and lived under the protection of Puloma, Bhrigu's wife.

The Devas once again attacked the Asuras. However, the Devas underestimated Puloma's strength. Through intense penance, Puloma had gathered immense powers. Using these yogic powers, Puloma defeated Indra. Seeing their king helpless and trapped under the effect of Puloma's spells, the Devas fled. They went to Vishnu for help. Vishnu knew that Puloma's capabilities were unsurpassed. There was only one way to rescue Indra: he would have to kill Puloma. So Vishnu went to the hermitage and using his Sudarshan Chakra, severed Puloma's head from her body. Bhrigu was so devastated when he heard of his wife's murder that he immediately cursed Vishnu.

"स्त्रियां हत्वा गम्भीरं पापं कृतं त्वया । त्वां शापयामि यत् त्वं मनुष्येषु पृथविया बहुवारं जायतं!"

"You have committed a grave sin by killing a woman. I curse you that you will be born several times on Earth among men!"

Bhrigu then muttered some incantations and connected his wife's head with her body. After sprinkling some water on her, the corpse miraculously came back to life. Puloma was reborn! But this incident is very important in Hindu mythology: because of Bhrigu's curse, Vishnu was born on Earth repeatedly whenever there was evil on Earth. This led to avatars of Rama, Krishna, Parshuram, and countless others.

BHRIGU VANSH

Bhriguvansh is one of the oldest dynasties in the world. In the oldest available book 'Rigveda', remembering Bhrigu as an ancestor at many places is a vivid proof of his antiquity. This dynasty had a relationship with the gods. Bhrigu's daughter Lakshmi was married to Shri Vishnu in Tridev. Thus Bhrigu was the father-in-law of sage Vishnu. Indra's daughter Jayanti was married to Bhrigu's son Shukracharya. These relations prove the importance of Bhrigu dynasty.

According to Manusmrti, Bhrigu was a compatriot of and lived during the time of Manu, the Hindu progenitor of humanity. Bhrigu had his Ashram (Hermitage) on the Vadhusara River, a tributary of the Drishadwati River near Dhosi Hill in the Vedic state of Brahmavarta, presently on the border of Haryana and Rajasthan. Along with Manu, Bhrigu had made important contributions to Manusmrti, which was constituted out of a sermon to a congregation of saints in the state of Brahmavarta, after the great floods in this area. As per Skandha Purana, Bhrigu migrated to Bhrigukutch, modern Bharuch on the banks of the Narmada River in Gujarat, leaving his son Chyavana at Dhosi Hill.

ATTEMPTED TO STOP MAHABHARTA

Maharishi (Sage) Bhrigu had the powers to travel in space like Rishi Durvasa Muni, Devarishi Narada Muni, etc. and he used to visit all the planets of the universe. Before the Battle of Kurukshetra, Maharishi (Sage) Bhrigu tried to stop the battle (Mahabharata war). Few times he instructed Maharishi (Sage) Bharadvaja about astronomical evolution, and he is the author of the great 'Bhrigu-Samhita', the great astrological calculation.

Maharishi (Sage) Bhrigu explained how air, fire, water and earth are generated from ether. Maharishi (Sage) Bhrigu described how the air in the stomach works and regulates the intestines. As a great philosopher, Maharishi (Sage) Bhrigu logically established the eternity of the living entity in the epic of Mahabharata.

Maharishi (Sage) Bhrigu was also a great anthropologist, and the theory of evolution was long ago explained by him. Maharishi (Sage) Bhrigu was a scientific profounder of the four divisions and orders of human society known as the 'varṇāśrama' institution. Maharishi (Sage) Bhrigu converted the Kshatriya King Vītahavya into a Brahmana (Brahmin).

GOTRAS

The real meaning of the word gotra was the place of cattle breeding. In very ancient times, whose animals were tied in the same school, they were called 'Sagotri'. Generally, due to the inclusion of children of the same ancestor in such people, the word 'Gotra' became the popular meaning of the dynasty. It has been said in the appendices of the sources, 'Yadapatya tadgotramityuchyate' means the children of those (sages) are called gotras. Panini has also said – Apatyam pautraprabhritigotram' means the children of the son, grandson etc. are the gotra. Earlier everyone used to live in one place. In course of time, when the number of people of the dynasty increased, then it became impossible for people to live at one place, so they separated and made separate places of their living, that is, gotras became branches. It is known from Rig-Veda that earlier there were four gotras, Bhrigu, Angiras, Atharvan and Vashishtha. People of Atharvan gotras went to Persia. Angiras gotras got absorbed in Bhrigu gotra.

The original gotra was Bhrigu. Due to 'Bhrigorapatyam' meaning 'child of Bhrigu', the place of 'Bhrigu' gotra was taken by 'Bhargava' gotra. As a result, the original gotra / vansh became 'Bhargava'. Due to the expansion of lineage, our ancestors settled in different places. In the name of those great forefathers (Rishigan), many branch-tribes were formed, whose details are as follows-

1. **Vats** - In the Bhrigu genealogy, the first name 'Vats' is found of Rishi who was the son of Dhatri Rishi. Their abode was East India A book written by him is found, whose name is 'Vats Smriti'.

2. **Vatsya**- He was a gotrakar of Bhrigukulotpanna. Many astrology books are available in his name. Unfortunately, this gotra merged into 'Vats' gotra.

3. **Vid** - His name 'Bid' is also available. This Bhrigukulotpanna was a gotrakar, he was Samadrashta Acharya. Panchvish Brahmin (13.11.10) and Gemini U. Bra. His full name 'Vidanvat Bhargava' has been mentioned in 3.1.

4. **Galav** - He was a famous sage. A book is found in his name, whose name is 'Galav Smriti'. as a breeder His name is 'Sangalav'.

5. **Gangey** - His real name was Gargya or Gagyayin. He was a gotrakar of Bhrigukul. Because of living on the banks of the Ganges, they were called Ganges. His composition is a book 'Gargya Smriti'.

6. **Kochasti** - He was the gotrakar of Bhrigukul, whose real name was Kochasti.

7. **Kashyapi** - Kashyapi is a Bhriguvanshi sage and gotrakar. Two books composed by him are found - 'Kashyapi Smriti' and 'Kashyapi Dharmashastra'.

8. Singh- It is written in old directories that this gotra is not found. At the time of the caste census of 1971, (Late) Naveen Chandra Bhargava, Delhi, found some families belonging to the Sihlas clan in the villages of Agra-Mathura. At that time they were counted in tens. There are people of this gotra in our caste. Although this gotra has not been mentioned in the texts like 'Gotra Pravardarpan', 'Gotrapravar Nirjan', 'Gotrapravarkarika', 'Gotrapravar Bhaskar', 'Gotra Pravar Manjari, Gotra Pravar Vivek' etc. Chaitr Vidhi Chaitra

GANA AND PRAVARA

At the time of Parashurama, the eight clans were divided into two clans

(a) Jamadagya clan
(b) Ajamadagya clan

Vatsa, Vatsya, Vid, Galav, Gangaiya and Kochahasti come under Jamadagya clan. The remaining two clans come under Kashyapi and Singh Ajamadgya Gana. Other names of Kashyapi gotra are Vaitahavya or Yasak.Similarly, the name of Gana of Singh gotra is also Arshtishen. The people of these gotras determined the number of Panch Pravar and Tripravar in the name of the best men of their respective gotras, such as-

Gotra - Vatsa, Vatsya, Galav, Gangey, Kochasti **Praver** - Bhrigu, Chyavana, Apravan, Urva, Jamadagni
   Gotra - Kashyapi **Praver** - Bhrigu, Vethavya, Savetas
   Gotra - Singh **Praver** - Bhrigu,Chyavana, Apravan, Arshtishen, Anoop
   Gotra - Vid **Praver** - Bhriguchyavan, Apravan, Urva, Bid

CHAPTER FIVE

CHYAVANA

Genealogy: Descending in order from Vishnu, Brahma, Bhrigu, Chyavana

Chyavana Rishi was the son of Sage Bhrigu, progenitor of the great lineage of descendants known as the Bhargavas (or Dhusars). The Mahabharata states that Chyavana was powerful enough to oppose the Vajra of Indra. He created the Mada demon to help the Ashvins get their fair share of the sacrificial offerings. He is also known for his rejuvenation, achieved through a special herbal paste known as Chyawanprash. This medication was first prepared for him some 10,000 years ago at his ashram on Dhosi Hill, in the state of Brahmavarta on the confluence of the sacred Saraswati and Drishadwati rivers at present in the Aravali mountains along the border of Haryana and Rajasthan. The Padma Purana **(Patala Khanda, Ch.8)** puts the Rishi's hermitage along the Satpura Range, near the river Payoshni.

Chyavana is mentioned in the Rig-Veda, which describes him as an aged and feeble person whose youth and strength was restored by the twin Ashvini Kumar brothers, who were the Rajya Vaid. According to a hymn of this text **(Rg X.61.1-3)**, Because he was closer to the Ashvins, Chyavana was apparently opposed to Turvayana, a Paktha king and Indra worshipper of the day.

BIRTH

According to the narrative, Puloma, who was once in love with Puloma, entered the ashrama while Bhrigu was away. Puloma noticed Agni, the God of fire, present in the fire-pit and questioned him about the true ownership of Puloma, who was married to Bhrigu. Agni, fearing Bhrigu's wrath, honestly explained that although Puloma was married to Bhrigu, it was not done according to the proper Hindu rites.

Upon hearing this, the demon Puloma transformed himself into a swine and took Puloma away. During their journey, Puloma gave birth to a son named Chyavana, who was described as brilliant as the sun. Frightened by the exceptional radiance of the child, the demon Puloma abandoned Puloma and the newborn baby on the way. Puloma returned to the ashrama with her child, weeping throughout the journey and creating a river of tears called Vadhusara.

It is noteworthy that Chyavana Maharishi, born from this union, became a renowned sage in his own right. This story highlights the trials and challenges faced by Puloma and the birth of Chyavana, who went on to make significant contributions in the field of spirituality.

Chyavana's birth is described in Mahabharata, Adi Parva, **Pauloma Parva (Chapters 5-6).** Accordingly, a Rakshasa named Puloma abducts Bhrigu's pregnant wife, also called Puloma. Assuming the form of a boar, he carries her off in the sky during which the child within Puloma forces himself out of the womb in anger, which came to be known as Chyavana.

ततःसगर्भोनविसन्कुक्षौभृगुकुलोद्वह।
रोषान् मातुश्च्युतः कुक्षेश्च्यवनस्तेन सोऽभवत्॥(1/6/2)

The protector of Bhrigu lineage, who was residing in that uterus, pushed himself out of his mother's womb in anger. Because of that he came to be known as Chyavana – the one who fell off from his mother's womb.

तं दृष्ट्वा मातुरुदराच्च्युतमादित्यवर्चसम्।
तद्रक्षो भस्मसाद् भूतं पपात परमिज्जय ताम्॥ (1/6/3)

Seeing that being shining like the Sun, slipping out of his mother's womb, the Rakshasa turned into ashes and releasing her, fell down.

BHRIGU CURSED AGNI

Upon Puloma's return to the ashrama, Sage Bhrigu questioned her about who told her that she was his wife. Puloma narrated the entire incident to Bhrigu, explaining what had transpired in his absence. Angered by the situation, Bhrigu summoned Agni and cursed him, saying, "May you consume everything on this Earth."

Deeply hurt by the curse, Agni withdrew and concealed himself. The absence of Agni caused great disturbance and disorder in all three realms—the heavens, the earth, and the netherworld. Recognizing the gravity of the situation, a delegation of affected beings approached Lord Brahma seeking a resolution. Brahma intervened and modified the curse by declaring that everything Agni touched would become pure.

Consoled by Brahma's modification of the curse, Agni resumed his responsibilities and began purifying things as he had done before. Thus, the balance and order in the worlds were restored, and Agni continued his essential role as the purifier.

ASWINIKUMARAS TESTED SUKANYA

The Devi Bhagavata contains a story of how the Aswini kumaras tested the fidelity of Sukanya, daughter of Saryati and made her old and senile husband into a young and virile one. Saryati, son of Vaivasvata Manu, had four thousand beautiful princesses as wives. But none had any children. When they were lamenting over this misfortune one of the wives gave birth to a girl and she was called Sukanya. The father and all his wives together brought up this daughter with great affection.

In the neighbourhood of the palace of Saryati there was a tapovana as good and grand as Nandanavana and it contained a lake similar to the Manasa Lake. In one corner of this tapovana a sage named Chyavana was doing penance. He had been sitting there for so long a period without food meditating on a goddess that he was covered with plants and shrubs had grown over him. He was unaware of the growth around him.

Once at this time Saryati with his wives and child and followed by a large retinue entered the tapovana for recreation. The King and his wives entered the lake and Sukanya with her friends moved about in the garden plucking flowers and playing. Moving about thus aimlessly Sukanya and party reached the place where Chyavana was doing penance. She saw the huge shrubby growth and while looking at it saw two gleaming points inside the shrubby heap. She was about to break open the thing when from inside she heard somebody addressing her thus: "Oh, innocent girl, why do you think of doing this mischief. Please do go your way. I am an ascetic. What wrong have I done to you for you to disturb me like this?" But Sukanya brought up as she was, as a very spoil girl did not like anybody advising her like this and so taking a pointed stick gave two pricks at the site of the gleam points and left the place arrogantly.

The gleam-points were the eyes of Chyavana and so he lost his eyes and suffered much from the pain. Though he felt angry he did not curse anybody. But slowly the country began to witness the evil effects of this cruel deed. People stopped passing urine or faeces. Even animals were affected. The King and his ministers were worried. People came on deputation to the King to describe the disaster that had gripped the state. The King began to doubt that somebody must have done some great injury to the sage, Chyavana. He started enquiries asking his subjects one by one about this. But everybody replied in the negative. He bribed, he threatened. The result was the same.

Then one day while the King and his courtiers were sitting despondent Sukanya approached her father and confessed what she had done. She said: "While I was playing with my friends in the tapovana I saw this huge shrub-heap and two points gleaming from inside. I took a pin-stick and pricked them both and on drawing it out I found it wet also. But I left the matter there and never made any enquiries thereafter". Saryati now knew the cause of this national disaster and so immediately rushed to the sage for forgiveness. Upon hearing Sukanya's confession, Saryati realized the cause of the calamities that had befallen the kingdom. Deeply remorseful, he immediately went to seek forgiveness from the sage Chyavana. Prostrating before the sage, Saryati pleaded for mercy and said, "O great sage, please forgive us for the unknowing harm that has been done. My daughter, who is innocent and playful, pricked your eyes in jest while she was playing in the garden with her friends. She had no knowledge of what she was doing. O revered sage, you possess great forgiveness, so I implore you to pardon this misdeed and bestow your blessings upon us."

Chyavana, who had been suffering from the pain and loss of his eyes, listened to Saryati's sincere plea. Despite his anger, he was moved by the king's humility and genuine remorse. Recognizing the innocence of

Sukanya's actions, he decided to forgive them. The sage responded, "O King, your daughter acted out of ignorance and innocence. I have witnessed your genuine remorse and humility. I forgive you and your daughter, and may the misfortune that has befallen your kingdom be lifted."

With the sage's forgiveness and blessings, the curse on the kingdom was lifted, and normalcy was restored. The people regained their ability to pass urine and feces, and the disastrous effects gradually subsided. Saryati and his family were grateful for the sage's mercy and continued to live in harmony, cherishing the lessons learned from this incident.

MARRIED TO SUKANYA

Chyavana replied that he would forgive if he gave Sukanya in marriage to him. Saryati was depressed. How could he give his only and beautiful daughter to this aged senile ugly and blind Rishi? Sukanya, understanding the gravity of the situation and the importance of her sacrifice for the welfare of the nation, willingly agreed to marry Chyavana. Despite the initial reluctance of her father, she reassured him and expressed her readiness to fulfill her duty. She said, "Dear father, please do not worry about me. I am willing to go as his wife. If it brings satisfaction to him and saves our nation from calamity, I am prepared to sacrifice my own happiness for the greater good. I am more than glad to do so."

With a heavy heart, Saryati gave his daughter in marriage to Chyavana, accepting her noble decision. Sukanya, after her marriage, devoted herself wholeheartedly to caring for her husband's well-being. She diligently served him by providing him with healthy and delicious fruits and vegetables, bathing him daily in hot water, arranging all the necessary materials for his rituals, and ensuring he had his meals. She sat by his side as he ate, and only after he was satisfied would she attend to her own needs.

After her own meals, Sukanya would return to her husband and sit by his side, giving him massages and attending to his comfort. In the evening, she would prepare everything needed for his worship, and after the rituals, she would nourish him with nutritious food. Whatever remained after his meal, she would consume. At night, she would sleep at the foot of her husband, always attentive to his needs. In the morning, she would diligently assist him with his ablutions and daily routine.

Sukanya lived with unwavering devotion to her husband, constantly striving to please him and ensure his well-being. Her selfless dedication and service were an inspiration to those around her, and she set an example of unconditional love and commitment in her role as a dutiful wife.

ASWINI KUMARAS

The Aswini Kumaras, impressed by Sukanya's beauty and intrigued by her circumstances, approached her and inquired about her situation. Sukanya explained that she was the daughter of Saryati and the wife of Chyavana, a sage who was old and blind. She shared how her father had arranged her marriage with the sage due to certain circumstances, and she had been living with him, dedicated to his well-being.

The Aswini Kumaras, being celestial beings, expressed their admiration for Sukanya's devotion and offered an alternative. They proposed that she should consider marrying one of them, as they believed she deserved a husband superior to the old and blind sage. However, Sukanya firmly rejected their advances and threatened to curse them if they persisted in such talk.

Surprised and somewhat fearful of her response, the Aswini Kumaras praised Sukanya for her righteousness and purity. They acknowledged her steadfastness in remaining faithful to her husband and offered her a boon. As divine physicians of the gods, they had the power to restore Chyavana's sight and rejuvenate him, making him young and virile again. However, they imposed a condition for granting this boon.

Sukanya, intrigued by the offer of the Aswini Kumaras, went back to the ashrama and shared the entire conversation with her husband, Chyavana. She informed him about the proposal and the condition set by the celestial beings. Although Sukanya was pleased with the prospect of seeing her husband young and handsome again, she sought Chyavana's guidance in making the decision.

Chyavana, wise and understanding, reassured Sukanya that there was no need for great deliberation. He instructed her to inform the Aswini Kumaras that she would comply with their wishes and bring them to the ashrama. Sukanya followed her husband's instructions and returned to the Aswini Kumaras, inviting them to visit the ashrama.

Upon their arrival, the Aswini Kumaras requested Chyavana to take a dip in the nearby lake, and they joined him in the waters. As they emerged from the lake, all three of them underwent a transformation, becoming young and handsome, indistinguishable from one another. Now, it was time for

Sukanya to choose her husband among the transformed Aswini Kumaras.

In her dilemma, Sukanya fervently prayed to her personal goddess, seeking the power to identify her true husband. Blessed with divine insight, she was able to recognize Chyavana amidst the identical forms of the Aswini Kumaras. Sukanya confidently chose Chyavana as her husband, and the Aswini Kumaras were pleased with her choice.

This incident is mentioned in the Seventh Skandha of the Devi Bhagavata, showcasing Sukanya's devotion, her husband's wisdom, and the divine intervention that enabled her to make the right decision.

ASWIN KUMARAS SOUGHT SOMA DRINK

After regaining his eyesight and youth, Chyavana fulfilled his promise to the Aswini Kumaras. When King Saryati and his wife visited the ashrama, they were astonished to find a young and handsome ascetic instead of the old sage. Initially, they had doubts about their daughter's situation, but soon their suspicions were dispelled, and they were overjoyed to see the transformation of Chyavana.

Chyavana then informed King Saryati about the request made by the Aswini Kumaras regarding their desire to drink the celestial Soma. The king, supportive of Chyavana and grateful for his daughter's well-being, promised to assist in fulfilling the Aswini Kumaras' request.

Upon their return to the palace, King Saryati arranged for a grand yaga (sacrificial ritual) and invited all the devas, including the Aswini Kumaras. Chyavana assumed the role of the priest for the yaga. However, when the time came to distribute the sacred Soma, Indra objected to the Aswini Kumaras partaking in it, citing their status as physicians of the devas.

Chyavana engaged in a fierce verbal debate with Indra, arguing that the Aswini Kumaras deserved to drink the Soma. Through his persuasive arguments, Chyavana managed to overcome Indra's objections and successfully enabled the Aswini Kumaras to partake in the celestial drink.

This event is mentioned in the Seventh Skandha of the Devi Purana, highlighting Chyavana's fulfillment of his promise and his ability to resolve the conflict between the Aswini Kumaras and Indra, ultimately securing their right to drink the Soma.

ANOTHER VERSION OF THE LIFE OF CHYAVANA

The story of Chyavan's rejuvenation and the involvement of the Aswini Kumaras is further elaborated in different texts, including the Satapatha Brahmanas and the Mahabharata. According to these accounts, Chyavana assumed a withered and abandoned form, which caught the attention of the sons of Saryati, who was a descendant of Manu. The sons playfully pelted clods at Chyavan's body, provoking his anger. To appease him, Saryati offered his daughter Sukanya to Chyavana in marriage.

In the Satapatha Brahmanas version, the Aswini Kumaras attempted to seduce Sukanya, but she remained loyal to her aged and withered husband. She challenged the Aswinis, stating that they were incomplete and imperfect, and offered to reveal their deficiencies if they could make her husband young again. They instructed Chyavana to bathe in a specific pond, and upon doing so, he emerged restored to the age he desired. Sukanya then informed the Aswinis that they were considered imperfect because they were excluded from a sacrifice performed by the other gods. The Aswinis heeded her advice, departed, and eventually succeeded in gaining admission to the other gods' sacrifice.

In the Mahabharata version, Chyavana sought Indra's permission for the Aswinis to partake in the soma libations, but Indra adamantly refused. In response, Chyavana commenced a sacrifice dedicated to the Aswinis, which resulted in the subjugation of the other gods, including Indra. Enraged, Indra attempted to crush Chyavana with a mountain and his thunderbolt. However, Chyavana sprinkled water on Indra, halting his attack, and created a fearsome monster named Mada, with colossal teeth and jaws capable of engulfing the earth and sky. The gods, including Indra, found themselves trapped at the root of the monster's tongue, akin to fishes trapped in the mouth of a sea monster. In this dire situation, Indra ultimately granted Chyavana's demand, leading to the Aswinis gaining the privilege of drinking soma.

These variations highlight the theme of Chyavana's rejuvenation, his connection to the Aswinis, and the circumstances that led to the Aswinis being granted the right to drink soma.

CHYAVANA AND KUSHIKA

Indeed, in the Anushasana Parva of the Mahabharata, there is a narrative involving Chyavana and King Kushika. Chyavana, having been pleased with their devotion and service, rewards the king and queen by creating a magnificent golden palace for them. He also predicts the birth of their grandson, who would possess immense power and ultimately attain the status of a Brahman. This grandson is none other than Vishwamitra, a prominent sage and a central figure in various stories and legends. Vishwamitra journey from being a king to becoming a revered sage is a significant aspect of Hindu mythology.

HERMITAGE

According to the **Padma Purana (Patala Khanda, Ch.8)**, his hermitage was on the Satpura Range, near the river *Payoshni*. According to another tradition, his hermitage was in Dhosi Hill in the Vedic State of Brahmavarta, near Narnaul in Mahendragarh district. Another place claimed to be the location of Chyavana's hermitage (ashram) is Chaunsa in Buxar district of Bihar.

CHAPTER SIX

AURVA

Genealogy: Descending in order from Vishnu, Brahma, Bhrigu, Chyavana, Aurva

BIRTH

Mahabharata, an ancient Hindu epic describes the story of Aurva, a descendant of the Bhrigu dynasty, and his conflict with the Kshatriya (warrior) kings.

According to the story, the Bhrigu dynasty's preceptors, known as the Bhargavas, became wealthy after educating Kartavirya, a famous king of the Haihaya dynasty. However, Kartavirya's sons grew envious of the Bhargavas' wealth and began hunting them down. Fearing for their lives, the Bhargavas fled and sought refuge in caves in distant mountains.

During this period, Arusi, the wife of Chyavana (a Bhargava), was pregnant. To protect her unborn child, she hid the pregnancy by concealing the fetus in her thighs while fleeing. However, a Brahmin woman discovered her secret and informed the Kshatriya kings. They apprehended Arusi, and in the process, her thigh broke, and a boy named Aurva was born.

Aurva, filled with resentment towards the Kshatriyas for the atrocities committed against his ancestors, embarked on rigorous penance. The intensity of his austerities caused the world to start burning. Worried about the consequences of his actions, the Pitrs (ancestors) appeared before him and urged him to stop his penance.

Aurva recounted his deep-seated hatred for the Kshatriyas, which he had developed even while in his mother's womb, upon hearing the cries of their mothers witnessing the beheading of their fathers. The Pitrs, astonished by the strength of his resolve and fearing the outcome of his penance, pleaded with him to desist. Yielding to their request, Aurva withdrew the fiery power of his penance and submerged it in the sea.

It is believed that this fire, in the form of a horse-head, resides beneath the sea and continuously emits heat. It is known as Badavagni.

PREDICTED SAGARA AS EMPEROR

There are various accounts from different Puranas (Hindu scriptures) regarding the interactions and relationships involving King Sagara, his wives Sumati and Kesini, the sage Aurva, and other figures such as Garuda and Parasurama. Here's a summary of the events described:

Subahu and Yadavi: Subahu, a celebrated king of the Ikshvaku dynasty, was defeated by King Talajamgha of the Haihaya dynasty. Subahu's wife, Yadavi, who was pregnant at the time, was poisoned by her jealous co-wives. Subahu and Yadavi sought refuge with Aurva in his ashrama. Subahu eventually died, leaving Yadavi grief-stricken. She was about to end her life, but Aurva stopped her, as she was carrying a child. After a few months, Yadavi gave birth to a son named Sagara, meaning "one with poison" due to the effect of the poison in her womb.

Sumati and Garuda: Sumati, the sister of Garuda (son of Vinata), was cursed by the sage Upaminyu. The curse stated that any Brahmin who married Sumati would have his head burst. To find a solution, Garuda sought the advice of Aurva, who suggested that Sumati marry a Kshatriya instead of a Brahmin. The people of Ayodhya, including Sagara, came in search of Subahu and Yadavi. Upon learning of Subahu's death, they were saddened but glad to find Sagara, Subahu's son. Garuda informed Aurva about Sumati's situation, and Aurva proposed that Sagara marry Sumati to overcome the curse. Sagara, along with the people of Ayodhya, returned to Ayodhya and eventually became the emperor of Bharatavarsha after defeating his enemies.

Sagara's sons: Sagara ruled the land for three thousand years, but he had no sons with either of his wives, Kesini and Sumati. Disheartened, he entrusted the administration to his ministers and went to Aurva's ashrama. Aurva blessed them and prophesied that Kesini would bear a son to continue the dynasty, while Sumati would give birth to sixty thousand sons who would not be of great use. As predicted, Kesini gave birth to a son named Asamanjas, and Sumati gave birth to a lump of flesh. Aurva instructed Sagara to cut the flesh into sixty thousand pieces and place each piece in a jar of ghee. Each year, one prince would be born from one of the jars, resulting in Sumati having sixty thousand sons.

Sagara's later life: In the later years of his life, Sagara stayed in Aurva's ashrama, where Aurva imparted divine knowledge to him. He taught Sagara about the importance of the four ashramas (stages of life), the rituals to be followed by the different castes (Brahmins, Kshatriyas, Vaishyas, and Shudras), and other divine subjects. Finally, Aurva granted Sagara Brahmajnana (knowledge of the Absolute).

Gathering of Bhargava Rishis: At one point, all the Bhargava rishis (sages belonging to the Bhrigu lineage) gathered in Aurva's ashrama. During that time, Parasurama, another renowned sage and an incarnation of Lord Vishnu, visited the ashrama and paid respects to Bhrigu, Khyati (Bhrigu's wife), Chyavana (Bhrigu's son), and Aurva (Chyavana's son)

Ayodhya was once ruled by a celebrated King of Iksvaku dynasty name Subahu. He had as his wife Yadavi a good natured and well behaved woman who was a gem among queens. One day Talajamgha a King of the Haihaya line of rulers who was then the King of Mahismati defeated Subahu in a battle. Yadavi was then pregnant. Jealous co-wives poisoned her; Yadavi did not die but the poison affected the child in the womb. After the defeat, Subahu and Yadavi went and stayed with Aurva in his ashrama. For seven years they lived there and then Subahu died. Grief-stricken Yadavi was about to jump into the funeral pyre and end her life when Aurva stopped her from the act pointing out that she was soon to deliver a child. After a few months she delivered a son and Aurva called him 'Sagara' meaning one with 'gara' (poison) in him. **(Brahmanda Purana, Chapters 16, 17).**

Garuda, son of Vinata, had a sister named Sumati. Upaminyu, a sage, wanted to marry her but neither she nor her relatives liked it. Enraged at this the sage cursed Sumati saying that the Brahmin who married her would have his head burst. The marriage of Sumati thus remained a problem for her parents. There was a friend of Vinata, a sannyasini, living in a forest and to find a way to escape from the curse Vinata sent Garuda to her. The sannyasini advised Garuda to approach Aurva to find a solution for the problem and Aurva was therefore approached for advice. It was at this time that the people of Ayodhya came in search of Subahu and Yadavi who had left them years before. When they knew of Subahu's death they were plunged in sorrow but were glad to know a son of Subahu, Sagara, had grown up to be a successor to Subahu. When Garuda made Aurva acquainted with the pitiable tale of his sister Aurva decreed that Sumati should marry a Kshatriya instead of a Brahmin and thus tide over the curse. He then asked Sagara to marry Sumati and blessed them saying that Sagara would one day become an emperor and perform an Ashvamedha yaga. Aurva then sent Sagara along with the people to Ayodhya where Sagara after defeating all his enemies became the emperor of Bharatavarsa. **(Brahmanda Purana, Chapters 18-21).**

Sagara ruled the land for three thousand years. He had besides Sumati another wife, Kesini. Both of them bore no sons for Sagara. Dejected he entrusted the administration of the state with his ministers and left for the ashrama of Aurva. Aurva blessed them and prophesied that Kesini would deliver a son to continue the dynasty and that Sumati would deliver sixty thousand sons of no great use at all. Sagara and his wives, returned to the palace and very soon both his wives became pregnant.

In due time Kesini delivered a son who was named Asamanjas. But Sumati gave birth to a lump of flesh. Greatly pained the King was about to throw it away when Aurva appeared there and stopped him from doing that. He directed him to cut the piece of flesh into sixty thousand pieces and put one piece each in a jar of ghee. Every year one prince would be born from one of them. Thus Sumati got sixty thousand sons. **(Brahmanda Purana, Chapter 92).**

In the evening of his life Sagara went and stayed in the ashrama of Aurva. Aurva gave him instructions on many a divine subject. He taught him about the importance of the four ashrama, the rituals to be practised by the different castes of Brahman, Ksatriyas, Vaisya and Sudra and many such other things. Finally Aurva gave Sagara Brahmajnana. **(Chapter 8, Ariisam**

3, Vishnu Purana).

All the Bhargava rishees together once stayed in the ashrama of Aurva. Parasurama visited the ashrama one day during that time and paid respects to Bhrigu, Khyati, wife of Bhrigu, Chyavana, son of Bhrigu and Aurva, son of Chyavana. **(Brahmanda Purana, Chapter 63).**

VADAVĀGNI

Later on, the sage Aurva engaged himself in a sacrifice to destroy the followers of Kārtavīryārjuna. He was however dissuaded from doing so. In this process Aurva discharged his anger into the sea, in the form of a horse. This submarine fire came to be known as 'Vaḍavāgni.'

CHILDREN

1. Rucheeka (son) –Grand Father of Parsurama
2. Kandalī (daughter)

AURVYOPAKHYANA: THE STORY OF AURVA
BY RAMESH BANADAKOPPA MANJAPPA

There was a celebrated king of the name of Kartavirya. That bull among the kings of the earth was the disciple of the Veda-knowing Bhrigu's. That king, after performing the Soma sacrifice, gratified the Brahmans with great presents of rice and wealth. After that monarch had ascended to heaven, an occasion came when his descendants were in want of wealth. Knowing that the Bhrigu's were rich, those princes went unto those best of Brahmans, in the guise of beggars. Some amongst the Bhrigu's, to protect their wealth, buried it under earth; and some from fear of the Kshatriya, began to give away their wealth unto other Brahmans; while some amongst them duly gave unto the Kshatriyas whatever they wanted. It happened, however, that some Kshatriyas, in digging as they pleased at the house of particular Bhargava, came upon a large treasure. The treasure was seen by all those bulls among Kshatriyas who had been there. Enraged at what they regarded as the deceitful behavior of the Bhrigu's, the Kshatriyas insulted the Brahmans, though the latter asked for mercy. Those mighty bowmen began to slaughter the Bhrigu's with their sharp arrows. The Kshatriyas wandered over the earth, slaughtering even the embryos that were in the wombs of the women of the Bhrigu race. While the Bhrigu race was thus being exterminated, the women of that tribe fled from fear to the inaccessible mountains of Himavat. One amongst these women, desiring to perpetuate her husband's race, held in one of her thighs an embryo endued with great energy. A certain Brahman woman, however, who came to know this fact, went from fear unto the Kshatriyas and reported the matter unto them. The Kshatriyas then went to destroy that embryo. Arrived at the place, they beheld the would-be mother blazing with inborn energy, and the child that was in her thigh came out tearing up the thigh and dazzling the eyes of those Kshatriyas like the midday sun. Thus deprived of their eyes, the Kshatriyas began to wander over those inaccessible mountains. Distressed at the loss of sight, the princes were afflicted with woe, and desirous of regaining the use of their eyes they resolved to seek the protection of that faultless woman. Then those Kshatriyas, afflicted with sorrow, and from loss of sight like unto a fire that has gone out, addressed with anxious hearts that illustrious lady, saying,

"By your grace, O lady, we wish to be restored to sight. We shall then return to our homes all together and abstain for ever from our sinful practice. It beholds you with your child to show us mercy. It beholds you to favour these kings by granting them their eye-sight."

The Brahman lady, thus addressed by them, said,

"You children, I have not robbed you of your eye-sight, nor am I angry with you. This child, however, of the Bhrigu race has certainly been angry with you. There is little doubt, you children, that you have been robbed of your sight by that illustrious child whose wrath has been kindled at the remembrance of the slaughter of his race. You children, while you were destroying even the embryos of the Bhrigu race, this child was held by me in my thigh for a hundred years! In order that the prosperity of Bhrigu's race might be restored, the entire Vedas with their branches came unto this one even while he was in the womb. It is plain that this scion of the Bhrigu race, enraged at the slaughter of his fathers, desires to slay you! It is by his celestial energy that your eyes have been scorched. Therefore, you children, pray you unto this my excellent child born of my thigh. Propitiated by your homage he may restore your eye-sight."

Hearing those words of the Brahman lady, all these princes addressed the thigh-born child, saying, "Be propitious!" And the child became propitious unto them. That best of Brahman Rishi's, in consequence of his having been born after tearing open his mother's thigh, came to be known throughout the three worlds by the name of Aurva (thigh-born). Those princes regaining their eye-sight went away. But the Muni Aurva of the Bhrigu race resolved upon overcoming the whole world. The high-souled Rishi set his heart, upon the destruction of every creature in the world. That scion of the Bhrigu race, for paying homage unto his slaughtered ancestors, devoted himself to the austerity of penances with the object of destroying the whole world. Desirous of gratifying his ancestors, the Rishi afflicted by his severe asceticism the three worlds with the celestials, the Asuras and human beings. The Pitrs, then, learning what the child of their race was about, all came from their own region unto the Rishi and addressing him said:

"Aurva, O son, fierce you has been in your asceticism. Your power has been witnessed by us. Be propitious unto the three worlds. Control your wrath. O child, it was not from incapacity that the Bhrigu's of souls under complete control were, all of them, indifferent to their own destruction at the hands of the murderous Kshatriyas. When we grew weary of the long periods of life allotted to us, it was then that we desired our own destruction through the instrumentality of the Kshatriyas. The wealth that the Bhrigu's had placed in their house underground had been placed only with the object of enraging the Kshatriyas and picking a quarrel with them. As we were desirous of heaven, of what use could wealth be to us? The treasurer of heaven Kubera had kept a large treasure for us. When we found that death could not, by any means, overtake us all, it was then, that we regarded this as the best means of compassing our desire. They who commit suicide never attain to regions that are blessed. Reflecting upon this, we abstained from self-destruction. That which, therefore you desire to do is not agreeable to us. Restrain your mind, therefore, from the sinful act of destroying the whole world. Destroy neither the Kshatriyas nor the seven worlds. Kill this wrath of yours that stains your ascetic energy."

Hearing these words of the Pitrs, Aurva, replied unto them to this effect:

"You Pitrs, the vow I have made from anger for the destruction of all the worlds, must not go in vain. I cannot consent to be one whose anger and vows are futile. Like fire consuming dry woods, this rage of mine will certainly consume me if I do not accomplish my vow. The man that represses his wrath that has been excited by adequate cause becomes incapable of duly compassing the three ends of life. The wrath that kings desirous of subjugating, the whole earth exhibit, is not without its uses. It serves to restrain the wicked and to protect the honest. While lying unborn within my mother's thigh, I heard the doleful cries of my mother and other women of the Bhrigu race who were then being exterminated by the Kshatriyas. You Pitrs, when those wretches of Kshatriyas began to exterminate the Bhrigu's together with unborn children of their race, it was then that wrath filled my soul. My mother and the other women of our race, each in an advanced state of pregnancy, and my father, while terribly alarmed, found not in all the worlds a single protector. Then when the Bhrigu women found not a single protector, my mother held me in one of her thighs. If there be a punisher of crimes in the worlds no one in all the worlds would dare commit a crime; if he finds not a punisher, the number of sinners become large. The man having the power to prevent or punish sin not does so knowing that a sin has been committed is he defiled by that sin? When kings and others, capable of protecting my fathers, protect them not, postponing that duty preferring the pleasures of life, I have just cause to be enraged with them. I am the lord of the creation, capable of punishing its iniquity. I am incapable of obeying your command. Capable of punishing this crime, if I abstain from so doing, men will once more have to undergo a similar persecution. The fire of my wrath too that is ready to consume the worlds, if repressed, will certainly consume by its own energy my own self. You masters, I know that you ever seek the good of the worlds: direct me, therefore, as to what may benefit both me and the worlds."

The Pitrs replied saying,

"Throw this fire that is born of your wrath and that desires to consume the worlds, into the waters. That will do you good. The worlds, indeed, are all dependent on water. Every juicy substance contains water, indeed the whole universe is made of water. Therefore, cast you this fire of your wrath into the waters. If, therefore, you desire it, let this fire born of your wrath abide in the great ocean, consuming the waters thereof, for it has been said that the worlds are made of water. In this way, your word will be rendered true, and the worlds with the gods will not be destroyed."

Then, Aurva cast the fire of his wrath into the abode of Varuna. And that fire, which consumes the waters of the great ocean, became like unto a large horse's head which persons conversant with the Vedas call by the name of Vadavamukha. And emitting itself from that mouth it consumes the waters of the mighty ocean.

CHAPTER SEVEN

RUCHEEKA (AJIGARTA) – HIS GRANDFATHER

Genealogy: Descending in order from Vishnu, Brahma, Bhrigu, Chyavana, Aurva, Rucheeka

In the world of sages and seers, there is a genealogy that traces its origins from Vishnu. From Vishnu, the lineage of Brahma and the Bhrigu lineage descended. The Bhrigu Vansha is highly revered and renowned, and its progenitor is Bhrigu Maharishi, who was born from the skin of the creator Brahma. All those belonging to this lineage are known as Bhargavas. Chyavana was the son of Bhrigu, and Aurva was Chyavan's son. Rucheeka, also known as Rucheeka Maharishi, was the son of Aurva. Rucheeka possessed immense tapas (deep and intense meditation) and was committed to truth. He had complete knowledge of Dhanurvidya, the Vedic science of archery. He held all four Vedas in his hands, metaphorically depicted as gooseberries. Rucheeka was the father of Jamadagni and the grandfather of Parasurama.

Rucheeka, the great Atharvan Rishi and revered fire worshipper of Aryavarta, was well-versed in Yantra Mantra Vidya and had complete authority over Atharvaveda. He was worshipped everywhere due to the eternal light emanating from his austere and powerful body. His curse fell upon King Mahismati and his Haihaya lineage, leading to the downfall of their religious principles and disorderly kingdom. Rucheeka, disdained by the Haihaya caste, settled on the banks of Saraswati. The thrones of mighty kingdoms used to bow before him, as he was the harbinger of spiritual purification and possessed Brahma Vidya (knowledge of the Supreme). His very breath emitted the sacred sound of Omkara. The curse he pronounced became the cause of the Haihaya caste's decline.

Jamadagni, the righteous son of Rishi Rucheeka, was a taponidhi (a treasure of penance) with pure and contemplative thoughts. He lived a secluded and conscientious life, dedicated to teaching and righteousness.

SOUGHT KINGS DAUGHTER HAND FOR MARRIAGE

In the lineage of Lunar Vansha, King Gaadhi, also known as Kusika, was the ruler. His daughter, Satyawati, possessed extraordinary beauty. One day, Rucheeka Maharishi, captivated by Satyawati's beauty, approached King Gaadhi and expressed his desire to marry her. He confessed that his heart, mind, and intellect were completely captivated by her. Though taken aback, the king could not deny the request of a Brahmin.

However, King Gaadhi, being aware of the Maharishi's power, cleverly placed a condition before granting his daughter's hand in marriage. He demanded that Rishi Rucheeka bring him 1,000 white horses with black ears. The king believed that the sage, being a poor Brahmin, would be unable to fulfill such a request.

Undeterred, Rishi Rucheeka agreed to the condition and departed. He went to the north bank of the river Ganga, bathed, and began to perform penance to Varuna, the deity associated with water and rivers. Varuna, pleased with the sage's devotion, appeared before him and granted him the ability to summon the horses whenever he desired. As a result, a thousand characteristic horses, white with black ears, emerged from the river Ganga.

With the horses created by him, Rishi Rucheeka returned to the king. King Gaadhi was astonished by the sage's ability but felt pleased to have such a son-in-law. He fulfilled his promise and performed the marriage between Rucheeka and Satyawati. Afterward, the newlywed couple went and settled in the forest.

As part of the dowry, Gaadhi presented Rucheeka with the 1,000 white horses with black ears, which were given to him by Varuna. The place on the banks of the Ganga where the horses rose up came to be known as "Asvatirtha." The wedding ceremony took place at a location called 'Kanyakubja'.

Rucheeka was given 1,000 white horses with black ears which could run fast, by Gaadhi as dowry. Varuna presented these horses on the bank of the river Ganga. The place in Ganga where the horses rose up came to be called "Asvatirtha". Gaadhi gave Satyawati to Rucheeka at the place called 'Kanyakubja'. **(M.B. Aranya Parva, Chapter 115)**

BIRTH OF JAMADAGNI

Upon hearing Satyawati's concerns about the lack of an heir to the throne, Rucheeka, being a wise and compassionate sage, understood her worries. Rucheeka belonged to a lineage of great Rishis and Gurus known as Bhrugukul, who were renowned for their wisdom and teaching abilities. In their lineage, the emphasis was on education and spirituality rather than ruler ship. During the Vedic period, the four-tier system of Varnas (social classes) did not exist, and individuals had the freedom to choose their Varna based on personal preference or family tradition. Women from influential families or clans such as Ikshwaku, Yadavas, Puru, Panchal, Chandravansha, and Atri often married Rishis from the Bhrugukul or Brahmankul.

Satyawati shared her desire with Rucheeka to have a son who could be an heir to the kingdom. Additionally, she requested that her mother be blessed with a son, so she could have a brother. Understanding her wishes, Rucheeka performed a homa (a sacred fire ritual) and prepared two rice balls. He infused one rice ball with "Brahmatejas" (the brilliance of Brahmins) and the other with "Ksatratejas" (the brilliance of Kshatriyas).

Rucheeka instructed Satyawati to eat one rice ball and give the other to her mother. However, due to a mistake, Satyawati consumed the rice ball meant for her mother, while her mother consumed the one intended for her. When Rucheeka learned of this error, he realized that Satyawati had consumed the rice ball with Brahmatejas, and her mother had consumed the rice ball with Ksatratejas.

In due course, both Satyawati and her mother gave birth to sons. Satyavati's son was named Visvamitra, who inherited the brilliance of Brahmins, and her mother gave birth to a son who possessed the brilliance of Kshatriyas.

This incident holds significant influence in the life of Lord Parashurama, who was born in the same lineage.

BLESS MY MOTHER TOO -TO HAVE A MALE OFFSPRING

The other version of the birth of Jamadagni says that once Rucheeka went to his ashram with his wife. Satyawati served him as an ideal wife. Time went by. The newly wedded couple longed to have a perfect son and performed a penance. One day the maharishi thought of begetting progeny (children). He went to his wife and told her that time is favorable for them and that she would become a mother. Satyawati was immensely pleased. She requested her husband for another blessing. "Swami! You have rich power of penance. You can do anything. My mother asked me to seek your blessing for her also. She has no male offspring. Bless her with your grace to have a son."

The Maharishi listened to his better-half request. Immediately he created with his powers two blessed food balls of boiled rice (Charuvus) and two havis (ghee in the yajna). Of these one Charuvus would give an effulgent son into tejas (great radiance) and the other a valorous and heroic son. One would be a pious and devout Brahmin and the other a warrior like Kshatriya. Showing the two blessed balls of cooked rice the maharishi told his wife. "While you are in your monthly period you embrace a fig tree. You ask your mother to embrace in her periods a Peepal tree. Later you take the ball of cooked rice which would make you give birth to an effulgent and devout Brahmin. Your mother takes the other ball of cooked rice which would make her give birth to a valorous and invincible Kshatriya like son." So telling the Maharishi went to the river for a bath. King Gaadhi and his queen came to sage Rucheeka ashram to see their daughter and son-in-law. Satyawati honoured her parents. She showed the blessed cooked rice balls to her mother. She told her what they were asked to do. Since both of them happened to be in their periods, they went to the trees to embrace them. By Gods will the fig tree that should be embraced by Satyawati was embraced by her mother. The Peepal tree that should be embraced by her mother was embraced by the daughter.

The mother and daughter also took the Charuvus wrongly. Maharishi Rucheeka returned to his ashrama and was happy to see his in-laws. While in conversation, the Maharishi saw in his divine vision (divya drushti) the mistake. The mother and daughter made the same mistake. He called his wife and told her: "The saying that one thinks of something God thinks of something and else is true. You and your mother have made an error in embracing the trees and taking the blessed cooked rice balls. For that reason there would be a difference in the sons you give birth to as prescribed. You give birth not to a splendid son with Brahmin effulgence-but to a cruel one, a killer of Kshatriya and your mother would give birth to a son with the radiance of a devout taapasvi.

Satyawati trembled listening to her husband's words. She broke into tears and fell at the rishi's feet, praying for his mercy and kindness. She prayed to him not to give her a son who would be cruel. The merciful Rishi took pity on his wife. But the blessed cooked rice balls he created will surely give the effect they believed to produce. The Maharishi thought that this was all Gods will and doing. Satyawati insisted upon having a Brahman son. However, Rucheeka Rishi denied the possibility. Now Satyawati requested to have at least the grandson should have the Brahman qualities if not the son. As a result of the exchange, after nine months at an auspicious moment, Satyawati and her mother delivered male babies. Gaadhi the king's son was named Vishwamitra. Rucheeka named his son Jamadagni. After Jamadagni, three more sons were born to Rucheeka. The eldest of them was named Sunahpuccha; the second was named Sunasgepha and the third, Sunolangula. Jamadagni was a born in Bhrigu clan so he spent his life in pious activities but he became hot tempered like a Kshatriya. His son Lord Parasurama had qualities of both the families. He is supposed to have both Brahma and Tej (Knowledge and Power). Rucheeka assured Satyawati that he would change the effect in another way. The cruelty would come to her grandson and not to her son. This comforted Satyawati a little bit.

SALE OF A SON FOR COWS

In this episode involving King Ambarisa, Indra, Rucheeka, and Visvamitra, it begins with King Ambarisa conducting a yajna (sacrificial ritual). However, Indra, feeling jealous of the king's prosperity, stole the sacrificial cow, which was considered an evil omen. The priests advised Ambarisa that either the lost cow must be found or a human substitute must be obtained to complete the yajna.

Ambarisa's men, in their search for the cow, eventually came across Rucheeka, who was deep in tapas (austerity) on the banks of the Bhrgutuiiga River. Rucheeka, in exchange for the price of 100,000 cows, sold his second son, Sunasgepha, to Ambarisa. The king took Sunasgepha with him and arrived at the Puskara tirtha (sacred place).

At Puskara tirtha, they encountered Visvamitra, who sympathized with Sunasgepha upon hearing of his plight. Visvamitra wanted to save Sunasgepha and offered to send one of his own sons in his place with Ambarisa. However, none of Visvamitra's sons were willing to oblige, and as a result, Visvamitra cursed them, transforming them into beings who consumed human flesh.

Visvamitra then turned to Sunasgepha and advised him that when he stood ready to be sacrificed near the altar, he should offer his prayers to Agni (the fire deity). He also taught him two songs of praise to Agni. Following Visvamitra's instructions, Sunasgepha recited the songs of praise to Agni while standing at the altar, prepared to be sacrificed.

As a result of Sunasgepha's prayers and invocations, Indra and the other gods appeared, saving him from the sacrificial fire. In recognition of Ambarisa's yajna and Sunasgepha's ordeal, the gods rewarded Ambarisa and brought a successful conclusion to the yajna.

This episode can be found in the Balakanda (Book of Youth) of Valmiki's Ramayana in the 62nd Sarga (chapter).

RUCHEEKA GOT A BOW FROM VISHNU

According to the stories mentioned in various scriptures such as the Ramayana and Mahabharata, Vishvakarma, the divine architect, created two powerful bows. One bow, known as Saivacapa, was given to Lord Shiva, while the other, called Vaisnavacapa, was given to Lord Vishnu.

The Devas (gods) wanted to determine who among Shiva and Vishnu was more powerful, so they instigated Brahma to create a conflict between them. Brahma succeeded in causing a quarrel between Shiva and Vishnu, leading to a fierce battle. Both Shiva and Vishnu wielded their respective bows, Saivacapa and Vaisnavacapa, in the fight. However, in the end, Vishnu emerged victorious over Shiva.

After the battle, Shiva gave his bow, Saivacapa, to King Devarata of Videha (also known as Janaka), and it eventually came into the possession of Janaka's daughter, Sita. The broken pieces of this bow were later witnessed at the Svayamvara (marriage ceremony) of Sita, where Lord Rama, an incarnation of Vishnu, demonstrated his strength by stringing and breaking the bow to win Sita's hand in marriage.

As for the Vaisnavacapa, after Vishnu's victory over Shiva, he gave his bow to the sage Rucheeka as a gift. Rucheeka, in turn, passed on the Vaisnavacapa to his son, Jamadagni. The bow then came into the possession of Parasurama, who confronted Sri Rama, another incarnation of Vishnu, when Rama returned from Sita's Svayamvara.

These accounts can be found in various chapters of the Ramayana, including the Balakanda, Sarga 75, as well as in the Anuasana Parva of the Mahabharata, Chapter 137, Verse 28.

ATTAINED VAIKUNTHA

According to the ancient scriptures, Rucheeka, a revered sage from the lineage of Bhrigu, achieved a great spiritual feat and attained Vaikuntha, the celestial abode of Lord Vishnu. His unwavering devotion and spiritual practices elevated him to the divine realm, where he would reside in eternal bliss.

During this transcendent journey, Rucheeka's devoted wife, Satyawati, who possessed immense virtue and righteousness, accompanied him. However, rather than transcending her earthly form like her husband, Satyawati chose to retain her physical existence and continue her divine journey in the mortal realm.

In the epic Mahabharata, specifically in the Asva medhika Parva, Chapter 29, Verse 23, it is mentioned that Satyawati, in her earthly body, joined Rucheeka in his ascent to Vaikuntha. This emphasizes her unwavering dedication and love for her husband, as she willingly embraced the path of accompanying him to the divine realm even while remaining in her human form.

In the Valmlki Ramayana, Balakanda, 34th Sarga, another facet of Satyavati's transformation is revealed. It is believed that after Rucheeka's ascension and her own accompanying journey to Vaikuntha, Satyawati transformed herself into a majestic river known as "Kausiki." This transformation allowed her to continue her divine presence in the mortal realm, albeit in the form of a sacred river.

The river Kausiki, flowing through the northern regions of India, became an embodiment of Satyawati's grace and spirituality. It served as a reminder of her remarkable journey and eternal connection with Rucheeka, as well as symbolizing her continued influence and blessings on the land she now traversed.

These accounts from ancient scriptures capture the ethereal nature of Rucheeka and Satyawati's spiritual attainment. While Rucheeka transcended his mortal form to reside in Vaikuntha, Satyawati, in her immense devotion, chose to remain in her earthly body and became a divine river, spreading her divine essence and bestowing her blessings upon those who encountered her sacred waters.

CHAPTER EIGHT

JAMADAGNI

Genealogy: Descending in order from Vishnu, Brahma, Bhrigu, Chyavana, Aurva, Rucheeka , Jamadagni

In the esteemed lineage of sages and seers, the genealogy traces its origins back to Lord Vishnu, the preserver of the universe. From Vishnu, the lineage branches out to include the esteemed lineage of Bhrigu, known as the Bhrigu Vansha. This lineage holds great reverence and renown among the spiritual and scholarly circles.

The progenitor of this illustrious lineage is Bhrigu Maharishi himself, who was born from the skin of Lord Brahma, the creator of the universe. All the descendants of this lineage are known as Bhargavas, honoring their connection to Bhrigu.

Chyavana, the son of Bhrigu, played an important role in continuing the lineage. He was succeeded by his son Aurva, who in turn had a son named Rucheeka. Rucheeka, known for his wisdom and spiritual prowess, carried the lineage forward.

Among the notable figures in this lineage is Jamadagni, a revered sage renowned for his extraordinary power and virtues. He was the son of Rucheeka and the father of Parasurama, an incarnation of Lord Vishnu. Jamadagni is referred to by various names, each signifying his exalted status. Some of these names include Arclka, Bhargava, Bhar-gavanandana, Bhrguiiardula, Bhrgusrestha, Bhrguttama, and Rclkaputra. These names were used by the sage Vyasa to describe Jamadagni in the epic Mahabharata, also known as Bharata.

The rich lineage of Bhrigu, spanning from Lord Vishnu to Bhrigu Maharishi and further down to Jamadagni, showcases the wisdom, spiritual strength, and noble character that flowed through generations. Their contributions to the spiritual and cultural landscape of ancient India continue to inspire and guide seekers on the path of righteousness and self-realization.

THE BIRTH OF JAMADAGNI

Indeed, the birth of Jamadagni, the renowned sage, carries an intriguing story. Rucheeka, his father, performed a sacred ritual known as homa, and following the ritual, he created two balls of rice with distinct intentions. He gave these rice-balls to his wife Satyawati, instructing her to consume one and offer the other to her mother.

In these rice-balls, Rucheeka had infused the divine brilliance of the Brahmins, known as "Brahmatejas," into one, and the radiant power of the Kshatriyas, called "Ksatratejas," into the other. However, a twist of fate occurred when Satyawati and her mother secretly swapped the pots containing the rice-balls, resulting in Satyawati consuming the rice infused with Kshatriya radiance, while her mother ingested the rice filled with the brilliance of Brahmins.

As the children grew within their respective wombs, the effects of the divine radiance became visible on their faces. Satyawati bore the appearance of Kshatriyateja, the radiance of the Kshatriyas, while her mother exhibited the glow of Brahmatejas, the brilliance of the Brahmins. Eventually, both Satyawati and her mother gave birth simultaneously. Satyawati became the mother of Jamadagni, embodying the Kshatriya radiance, while her mother gave birth to Visvamitra, who possessed the divine brilliance of the Brahmins.

Due to this unique circumstance, different Puranas present varying accounts of their relationship. Some Puranas describe Visvamitra as the uncle of Jamadagni, highlighting their distinct lineages, while others depict them as brothers, acknowledging their shared heritage and the intertwining of their destinies.

This tale showcases the intricate interplay of divine radiance, the consequences of hidden actions, and the subsequent birth of two extraordinary beings that left an indelible mark on the annals of mythology and spirituality. **(Brahmanda Purana, Chapter 57)**

HIS MARRIAGE

When Jamadagni grew up he made a tour and visited the holy places one by one and reached the palace of King Prasenajit of the family of Iksvaku dynasty. He saw Renuka the beautiful daughter of King Prasenajit and fell in love with her. He requested Prasenajit for the hand of Renuka. The King, without raising any objection gave his daughter Renuka in marriage to Jamadagni. The couple came to the bank of the river Narmada and erecting a hermitage began 'tapas' (penance). Four sons, Rumanvan, Suhotra, Vasu and Visvavasu were born to Jamadagni by Renuka. **(Brahmanda Purana, Chapter 58)** .

After their marriage, Jamadagni and Renuka settled on the banks of the river Narmada, where they established a hermitage and devoted themselves to penance and spiritual practices. In due course, they were blessed with four sons named Rumanvan, Suhotra, Vasu, and Visvavasu, who would play significant roles in their future lineage.

Meanwhile, Maharshi Rucheeka, Jamadagni's father, embarked on his own spiritual journey. He initially resided at Kotitirtha, situated along the banks of the river Godavari in present-day Andhra Pradesh. Spending several years in prayer and meditation at his ashram, Rucheeka eventually traveled northward and continued his tapas (meditation) on the banks of the river Ganga.

During this time, the region was under the rule of King Renu. Maharshi Rucheeka, recognizing the virtues of the king's daughter, Princess Renuka, advised the king to organize a svayamvara, a grand ceremony where eligible suitors would compete for the hand of the princess. Numerous kings and gods attended the event, all vying for Princess Renuka's hand in marriage. However, she chose Rishi Jamadagni as her husband, following her heart's desire.

In recognition of their union, Princess Renuka received precious gifts from the king of gods, Lord Indra. Among these divine gifts were the Kalpa Vriksha, a wish-fulfilling tree, the Chintamani, a mystical gem capable of granting any desire, and the Kamadhenu, a sacred cow known for its ability to provide endless abundance and fulfill all needs. These gifts would later play significant roles in the life of Lord Parashurama, one of the sons of Jamadagni and Renuka.

Jamadagni, entrusted by his father, took on the responsibility of managing the various ashrams scattered throughout the country. One of these ashrams was located on the banks of the river Malaprabha, near Belgaum-Saundatti in present-day Karnataka. While Renuka oversaw the affairs of this ashram, Jamadagni would travel to other ashrams, fulfilling his duties and spreading the teachings of their lineage.

THE SUN GAVE JAMADAGNI AN UMBRELLA AND SANDALS

The story of Lord Surya gifting an umbrella and a pair of sandals to Jamadagni is indeed mentioned in the Mahabharata, specifically in the Anusasana Parva (Chapter 95-96) of the Dana Dharma Parva.

During one of Jamadagni's archery practice sessions, he requested his wife Renuka to retrieve the arrows he shot. On this particular day, the sun's rays were exceptionally intense, causing Renuka's head and feet to be scorched by the heat. Despite the pain, she managed to bring back the arrows but was delayed.

Upon seeing this, Jamadagni, in his anger, questioned Renuka about her delay in returning with the arrows. Renuka explained the ordeal she faced due to the intense heat of the sun's rays, which made her seek shelter under a tree. Understanding her plight, Jamadagni decided to destroy the sun with his powerful arrows.

However, Lord Surya, witnessing Jamadagni wrath, assumed the form of a Brahman and approached the sage. He explained the importance of the sun for sustaining life on Earth. But despite the explanations, Jamadagni insisted on bringing the sun down.

In response, Lord Surya, out of respect for Jamadagni's power, placed himself under the sage's protection. Jamadagni then requested a remedy to alleviate the intense rays of the sun that affect people. In response to his plea, Lord Surya presented Jamadagni with an umbrella and a pair of sandals as a solution to protect people from the scorching heat of his rays.

This divine gift from Lord Surya, the umbrella to shield the head and the sandals to protect the feet, served as a remedy to mitigate the harmful effects of the sun's intensity and ensure the well-being of people on Earth.

एतावदक्कृत्वा स तदा तूष्णमिासदि् भगृतु्तम : |
अथ सूर्योऽददृत तसृमै छतृरो पानहमाशृवै ||13 ||

'So saying, that excellent descendant of Bhrigu remained silent for a while, and Surya forthwith made over to him an umbrella and a pair of sandals.'"

सूर्यउवाच
अदृयपृरभतृर चिवैहृ लोके संपृरचरषिृयति ||
पुणृयकषेृ च सरृवेषृ परमकृषयृयमवेच ||15 ||

Surya said, 'Do thou, O great Rishi, take this umbrella wherewith the head may be protected and my rays warded off. This pair of sandals is made of leather for the protection of the feet. From this day forth the gift of these articles in all religious rites shall be established as an inflexible usage!'"

This custom of giving umbrellas and shoes was introduced by Surya! O descendant of Bharata, these gifts are considered meritorious in the three worlds. Do thou, therefore, give away umbrellas and shoes to Brahmans? I have no doubt that thou shall then acquire great religious merit by the act.

This story is mentioned in **MahabharataChapters 95 and 96, Anusasana Parva, M.B** of how footwear and umbrella were born. Once the heat of the Sun became unbearable to Jamadagni and enraged at this the sage started sending arrows against the Sun. His wife Renuka was supplying him with arrows. When a set of arrows was finished Renuka brought another set. This continued without break and the Sun began to feel the attack. Unable to do anything against the sage the Sun heated the head and foot of Renuka on her way to supply the arrows so fiercely that Renuka fell down under a banyan tree exhausted. When she became well enough to walk, she took the arrows to her husband who was very angry for her being late. She then explained to him how because of the extreme heat of the sun she fell down on the way. Jamadagni then started with increased fury his shower of arrows and the Sun in the disguise of a Brahmin approached and advised him that it was not possible to strike down the Sun because he was a swift-mover in the sky and so it was better to withdraw from that attempt. But Jamadagni said the Sun would be stationary for some time at midday and then he would hit the Sun down. When the Sun found that Jamadagni would never drop his attempt he accepted defeat and presented Jamadagni with a pair of sandals and an umbrella to protect against the heat from below and above. From that day onwards footwear and umbrella came into vogue. The practice of presenting sandals and umbrella is being carried down from generation to generation and even today it is being followed; these two are given as gifts on the 'Sraddha' day.

THE TEMPTATION OF DHARMA

Jamadagni is indeed a prominent figure in Hindu mythology and is mentioned in various ancient texts, including the Rig-Veda, Atharvaveda, Yajurveda Samhitas, and the Brahmanas. He is depicted as a revered sage and is associated with several other renowned sages such as Visvamitra, Vasishtha, Atri, Kanva, Asita, and Vitahavya.

In the Rig-Veda, Jamadagni is mentioned both as the author of hymns and as an individual referred to in different contexts. He is sometimes linked with Visvamitra, indicating a close association or collaboration between the two sages.

Jamadagni's ritual prowess is highlighted in the texts, particularly his family's successful performance of the "catūrātra" or "four-night" ritual. This ritual played a significant role in their prosperity and spiritual accomplishments.

Additionally, Jamadagni is mentioned as an adhvaryu priest during the proposed sacrifice of Sunahsepa in the Atharvaveda. His association with other revered sages suggests his active participation in Vedic rituals and scholarly pursuits.

According to the Mahabharata, Jamadagni delved deeply into the study of the Vedas and gained comprehensive knowledge of these sacred scriptures. His devotion to learning and his mastery of the Vedas earned him great respect and recognition.

Overall, Jamadagni is depicted as a highly esteemed sage, renowned for his rituals, knowledge of the Vedas, and associations with other prominent sages in Hindu mythology.

JAMADAGNI VISITED RAJA RAM ON HIS RETURN

As per Uttar Ramayana, Jamadagni was one of the hermits, who visited Sri Rama on his return from forest life. The hermits who came to Ayodhya from the North were, Kasyapa, Bharadwaja, the Sanakas, Sarabhariga, Durvasas, Matanga, Vibhandaka, Tumburu and the Saptarsis (the seven hermits).

UDAYANA GREW UP IN THE HERMITAGE OF JAMADAGNI.

The Vasavadatta episode is a well-known and captivating story in the life of King Udayana (formerly known as Sahasranika) of Vatsa. It revolves around his love affair with Princess Vasavadatta, the daughter of King Pradyota of Avanti.

One day, Udayana sees a painting of Princess Vasavadatta and falls deeply in love with her. He becomes obsessed with the desire to marry her. However, the king of Avanti, King Pradyota, is known for his arrogance and has set a challenge for any suitor who wishes to marry his daughter. The challenge is that the suitor must solve a series of riddles posed by Vasavadatta herself, and failure to answer them would result in death.

Undeterred by the challenge, Udayana, with the help of his minister, Vasantaka, sets off to Avanti to win the hand of Princess Vasavadatta. Along the way, they encounter various adventures and obstacles. Udayana's intelligence, wit, and bravery are put to the test as he overcomes these challenges.

When Udayana finally reaches Avanti, he faces the riddles posed by Vasavadatta. With his sharp intellect and quick thinking, Udayana successfully answers all the riddles, impressing Vasavadatta and earning her admiration.

The love between Udayana and Vasavadatta blossoms, and they are married amidst great joy and celebration. The story highlights their deep love, loyalty, and the triumph of Udayana's intelligence and perseverance.

The Vasavadatta episode is a popular tale of love, adventure, and wit, showcasing the extraordinary qualities of King Udayana and the power of true love. It is often celebrated for its romantic and dramatic elements and has been a subject of numerous adaptations in literature and performing arts throughout history.

JAMADAGNI & MAHABHARTA

Jamadagni was present at the Janmotsava (birth celebration) of Arjuna son of King Pandu and Kunti. **(M.B. Adi Parva, Chapter 122, Stanza 51)** . Jamadagni is a luminary in the assembly of Brahma. **(M.B. Sabha Parva, Chapter 11, Stanza 22)**.During the time of the battle of Mahabharata, Jamadagni visited Kuruksetra and advised Drona to stop the battle. **(M.B. Drona Parva, Chapter 190, Stanza 35)**. Jamadagni once delivered a speech on the bad sides of accepting rewards, to the King Vrsadarbhi.**(M.B. Anusasana Parva, Chapter 93, Stanza 44)** .

JAMADAGNI VOWED HIS INNOCENCE OF STEALING OF AGASTYA'S LOTUS

It is indeed an interesting episode involving Agastya, Indra, and the hermits. In this tale, Agastya grows lotus flowers at Brahmasaras, a holy place in the Kausiki region. When a group of hermits, led by Indra, arrives there during their pilgrimage, they secretly pluck and eat the lotus flowers.

Agastya, upon discovering the theft, becomes furious and begins searching for the culprit. However, none of the hermits confess to the theft, denying any involvement. Eventually, Agastya catches hold of Indra and accuses him of being the thief. In response, Indra explains that he was driven by his eagerness to listen to Agastya's teachings on duty, which led him to take the lotus flowers.

Realizing Indra's sincerity and his eagerness to learn, Agastya is pleased. Indra returns the lotus flowers, and Agastya allows him and the other hermits to leave peacefully, without any further repercussions.

This story highlights the theme of humility and the importance of seeking knowledge. Indra's eagerness to learn from Agastya and his sincere admission of his actions reflect his humility. Agastya, in turn, recognizes Indra's sincerity and forgives him, emphasizing the value of forgiveness and understanding.

These tales from Hindu mythology often carry deeper moral and philosophical lessons, encouraging virtues such as humility, forgiveness, and the pursuit of knowledge.

Jamadagni vowed that he was innocent in the affair of the stealing of Agastya's lotus. Once Bhrigu, Vasiṣṭha and other hermits went on a pilgrimage, with Indra as their leader. On the way they reached Brahmasaras, in the holy place of Kausiki. Agastya had grown some lotus flowers there. The pilgrims plucked stealthily all the lotus flowers nurtured by Agastya and ate them. The furious Agastya got into the midst of the hermits in search of the culprit. None admitted the theft. Finally he caught hold of Indra, as the thief. Indra said "O, Lord, had it not been for my eagerness to hear discourses on duty from your face, I would not have stolen your lotus flowers." Saying thus Indra returned the lotus flowers. Agastya was pleased and let Indra and the hermits depart in peace. **(M.B. Anusasana Parva, Chapter 94, Stanza 25)**

CHAPTER NINE

THE BIRTH OF RAMA

The birth of Parashurama, also known as Rama Jāmadagnya, was an extraordinary and joyous occasion that filled the air with a sense of celebration and anticipation. According to the revered lineage of Bhrigu, Parashurama's origins can be traced back to Vishnu himself, with Bhrigu Maharshi being the progenitor of this illustrious lineage. Born from the skin of the creator Brahma, Bhrigu Maharshi held a special place in the Bhargava lineage, and all those descended from him were known as Bhargavas.

Parashurama's father, Jamadagni, was a revered sage of great power and wisdom. His mother, Renuka, possessed immense purity and devotion. As the day of Parashurama's incarnation arrived, it brought immense happiness and excitement to the household of Maharishi Jamadagni and Renuka. The atmosphere was filled with joy and anticipation as the brahmacharis blew their conch shells, announcing the auspicious occasion. Sages and their wives joined in the celebration, singing melodious songs of blessings and auspiciousness. Aryavart's renowned poet and fierce commander, Kavi Chaiman, offered Arghya, a ritual offering, to the gods, adding to the divine ambiance.

The entire ashram seemed to come alive with the news of Parashurama's birth. The sky was clear, and the surrounding greenery appeared more vibrant and animated than ever before. The joyous sounds reverberated through the air, enveloping the ashram in an enchanting aura. It was as if the world itself was celebrating the birth of Parashurama, the embodiment of divine grace and power.

Parashurama, even as an infant, exuded a unique aura. He brought immense joy to his parents, filling their hearts with love and pride. With each passing day, he grew in strength and vitality. His playful nature and innocent laughter echoed throughout the ashram, bringing happiness to all who beheld him. Sometimes cradled in his mother's loving embrace, sometimes within the sanctity of his father's meditation chamber, and sometimes perched upon the shoulders of Kavi Chaiman, Parashurama explored the world around him, radiating pure bliss.

The blood of the Bhargavas, known for its majestic lineage, coursed through Parashurama's veins. As he grew older, his footsteps echoed with a powerful and confident gait. With each stride, he seemed to embody the strength and courage of a lion. Even as a child, his presence evoked both reverence and awe.

Parashurama's birth marked the beginning of an extraordinary journey that would see him become a revered figure in Hindu mythology. His valiant deeds and divine purpose would unfold in time, leaving an indelible mark on the world. The early days of his life, as described, capture the essence of his divine nature and the extraordinary destiny that awaited him.

Parashurama's story continues to inspire and fascinate devotees and seekers of truth, as he remains an embodiment of devotion, strength, and righteousness in Hindu mythology.

BIRTH OF RAMA

Because of the wickedness of the Ksatriyas Kings, the goddess Earth became miserable. She made a representation to Brahma who took her to the sea of Milk and told Mahavishnu every-thing. Mahavishnu promised to take an incarnation as the youngest son of Jamadagni and destroy all the wicked Kings. Accordingly Renuka gave birth to Parasurama, who was an incarnation of Mahavishnu. **(Brahmanda Purana, Chapter 59).**

The couple had five sons- Vasu, Vishwavasu, Bruhadbhanu, Bruhatkanva and Bhargavram (Parshuram). Parshuram's original name was only Ram but he is also known by the names Jamdagnya Ram, Bhargavram, and Renukanandan.

नसः । इंद्र द्वुस्युव्रादनों वैश्ववदेवं त्वु वट्विृतं'। उश्धुयमं बध्रः सौम्य ऋत्वक्सित्तुर्स्वा नवम्यंत्ये'जगत्यौ गाययोर्मध्ये'पंचमी गहू- ती ते'मुली भाची दृध्सने षमव चार्ज जगायेति दुरौघण' वाद्या तत्रीयांत्या च' बहूत्यः । चशंु सप्तोनेंद्रो ऽप्रति- रमचतुर्थी बार्हस्पत्योपांत्याम्वादेष्यत्यानुष्टुम्मारुती वा । सा- व्येकादशाष्टको वैचामषिः कदा फोन्सो दुरुमची नाम्रा सुम्त्रिो गुणतः सुमची वा नाम्रा दुरुमची गुणत औष्णहिं'हरी वर्ज पपीलकिमध्ये'पट्टितुयाद्या गायची वा ॥

उभौ भूताशः काश्यप आश्वनिं । " आवर्दिष्यियो दक्षणिा वा प्राजापत्या दक्षणिा' तदातत्तूवास्तीचतुरूथी जगती। कमिि छंती पणभिरिमुरुरैनरिल्हा' गा अन्वेष्टुं सरमा' देवश्नीमदिरेण प्रहतिमयंगुभिः पणयो मशिृरीयंतः पुरोचुः सा' तान्यगुमांत्याभिरि नचिछंती पुरत्याचष्ट टेऽवसन जहूमंझनामा बाझो वो नाभा वैश्ववदेव'धनुष्टव्वं। **समटि एकादश जमदि वा राम साप्ररयिः** परं'चलारो वैरूपाः मनीषयियो दशा- ष्टादष्ट्रुरः" । " इंदुर पबि नभः पुरभदेनः । " तमस्य शतप्रभदेनोऽत्या तुरष्टिटुपु"। " धर्म सपुरस्तिापसी वा धर्मों'वैश्ववदेव'चतुरूथी जगती। चतिर इव वारविय उपसुततु साय'जागत'त' ॥

HIS BIRTH

Parashurama was born in the first quarter of the night in Purnavasu Nakshatra with the Putreshti Yajna. There is also a belief that the virtue is given on this day never ends. Parasurama was born as fifth son to sage Jamadagni and Renuka Devi. They had four sons Rumanvan, Suhotra, Vasuand Visvavasu even before the birth of Parasurama **(Chapter 58, Brahmanda Purana).**

It is true that different versions and locations have been associated with his birth in various sources and traditions.

One prominent belief is that the birthplace of Parashurama is in the Haihaya Kingdom, which is located in the present-day region of Maheshwar on the Narmada Plateau. This historical lineage of Parashurama's ancestors is said to have unfolded in this region.

Another place associated with his birth is Janapav Hill, situated in Janapav village, approximately 50 km from Indore on the Mumbai highway. This hill, elevated at 900 meters above sea level, is believed to have been the birthplace of Parashurama according to some traditions.

Furthermore, there are mentions of Parashurama's birth taking place at Renuka Tirtha in Sirmour district, Himachal Pradesh. It is considered as the sixth incarnation of Lord Vishnu and holds significance in that region. The story behind this birthplace involves Jamadagni and Renuka meditating at Tape Ka Tiba near Renuka Lake, seeking divine blessings before the birth of their fifth son.

The various versions and locations associated with Parashurama's birth showcase the diverse narratives and beliefs surrounding this revered figure in Hindu mythology. Each of these places holds its own cultural and spiritual significance, adding to the richness of Parashurama's story and the devotion he inspires among his followers.

In Chapter 6 of the Devi Bhagavata Purana, he is born from the thigh with intense light surrounding him that blinds all warriors, who then repent their evil ways and promise to lead a moral life if their eyesight is restored. The boy grants them the boon. **In Chapter 4 of the Vishnu Purana,** Rucheeka, his grandfather prepares a meal for two women, one simple, and another with ingredients that if eaten would cause the woman to conceive a son with martial powers. The latter is accidentally eaten by Renuka, and she then gives birth to Parashurama. In **Chapter 2 of the Vayu Purana,** he is born after his mother Renuka eats a sacrificial offering made to both Rudra (Shiva) and Vishnu, which gives him dual characteristics of Kshatriya and **Brahmin. Brahmanda Purana, Chapter 59** mentions that, because of the wickedness of the Ksatriyas Kings, the goddess Earth became miserable. She made a representation to Brahma who took her to the sea of Milk and told Mahavishnu everything. Mahavishnu promised to take an incarnation as the son of Jamadagni and destroy all the wicked Kings. Accordingly, Renuka gave birth to Parasurama, who was an incarnation of Mahavishnu.

CHILDHOOD AND EDUCATION

During his boyhood, Parasurama resided with his parents in the ashrama, where he received guidance from his father, Jamadagni. Although there is no explicit mention of him studying the Vedas, it is believed that he may have received Vedic instructions from his father during their time together.

From a young age, Parasurama displayed a keen interest in weaponry and martial skills. He was particularly drawn to the art of archery and sought to acquire proficiency in it. To fulfill his desire, he embarked on a journey to the Himalayas and engaged in intense penance to please Lord Shiva. He dedicated several years of his life to this pursuit, honing his skills in archery and other related disciplines.

While Parasurama excelled in archery, it is important to note that he did not spend his entire life solely as an archery instructor. He lived with his parents and siblings in the ashrama, situated in a forest away from bustling cities. However, due to his exceptional combat skills, he often came to the aid of Brahmins residing in small forest ashrams who faced threats from wild animals or other aggressors.

Apart from archery, Parasurama received instruction in various other disciplines such as wrestling, sailing, and horse-riding from the poet Chaiman. He also sought wisdom and knowledge from revered sages like Vashisht, Vishwamitra, and his own father, Jamadagni. Through rigorous practice, penance, and the accumulation of knowledge, Parasurama achieved great success. His physical form became strong and graceful, resembling an exquisite marble sculpture. His eyes radiated the bliss of winter, the smile of spring, the scorching heat of summer, the flicker of lightning, and the rush of a flowing river. At times, he appeared as the embodiment of Tripurari, absorbed in fierce determination.

During his teenage years, Parasurama demonstrated his strength by slaying a ferocious wolf, thus passing a test of power. His silent yet majestic aura left a lasting impression in the hearts of all who encountered him, evoking deep admiration and reverence.

HIS SIBLINGS

Parasurama was born as fifth son to sage Jamadagni and Renuka Devi. Five sons named Rumanvan, Suhotra, Vasu, Visvavasu and Parasurama were born to Jamadagni by his wife Renuka (**Brahmanda Purana, Chapter 58).**

RUMANVAN

The eldest of the five sons born to Jamadagni by his wife Renuka. It was

Rumanvan that Jamadagni ordered to kill Renuka who was late in fetching water from the river. But Rumanvan did not obey his father. The angry hermit cursed Rumanvan. According to the curse Rumanvan became dull-witted like birds and beasts. (**M.B. Vana Parva, Chapter 116, Stanza 10).**

SUSENA IV/ SUHOTRA I

The Sage asked Susena to kill his mother, but he did not obey his father. Jamadagni, therefore, cursed him and Parasurama redeemed him from the curse. **(Vana Parva, Chapter116).**

VASU IV.

A Vasu is mentioned in **Brahmanda Purana Chapter 58,** as the brother of Parasurama.

VISVAVASU I/BASU

The concept of the Basudev is actually linked to this Basu. In time the Basus became powerful worshippers of Lord Vishnu & they had a say in electing the Basudev, who was considered an avatar of Lord Vishnu & regarded as the spiritual head of the Vaishnavs. Krishna was elected one such Basudev. Thus the Basus & the Parashurama's were closely associated, while the former had an important say in the political setup of the country, the latter were innovators of new weapons & other innovations.

CHAPTER TEN

RENUKA THE MOTHER

Renuka, also known as Renuga or Renu, holds a significant place in the mythology and worship of certain regions in Maharashtra, Karnataka, Tamil Nadu, Andhra Pradesh, and Telangana. She is revered as the mother of Parashurama, and her abode is believed to be in Mahur, located in the Yavatmal district of Maharashtra. Renuka is often depicted riding a lion, symbolizing her strength and divine power.

According to the legends, Renuka was born as the daughter of King Prasenajit, who was conducting a sacred yajna to ensure peace and well-being for his family and kingdom. During this ritual, Renuka emerged from the flames of the yajna as a divine blessing. She grew up to be a grounded, humble, active, and intelligent child, and she was greatly loved by her parents.

Sage Agastya, who was married to Lopamudra, advised King Prasenajit to arrange Renuka's marriage with sage Jamadagni when she came of age. Recognizing the wisdom and virtue of sage Jamadagni, King Prasenajit readily agreed to the proposal. As Renuka reached the appropriate age, her marriage was solemnized with sage Jamadagni.

The union of Renuka and Jamadagni resulted in the birth of their renowned son, Parashurama. Renuka's devotion, virtues, and role as a mother hold a special place in the hearts of devotees, and she is honored and worshipped in various temples and shrines across the regions where her reverence is prevalent.

As per Brahmanda Purana, Chapter 58, When Jamadagni grew up he made a tour and visited the holy places one by one andreached the palace of King Prasenajit of the family of Iksvaku. He saw Renuka the beautiful grand –daughter of Sarhhitasva and daughter of Prasenajit and fell in love with her. He requested Prasenajit for the hand of Renuka. The King, without raising any objection gave his daughter Renuka in marriage to Jamadagni. The couple came to the bank of the river Narmada and erecting a hermitage began'tapas' (penance).Once, Jamadagni abandoned the beautiful Renuka but fearing a curse Prasenajit gave her again to Jamadagni.

Jamadagni and Renuka lived happily in the Ramshrung Mountains which are located near the Saundatti area in the Belgaum district. Renuka was a devoted wife and she helped Jamadagni from time to time in performing and fulfilling his duties. She also helped him in performing rituals, prayers, offerings etc. Just like her parents, she soon became the favourite of Jamadagni as well. They got very close and became dear to each other. Renuka was blessed with a daughter – Anjana who was later known as Anjana Devi.

Renuka was known to be extremely devotional to her husband. So much so that she used to fill up water in a pot created of sand every day and it used to hold water. This was all only because of her devotion and love for her husband. Renuka had a ritual of bathing early in the morning in the Malaprabha river. She made sure her concentration and devotion were complete and totally towards her husband. She brought water for her husband in a pot made of sand and helped him with his rituals.

DEATH & REBIRTH OF RENUKA

Renuka had five sons along with Parashurama who was the youngest. One fine day, Renuka encountered Gandharvas who was flying over the pond with his wife when she went to the pond for her bath and got distracted. Their pleasure made her feel envious, so she was "denied by unworthy thoughts, and returned wetted but not purified by the stream." Her husband beheld her "fallen from perfection and shorn of the lustre of her sanctity." So he reproved her and was exceeding wroth. As she thought about another man, she lost devotion, concentration and love for her husband which led to her losing the power of gathering water in the unbaked pots. Jamadagni had seen the happenings through his yogic power and was bursting with fury.

Jamadagni sons came into the hermitage in the order of their birth, and he commanded each of them in succession to kill his mother. Influenced by natural affection, four of them held their peace and did nothing. Their father cursed them and they became idiots bereft of all under- standing and another version says that Jamadagni had turned the Vasus into stones for not following his orders. When Renuka came to know what was going to happen, she hid in a small hut by the river and requested the fisher couple to help her out. He ordered Parashurama to kill Renuka and punish her for what she had done.

Parasurama obeyed his father's order and struck off his mother's head with his axe. Parashurama was filled with rage and wanted to obey his father's instructions. The deed assuaged the father's anger. Rishi Jamadagni was pleased and Parasurama was blessed with two Varas (wishes) by him. Lord Parasurama asked his mother's and brothers' life through one wish. Then he wished that his mother and brothers should not have any memory of the event. The wishes were granted but Parasurama remained guilty of killing his mother and brothers. He had sinned though his mother restored to life in purity, and that his brothers regain their natural condition. All this the father granted. Parasurama got them back to life as well and wiped their memory of being dead.

A version says that, when the resurrection of Renuka happened, her body was switched with that of the fisherman's wife and the fisherman's wife got the body of Renuka. Here is where the phenomena of Renuka and Yellama came into being. Renuka and Yellama are extensively worshipped in today's time differing from state to state.

Another version: Renuka was known for her chastity and devotion to her husband. Such was her faith, that she was able to fetch water from the river in a pot of unbaked clay, with the pot held together only by the strength of her devotion. The pot is wet but water will not spill out and bring the water for her husband to do the Vedic rituals. Renuka Devi a pativrata used to have a bath in the river and make a mud vessel with clay every day.

One day while getting water from river she happened to see some gandharvas passing in a chariot and for a moment she thought of gandharvas beauty. Filled with desire for only a moment, the unbaked pot she held dissolved in the river. Afraid to return to her husband, she waited at the river bank, uncertain of what to do next as the wet mud pot discharged and water were spilled out. She tried to do fresh pot but could not and without knowing what to do she held back in the river shore itself. The sage waiting for his wife had observed through his yogic powers what had happened and asked his elder son to cut the throat of mother with axe. The boy terrified with his father's order and refused to kill the mother.

Sage Jamadagni asked next and next but all the four sons refused to obey the order. The sage cursed the brothers to convert as stones. Finally sage called the Parasurama who went to collect samidhas to forest and asked to cut the neck of his mother. Parasurama always obeys his father's words with utmost care. Without any hesitation, Parasurama taken the axe and cut the neck of his mother and came to his father and said that he has carried out the order. The beheading his mother was only because he was bound by the words of his father. If Parasurama had opposed the words of his father, Jamadagni anger would not have been appeased and he would have cursed Parasurama along with the other brothers.

Sage Jamadagni pleased with Parasurama and asked him to have two boons. The first boon he asked his father was restoration of his mother's and brothers' lives and complete forgetfulness of the incident. That was his love for mother and also requested his father to make the brothers from stone to flesh. So he did a very tactical move. He appeased Jamadagni and restored the lives of his brothers and mother. Jamadagni was impressed by the affection and devotion of his son, Jamadagni granted his request.

Another version; When, Parasurama became fourteen years old. Jamadagni went to the forest to gather fruits, roots etc. After completing the cleansing work of the hermitage, leaving Parasurama in the forest, Renuka went to the bank of the river Narmada (Reva) to fetch water. When she reached the river, Kartaviryarjuna and his wives were playing in water. She waited for them to go.

When they were gone she got into the river. But as the water was muddy because of the play, she walked a little to the east where there was pure water. She saw Chitraratha the King of Salva playing with his wife in the water. How beautiful they were! She had never seen so beautiful a woman or so handsome a man. She stood there looking at them for a while. A sight of the connubial endearments of Bang Chitraratha and his wife inspired her with impure thoughts, and her husband, perceiving that she had fallen from perfection. It was only after they had departed that she was able to return to the Ashrama with water.

When she reached the hermitage with water, Jamadagni had already returned a long while ago. He had returned weary and tired of the heat of the midday-sun. He did not see his wife in the hermitage. He had been sitting very angry when Renuka returned with water. She put the pot down and bowed before her husband and told him the reasonfor her being late. When he heard the reason his anger blazed.

He called his sons one by one and ordered them to kill her. But the four elder sons did not dare to execute his order saying that slaughter of a woman was a great sin. But Parasurama came forward and by a cutting-arrow cut off the head of his mother. The father called the four sons who disobeyed him and cursed them thus:"Since you have disobeyed the order of your father, because of your ignorance, you shall become foresters and live in forest."Being overwhelmed with sorrow at the death of his mother, Parasurama swooned and fell down.

When his anger subsided, discretion dawned on Jamadagni.He aroused his son and took him on his lap and asked him what boon he wanted for having accomplished the accomplishable task. Parashurama's request was that his mother should be brought to life again. The hermit was pleased and he brought Renuka to life again. **(Brahmanda Purana, Chapter 60).** It is also mentioned that he asked for four boons. Parasurama sought the Mother be revived, Let her not remember to die, Brother become normal and I will be eternal. Jamadagni granted him all four boons.

In some versions, he even kills his own mother because his father asks him to and because to take his test obeisance towards his parents. After Parasurama obeys his father's order to kill his mother, his father grants him a boon. Parasurama asks for the reward that his mother be brought back to life, and she is restored to life. Parasurama remains filled with sorrow after the violence, repents and expiates his sin.

After his Mother comes back to life, he tries to clean the blood-stained axe but he finds a drop of blood which he was unable to clean and tries cleaning the blood drop in different rivers. This is when he moves towards the south of India in search of any holy river where he could clean his axe, finally, he reaches Tirthahalli village in Shimoga, Karnataka and tries to clean the axe and to his surprise, the axe gets cleaned in the Holy river of Tunga. With respect towards the holy river, he constructs a Shiva linga and performs pooja and the temple is named as Rameshwara temple. The place where Lord Parashurama cleaned his axe is called Ramakunda.

The another Sanskrit version mentions that the pious sage had, on one occasion, reason to be dissatisfied with the conduct of his wife, and asked his sons to cut off her head. Each and all of them refused, except Parasurama, who, subordinating feeling to obedience and filial duty, without hesitation beheaded her with the Parasu, (axe)— the gift of his patron deity Mahadeva. Highly pleased with his son's sense of duty, Jamadagni wished him to request a boon. He prayed that his mother might be brought back to life, and that he might enjoy long life and prove invincible in war. The request was granted. In order to atone, however, for the sin of matricide, Rama went to Mount Kailash where he remained absorbed for years in meditation and prayer.

THE STORY VERSION OF RENUKA KILLING

As Ram listened to the news from Acharya Vimad Bhargava, a wave of sadness swept over him. The weight of the Dashragya war and the losses suffered by his family weighed heavily on his heart. The mention of his beloved father, poet Chaiman, having passed away and Maharishi Jamadagni wandering alone only deepened his sorrow.

Ram's thoughts turned to his elder brother, Vidvant, who was preparing to join the war. The news of his other two brothers being killed in the battle filled him with grief and anguish. The absence of his mother, Mataji, who had left the ashram and gone to Gandharvaraj's place, further added to the sense of loss and separation.

Tears welled up in Ram's eyes as he realized the extent of the tragedy that had befallen his family. Yet, even in the midst of his sorrow, his determination and resilience remained unwavering. He resolved to honor the memory of his father and brothers, and to carry forward their legacy.

With a heavy heart, Ram sought solace in his duties and the teachings of his revered gurus. He knew that he had a responsibility to uphold the principles and values instilled in him by his father, Maharishi Jamadagni, and the guidance of Acharya Vimad Bhargava.

Though burdened by grief, Ram gathered his strength and prepared himself to face the challenges ahead. The news of the war and the loss of loved ones had left an indelible mark on his soul, but he knew that he must carry on, driven by a sense of duty and the determination to protect righteousness and justice.

As Bhargava, filled with grief and anger, mounted his fierce black horse, a sense of foreboding spread through the deserted ashram of Jamadagni. The earth trembled beneath his powerful presence, and his determination to seek his father burned like embers in his eyes. With his sword gleaming at his side, he embarked on his journey, urging his family to seek refuge in the ashram.

The ashram, once a place of tranquility, seemed to hold its breath, as if aware of the impending upheaval that would follow in Bhargava's wake. His horse thundered through the hermitage, its hooves echoing like the roar of a lion. Bhargava, with his black hair flowing and his eyes ablaze, resembled the mighty Trilochan, the three-eyed deity of destruction.

Bhargava's heart raced as he hurriedly made his way to his father's hut. There, at the entrance, sat an elderly Tapasvini, tears staining her lap. Ram, desperate for news of his father, approached her with urgency and desperation in his voice. The woman cried, her voice choked with sorrow, and she clung to Ram, cautioning him not to engage with anyone.

Without a moment's hesitation, Parashurama leaped, propelled by his fierce determination, and reached the banks of the river. His eyes scanned the surroundings, searching for any sign of his beloved father. His heart filled with a mixture of hope and fear, knowing that the fate of his family and the weight of his responsibility rested on finding Maharishi Jamadagni.

In that moment, as Parashurama stood on the riverbank, his resolve hardened like steel. The river flowed before him, separating him from the answers he sought. With determination burning in his veins, he steeled himself for the challenges that lay ahead, ready to confront any obstacle that stood between him and his father.

Parashurama, the fierce warrior with unparalleled strength and unyielding devotion, embarked on his quest to find Maharishi Jamadagni. His journey would test his mettle and shape his destiny, as he sought to restore balance and seek justice in a world filled with turmoil and suffering.

Overwhelmed with grief and anguish, Jamadagni stood beneath the shade of a towering banyan tree, his frail form draped in tattered skins and bones. His once majestic appearance had withered, and his eyes, like flickering lamps in a dark cave, bore the weight of untold suffering. Bhargava's heart shattered at the sight of his father's pitiable state. He cast aside his weapon, the parasu, and rushed to his father, clasping his feet.

But Jamadagni, lost in his suffering, seemed to have forgotten his own son. His sunken eyes stared blankly, as if he knew not the love and bond they once shared. Bhargava's anguish intensified, and tears streamed down his face as he pleaded with his father, "Father, I am your son Ram, do you not recognize me?"

With a voice heavy with sorrow, Jamadagni responded, "I am nobody's father, I have no son. Who are you? I do not know you." Bhargava, his heart breaking, stood up and humbly folded his hands, desperately trying to rekindle the connection that had been lost. "Father, I am your youngest son Rama, who was taken away by Sahasrarjun. Please, recognize me."

Ram's eyes filled with tears, his heart aching at the thought of his father's memory fading away. But Jamadagni, with a solemn expression, uttered words that pierced Bhargava's soul, "If Ram is truly my son, then behead his mother Renuka. She has transgressed the boundaries of Aryatv."

The weight of the command hung heavy in the air, and Bhargava, torn between his love for his mother and his duty as a son, made a solemn vow to fulfill his father's demand. Determined, he took up his parasu once again and mounted his horse, setting forth on a journey that would test the limits of his resolve.

The powerful horse thundered through the land, its hooves shattering stones upon the Himalayas. Bhargava arrived at the city of the Gandharvas, and as he dismounted, the horse let out a relieved neigh, as if releasing the burden it had carried. It was there that Bhargava caught sight of his mother Renuka descending from the hill.

His gaze grew stern as he observed her condition. Renuka's once lustrous hair had turned white, her once graceful body had withered, and an indelible sorrow marked her face. She appeared as if she had been crafted from the tears of a grieving widow. As Bhargava approached, Renuka recognized her son, and a glimmer of recognition and love flickered in her eyes.

As happiness bloomed on Renuka's face, her eyes danced with joy. Uttering the words "Mere Ram," she moved forward, filled with love for her son. Ram, on the other hand, stood firm and cold-hearted. Renuka sensed the gravity of the situation and hesitated, her face reflecting a sense of despair. His expression turned dull, as if he had lost consciousness.

"Father has sent me," roared Ram's voice. Renuka replied, "Your father sent your brothers to kill me, but they did not dare to. Did he send you for the same purpose?" Ram's demeanour remained stern as he responded, "He did not ask me to kill you, I have come to kill you. It is the righteous duty to eliminate a woman who has transgressed the boundaries of Aryatv."

"Bhrgusrestha is a righteous soul, a master of knowledge and penance. I believe I have lost my righteousness. It never troubled him. You are my beloved son, but you refuse to acknowledge that. I am not afraid of death. The day my husband renounced the world, I died with him. If you have come as Kaal, then kill me. I bow down before you."

Ram's eyes welled up with tears upon hearing these heart-wrenching words. "Then why are you still here? Go back to the ashram! I do not wish to stain the purity of Bhrugukul. My unrighteousness will corrode Aryatv. There is no place for me in Pitralok; the fierce dogs of Yama guard that realm."

"I won't let that happen." "Amba! Amba! Knowing everything, why did you tarnish our father's glory?" Ram cried out. "I abandoned our ancestral religion to follow another. It is the fault of the compassion that arose within me." "For which religion did you forsake our lineage?" "Come, I will show you my religion. The one who showed me the stone house ahead, I have embraced another religion there."

Mother and son entered a hut made of rough stones. Inside, a scene of horror unfolded. The room was filled with the repulsive stench of leprosy. Bhargava covered his nose in disgust. The patients within cried out, "Amba, give me water, shoo away the flies. Mother, you have come!" Some had lost their hands, others had buzzing feet. Some had lost their nose and lips, leaving only yellowing teeth visible. Amidst the cries, Amba rushed around, tending to the sick, driving away flies, and offering solace to those suffering on dirty, makeshift beds.

Limbs had been lost, urine flowed freely. Yet, when they saw Amba, they found solace. "Amba, Amba, my Amba! Give me a sip of water," one of them cried, joining their weakened hands together. With her hands, she aided them in drinking water and said, "Gandharvaraj, my youngest son has come to meet me. I have brought him here to meet you."

Bhargava's hardened heart melted at the sight. He covered his eyes with both hands and cast aside his parasu in remorse.

Amba, Amba, forgive Kalyani, forgive me. It's Jaggajni, not only mine; you are everyone's mother, but come with me from here." Bhargava took his mother's hand and led her away. After walking some distance, Parashurama said to his mother, "Mother, I left my parasu there, let me retrieve it. Please sit down." Parashurama returned with a composed mind after an hour, and he lifted his mother as if she were a ball and mounted the horse. The horse galloped, and Renuka began to cry, hitting Ram's chest. "Who will give water? Who will provide medicine to my helpless patients in Gandharvaraj's place?"

"Quiet, mother. Those ignorant people went to Yampur and were killed by my parasu. There is no fault in killing dear ones who cannot live. Mother, your tears are meant to give strength to the strong, to the death of a dying creature, not to mark the passage of time."

"Oh, my fierce son, are you now leading me into the fire of disobedience?" Parashurama's voice tinkled, its tone infused with untouchable sharpness like Gaurishankar. "Mother, I will establish righteousness. Without following it, there is no salvation for the world." A sense of pure religion awakened in Renuka's heart.

Word had spread to every household that Ram was coming with his mother Renuka. An unimaginable and terrible event was about to take place. Ram would kill his mother Renuka in front of everyone, and after killing her, he himself would relinquish his own life. This worry had thrown everyone into turmoil. Mantras were not chanted in the ashrams, the smoke from the yajnas did not rise, the scholars did not study. Everyone was waiting with heavy hearts for Parashurama's arrival.

Sage Vashisht remained silent in the midst of his disciples, but his silence spoke volumes. Benevolent wishes for the welfare of the world shone on his face, and blessings for the Bhrigu dynasty emanated from his entire being. His mind chanted for the well-being of Parasurama and Renuka. The thundering hooves of the restless horse could be heard approaching. The sound was fiercer than Yama's footsteps. Tears welled up, women cried out. Bhrigu Shrestha's determination could not be swayed, and Ram's vow could not be averted. Such thoughts filled the people with anguish.

Amidst the rustling and roaring, Ram's horse drew nearer. Tornadoes of dust arose everywhere. In the whirlwind of dust, only the radiance of Bhargavas wings, the intensity in Arun's dilated eyes, and Renuka's flowing white hair, filled with desperation, were visible.

Like the speed of a storm, that intoxicated horse reached Bhrigu Shrestha's. Parashurama got down from the horse, carrying Amba in his hand like a flower-kanduk. Keeping the mother at the feet of the father, she said eagerly, "Father, father! I have brought Amba lying at your feet." Bhrigu Shrestha's started trembling. "Ram you have come."

He closed his listless eyes. "Father, father, your youngest son I have brought Bhagwati Amba." The whole crowd was watching with bated breath, speechless, Ram's agitation and Maharishi's indifference. Rishi's eyes opened. Seeing Renuka, he trembled with unbearable guilt.

"Ram ! Ram ! you are my son So cut off your mother head now." Maharishi Vashisht came in front. "Be careful Bhrgusrestha Jamadagni, Ram! Wait." "Brahmarishi Shrestha's, it has not been seen or heard anywhere in Arya life that a woman of any clan-husband has adopted another man, I am seeing that in my own house, Ram, act now and kill this evil character."

"Son, I wanted to die by your hands, I bow my head. Cut the body from which I gave birth to you and throw it in front of the dogs." Renuka bowed her head. Parshu's lightning started flashing in Ram's hands. Sobbing said - "Father, I will kill Amba now, after that I will end my life as well. I do not want to live the life of a Chandal by killing my mother, understand this also, I will never be born in your dynasty, nor will I be born in your family." I will meet the ancestors.

"Son, why do you want to die?" Son Jamadagni said. Ram replied, because it is better to die than to live a tarnished life like a fowl amidst the anger and hatred of the society. Bhrigu Shrestha's! I will say what I do not want to say. You are proud of Aryanism, but do not know what Aryanism is.

On earth Discord kept spreading and you kept running away with the power of Aryatv. If you wanted, you could have tied Aryavarta in a thread. You could have saved the struggle of Guru Vashisht and Vishwamitra. The foundation of Dashragya would not have been laid, nor there is such a big struggle.You stuck on the body of Amba, not knowing the life inside her. If you knew, then you would not have been hungry for Amba's life. Dharma is not protected by pride. For so many days, did penance, served knowledge, followed the truth, tried the mantras, but did not make any path of your own, kept following the path of others.

Bhargava addressed his father in a somewhat angry voice - "You have questioned Amba's chastity. You sent your four sons each to kill her, but did not walk on your feet to see which Gandharvaraj's Amba belonged to. The one who serves the screaming lepers lying on the deathbed with rotting hands and rotting feet, has become Arya Aranya? Father, sin does not reside in conduct; it resides in the eyes lying behind it. On the other hand, Sahasrarjun Aryavarta Coming to destroy us, here you are bent on making your own house a slaughterhouse

Renuka stood up seeing her brilliant son's eloquence not stopping. His lips started trembling. "Son, are you omitting the recognition of the father that too in front of Guru Vashisht. You have become so big; the difference between father and son is not known to you? The son's head adorns the feet of the father's religion.

Ram, you fall at the feet of father and ask for forgiveness. Ram kept looking fiercely like a lion. "Son, leave your pride, leave it, otherwise I will die by consuming poison before you kill me." Bhargavas vision became pure. The fierceness disappeared. Keeping his head on the feet, said in a trembling voice - "Father has become very impudent, forgive him for what he said. Anger is the root of disaster. Only the father forgives the son's crime." Jamadagni became alert.

Tears were dripping from his eyes. He bowed down and hugged his son. "Son, religion is not protected by pride. Without power Aryatv is motionless, how true is this statement of yours. Sin remains in the vision lying behind it, not desire. This is the seed mantra of Aryatv. Renuka! Renuka!" Weeping, Jamadagni said - "I got you killed, but your son gave me life. The speed of religion is very subtle, Renuka. Ram, you throw away your Parshu, I will return my promise. He lifted Renuka lying on his feet. Tears of joy started falling from the eyes of the people and started shouted admiring the conduct of Rama from all the directions.

CHAPTER ELEVEN

DHARANI

Dharani, as the wife of Parashurama, represents an intriguing aspect of the divine manifestation of Lakshmi, the consort of Vishnu. In the various avatars of Vishnu, Lakshmi assumes different forms and roles, aligning herself with the nature and purpose of each incarnation. When Vishnu took the form of Parashurama, Lakshmi appeared as Dharani, a mortal woman who became his devoted companion and partner.

The concept of Lakshmi adapting her form according to Vishnu's avatar is a fascinating aspect of Hindu mythology. In celestial forms, Lakshmi manifests as a divine and celestial being, reflecting the divinity of Vishnu's avatar. However, when Vishnu takes on mortal forms, such as Parashurama, Lakshmi also assumes a mortal form to accompany him on his earthly journey.

The role of Dharani as the wife of Parashurama signifies the significance of partnership and companionship in the human realm. As a mortal, Dharani shares in the joys, challenges, and experiences of Parashurama's life. She stands by his side, supporting him in his endeavors and assisting him in fulfilling his divine purpose.

While some interpretations consider Dharani to represent Mother Earth, symbolizing the connection between Parashurama and the natural world, it is also plausible to view her as an incarnation of Lakshmi herself. As the embodiment of Lakshmi, Dharani brings her qualities of prosperity, abundance, and grace into Parashurama's life and the world around them.

The presence of Dharani as the wife of Parashurama highlights the deep bond between Vishnu and Lakshmi and their commitment to each other across different incarnations. It signifies the divine harmony and synergy between the masculine and feminine aspects of the divine, reflecting the eternal cosmic balance.

Overall, the inclusion of Dharani as Parashurama's wife expands the understanding of Lakshmi's role in various avatars of Vishnu and emphasizes the importance of partnership and companionship in fulfilling divine missions on Earth. Dharani's character showcases the ever-present love and support of Lakshmi as she accompanies Vishnu in his mortal journeys, embodying the qualities of devotion, loyalty, and strength that are inherent in the divine feminine.

Lord Parashurama is considered to be a lifelong celibate by most people. The general idea is that he is an ascetic who meditates and prays for the greater good of the world. There are no mentions of Parasurama being married in Sreemad Bhagavatham either. In the **Vishnu Puranam** though, it is mentioned that Dharani was the wife of Parashurama.

पुनश्चपद्मासम्भूतायदाऽदतियोऽभवद्धरिः।
यदाचभार्गवोरामस्तदाभूद्धरणीत्वयिम्॥

Padma was born when Hari became Aditya (The son of Aditi) and when he became Bhargava Rama, she came as Dharani.

LAKSHMI

Lakshmi, the goddess of fortune and prosperity in Hindu mythology, holds a significant place in the religious and cultural traditions of India. Her origins and depictions have evolved over time, encompassing various legends and symbolisms.

The Rig-Veda, one of the oldest sacred texts of Hinduism, mentions the concept of good fortune associated with the word "Lakshmi." In the Atharvaveda, this idea becomes personified in female form, representing both auspicious and inauspicious aspects. This development reflects the human inclination to attribute personal qualities to abstract concepts.

In the Taittiriya Samhita, an important Vedic text, Lakshmi and Sri are described as the two wives of Aditya, the sun god. This association signifies the divine connection between wealth, prosperity, and the radiance of the sun. The Satapatha Brahmana further expands on Lakshmi's lineage, presenting her as emanating from Prajapati, the lord of creatures.

The Ramayana, a revered epic, narrates a popular legend regarding Lakshmi's birth. According to this tale, during the cosmic event known as the churning of the ocean (Samudra Manthan), the gods and Asuras (demons) joined forces to extract the nectar of immortality from the depths of the ocean. As they churned the waters vigorously, a divine lotus emerged, and from its petals, the resplendent goddess Lakshmi appeared. She emerged in her full beauty, holding a lotus in her hand, captivating all who beheld her.

Another variation of Lakshmi's origin story portrays her as being born from the sea of milk (Kshirabdhitanaya), a metaphorical representation of the cosmic ocean. Her connection with the lotus, symbolizing purity and divine transcendence, led to her epithet Padma, meaning "lotus-born." The lotus, rooted in the muddy depths but blossoming above the water's surface, signifies spiritual enlightenment rising above worldly existence.

In the Puranas, ancient Hindu scriptures, Lakshmi is described as the daughter of Bhrigu, a revered sage, and his consort Khyati. These texts provide further details on her divine attributes and associations. According to the Vishnu Purana, Lakshmi's various manifestations are connected to different avatars of Lord Vishnu, the preserver of the universe. When Vishnu took the form of a dwarf (Vamana), Lakshmi appeared as Padma or Kamala from a lotus. In Vishnu's incarnation as Rama, Lakshmi assumed the form of Sita, his devoted and virtuous wife. And in Krishna's avatar, she manifested as Rukmini, Krishna's beloved queen.

It is important to note that Lakshmi is not limited to these particular forms but is considered to be a universal goddess of fortune, associated with abundance, wealth, and auspiciousness. Her presence is not confined to temples but is believed to permeate the entire universe, blessing devotees with prosperity and well-being. Lakshmi is often depicted with multiple arms, symbolizing her ability to bestow blessings and fulfill the desires of her worshippers.

Various names are attributed to Lakshmi, each highlighting a particular aspect of her divine nature. Hira and Indira emphasize her radiant beauty and charm, while Jaladhija portrays her connection with the ocean's depths. Chanchala or Lola refers to her fickle nature as the goddess of fortune, symbolizing the unpredictable nature of wealth and prosperity. Loka-mata, meaning "mother of the world," underscores her role as a nurturing and benevolent deity, providing for the needs of all beings.

Throughout history, Lakshmi has remained a beloved and revered goddess in Hinduism. Her worship is central to festivals such as Diwali, the Festival of Lights, where devotees seek her blessings for wealth, well-being, and spiritual abundance. Lakshmi symbolism goes beyond material prosperity, encompassing spiritual and emotional fulfillment as well. As the goddess of fortune, she continues to be cherished and venerated, reminding people of the potential for abundance and the significance of gratitude and devotion in their lives.

CHAPTER TWELVE

COW SURBHI

Parasurama father hermit Jamadagni had been living there with his wife Renuka and his sons. There were many others habitants in the ashrama at the bank of Narmada. Surabhi- Sushila - Nandini, the calf of Kamadhenu was acquired by the sage Jamadagni after years of penance. Once, Kartaviryarjuna and his retinue were roaming in the Vindhya forests in search of game. At noon after, a refreshing bath in the clear waters of the river Narmada, when they were preparing to return, they saw Jamadagni Ashrama. After asking his men to wait at the river-bank, Kartaviryarjuna went alone to the Ashrama. Kartaviryarjuna paid his respects to the sage and after their usual greetings, Jamadagni asked him to call his followers also to the Ashrama.

When all of them arrived the sage arranged for their sumptuous feast through his divine cow Kamadhenu (wish-yielding cow), which provided the King and his followers with a very good supper. The cow was also named as Susila- the sister of Cow Surabhi. She was in service for all kind of auspicious offerings made in the ashrama of the sage Jamadagni.

Kamadhenu was acquired by the sage Jamadagni after years of penance at Goloka and pleased Surabhi by his penance and she gave him Susila, her sister.

The cow was playing the important role of providing milk and milk products to be used in her sage-master's oblations and she was also capable of producing fierce warriors to protect him. Jamadagni gave the cow (Susila) to Renuka as a token of love. As Jamadagni gave a feast to the King and his followers, Kartaviryarjuna wondered how the sage managed to provide all the rare articles of food to his number of guests. Jamadagni told him about the cow capable to feed the unlimited. Though, the king came with his massive entourage, the sage able to give good sumptuous feast to them in a short notice. The king asked the sage how he could able to arrange in a short notice and the sage said he had a calf of Kamadhenu offered by Indra so that he is able to feed them.

When after the meals were over, they started to take leave of the sage, Chandragupta, a minister of Kartaviryarjuna brought to the notice of the king the superior powers of the Kamadhenu (Susila). Kartaviryarjuna grew greedy and wanted to get the cow and asked Chandragupta to tell the sage about it. Wanting the Divine Cow "Kamadhenu" for himself, the king offered wealth to Jamadagni which he refused.

Despite Kartaviryarjuna greed and desire to possess the divine cow Kamadhenu, Jamadagni, being a sage of high virtue, refused the king's offer of wealth. Jamadagni was content with the presence of Kamadhenu and her sister Susila in his ashrama, and he recognized their significance in his spiritual practices and offerings.

However, Kartaviryarjuna desire for power and material possessions continued to grow. Frustrated by Jamadagni refusal, the king became consumed by envy and hatched a plan to seize the sacred cow by force. He sent his men to the ashrama to forcefully take Kamadhenu and eliminate any obstacles in their path.

When the soldiers arrived at the ashrama, they encountered Jamadagni's sons, including Parasurama, who were prepared to defend their father and the divine cow. Parasurama, known for his exceptional skill in combat and his unwavering devotion to his father, stood fearlessly against Kartaviryarjuna's men.

A fierce battle ensued between Parasurama and the soldiers. With his unmatched prowess and divine strength, Parasurama single-handedly defeated the entire army sent by Kartaviryarjuna. His skill with the axe, a weapon he wielded with exceptional precision, earned him the title "Parasurama" (Rama with the axe).

As per some hindu scriptures, Kartaviryarjuna was killed by Parashurama at this conflict at Ashrama. However majority of the scriptures mentioned Parashurama Kartaviryarjuna battle at former place . Upon learning of the defeat of his soldiers, Kartaviryarjuna himself came to confront Parasurama. However, he too fell before the might of Parashurama's axe. Parasurama, driven by his duty to protect his father and the sanctity of the ashrama, struck down Kartaviryarjuna, bringing an end to his tyranny.

The news of Kartaviryarjuna demise spread far and wide, creating ripples of both fear and admiration for Parashurama's velour. Parashurama's victory not only safeguarded the ashrama and Kamadhenu but also established him as a formidable warrior and protector of dharma.

The episode of Kartaviryarjuna defeat at the hands of Parasurama marked a significant event in Hindu mythology. It highlighted the importance of righteousness, devotion, and the divine intervention that supports those who stand up against injustice. Parashurama's act of defending his father and upholding righteousness against a powerful ruler exemplified the triumph of good over evil.

Parashurama's journey continued beyond this incident, as he embarked on further adventures and played a crucial role in the lineage of the avatars (incarnations) of Lord Vishnu. His unwavering dedication and his exploits in subsequent tales further solidified his status as a revered figure in Hindu mythology.

THE KILLING OF JAMADAGNI

Despite the sage Jamadagni's refusal to part with the sacred cow Kamadhenu, Chandragupta, driven by his desire to possess her, persisted in his demands. He tried to persuade the sage through appeals, forceful tactics, and even begging, but Jamadagni remained resolute in his decision.

Frustrated by the sage's unwavering stance, Chandragupta resorted to violence. He forcibly seized the calf of Kamadhenu, intending to provoke Jamadagni into a battle to reclaim it. However, as the king's men tried to capture the calf, both the calf and the divine cow vanished into the sky, eluding their grasp.

Jamadagni, determined to protect Kamadhenu, stepped forward to prevent the king's men from further aggression. But in his valiant attempt, he was overpowered and beaten. However, to the astonishment of all present, the cow and calf reappeared before them.

Assuming an extraordinary size, the divine cow displayed her power and ferocity. With a bold front, she fiercely attacked the king and his followers, causing chaos and havoc. Many of them met their demise, either gored to death or fleeing in fear.

Meanwhile, Jamadagni, with a heart filled with sorrow, followed the cow, desperately pleading for her return. His cries echoed through the air as he pursued the divine creature, witnessing the destruction left in her wake.

However, the story does not end here. The divine intervention of Sukramuni, an enlightened sage, played a crucial role in the events that followed. He appeared at the scene and, invoking the ancient art of Mrtasanjivani, the ability to revive the dead, brought Jamadagni back to life.

Revived and restored, Jamadagni was once again among the living. Sukramuni, having fulfilled his purpose, departed from the scene, leaving the sage and his wife Renuka to grapple with the consequences of the fateful encounter.

It is worth noting that Hindu scriptures often highlight the significance of Kamadhenu in the possession of sages such as Jamadagni and Vashisht. The cow's role in providing essential milk and milk products for sacred rituals and her ability to produce formidable warriors to protect her master add to her revered status. Those who dared to steal Kamadhenu from the sages often faced dire consequences for their actions, serving as a reminder of the sanctity and power associated with these divine beings.

After the altercation between Chandragupta (or the minister) and Jamadagni, where the cow and calf reappeared and caused chaos, Jamadagni's wife Renuka went in search of her husband. Sadly, she found him lying lifeless, having been beaten to death by Chandragupta (or his men).

In grief and despair, Renuka and the other members of the ashrama performed the final rites for Jamadagni. They placed his body on a funeral pyre, and as they were about to light the fire, Sukramuni, an enlightened sage, appeared at the scene.

Sukramuni possessed the ancient knowledge of Mrtasanjivani, the ability to revive the dead. Moved by the devotion and righteousness of Jamadagni, he invoked this mystical art and brought Jamadagni back to life, reversing the tragic outcome. After successfully restoring Jamadagni's life, Sukramuni left the scene, having fulfilled his divine purpose.

It's important to note that the story of Jamadagni and Kamadhenu is often portrayed as a moral lesson, emphasizing the consequences of greed and the sanctity of divine beings. While the specific details may vary across different versions and interpretations, the underlying teachings and themes remain consistent.

In Hindu scriptures, Kamadhenu is often associated with the sage Jamadagni or his counterpart, sage Vashisht. Kamadhenu is revered as the divine wish-fulfilling cow, capable of granting any desire.

According to these scriptures, Kamadhenu played a crucial role in the ashram of the sage-master. She provided abundant milk and milk products that were used in sacred rituals and oblations performed by the sage. Her milk was considered pure and auspicious, and it played a significant role in the spiritual practices and offerings of the sage and his disciples.

Furthermore, Kamadhenu possessed mystical powers beyond providing nourishment. She had the ability to generate and produce fierce and powerful warriors to protect her sage-master and his ashram. These divine warriors would emerge from her and stand guard, ensuring the safety and sanctity of the sacred space.

Given Kamadhenu's divine nature and the blessings she bestowed upon the sage, kings or individuals who attempted to steal or harm her often faced severe consequences for their actions. These consequences could range from personal misfortune to divine retribution, serving as a cautionary tale against greed, disrespect, and the violation of the sacred bonds between sages and their divine companions.

CHAPTER THIRTEEN

KARTAVIRYARJUNA

Kartaviryarjuna, also known as Arjuna, was a prominent king of the Haihaya dynasty. The Haihayas were a race or tribe of people who were associated with borderers and outlying tribes. While the Vishnu Purana suggests that they were descendants of Haihaya of the Yadu race, they are also believed to have Scythian origins.

According to the Vayu and other Puranas, the Haihaya tribe was divided into five major divisions: Talajangha, Vitihotras, Aventis, Tuwrfikeras, and Jatas (or Sujatas). They were known for their conquests, and they managed to conquer Balm or Bahuka, a descendant of King Harischandra. However, they were later defeated by King Sagara, son of Bahu, along with several other barbarian tribes.

The Mahabharata mentions that the Haihayas traced their ancestry back to Saryati, a son of Manu. They frequently made incursions into the Doab region and successfully captured the city of Kashi (Benares), which had been fortified against them by King Divodasa. Nonetheless, Pratardana, the grandson of Divodasa, eventually destroyed the Haihayas and restored the kingdom of Kashi.

Kartaviryarjuna, who was also known as Arjuna, was a renowned king among the Haihayas. He was believed to be an incarnation of the Sudarshana Chakra of Lord Vishnu, who took a human birth. Kartaviryarjuna was known for his extraordinary strength and prowess in battle, with the Mahabharata describing him as having a thousand arms.

A WARRIOR WITH THOUSAND HANDS

According to this version, Kartaviryarjuna's mother was initially unable to conceive a child. Anusuya, a wise woman, advised her to undertake a vrata (a religious vow) dedicated to Lord Dattatreya. Dattatreya is considered a combined incarnation of three deities, with Vishnu being the main avatar for the Vaishnava sect. In response to the mother's vrata, Dattatreya appeared and granted her a boon, stating that her son would be powerful and could only be killed by Dattatreya himself.

Kartaviryarjuna was born with defective limbs, which brought him great distress. He embarked on a severe penance dedicated to Dattatreya, seeking a remedy for his physical condition. In response to his devotion, Dattatreya appeared again and bestowed upon Kartaviryarjuna a thousand arms, curing his physical ailment. From that point onwards, Kartaviryarjuna became a devoted follower of Dattatreya.

As a result of his newfound power and devotion, Kartaviryarjuna became the ruler of the entire world, and the earth flourished under his reign. His fame and influence even surpassed that of Indra, the king of the gods. He was said to have defeated Ravana, the demon king of Lanka, with ease.

However, as time passed, Kartaviryarjuna's power and success led him down a tyrannical path. Intoxicated by his own might, he gradually lost control and his rule became oppressive. His sons and subordinate kings, influenced by their invincibility, started committing mistakes and wrongdoings against other social groups (varnas).

Another version is that, Once Kartaviryarjuna pleased the hermit-sage Dattatreya the son of Atri, by doing penance sought and obtained these boons, viz.,

-He should have a thousand arms and a golden chariot that went where so ever he willed it to go;

- The power of restraining wrong by justice/ the conquest of the earth and the disposition to rule it righteously;

-He should be invincibility by enemies, and death at the hands of a man renowned over the whole world.

By him this earth was perfectly governed, and of him it is said : —" No other king shall ever equal Kartaviryarjuna in regard to sacrifices, liberality, austerities, courtesy, and self-restrain "so he was ruling, with unbroken health, prosperity, strength, and valour. " All the Kings in the world acknowledged the supremacy of Kartaviryarjuna Triumphal March. **Brahmanda Purana, Chapter 16**, defines that Kings of the solar dynasty like Trayyaruna, Hariscandra, Rohitasva and Cuncu were defeated by Kartaviryarjuna. In his golden chariot he went about defeating Devas, Yaksas, Rishi's and others. He challenged even Vishnu. He insulted Indra in the company of Indrani. **(Vana Parva, Chapter 115).**

With these boons, Kartaviryarjuna became immeasurably powerful, conducting many military conquests. Kartaviryarjuna military conquests were unbeatable because of the alliances he formed. It mentions the support he received from the military corporations of the Shakas, Yavanas, Kambojas, Pahlavas, and Paradas, known as the Five Hordes. These alliances strengthened the Haihaya and Talajamgha factions.

The Haihaya dynasty, belonging to the Lunar Dynasty, led by Kartaviryarjuna, sacked the city of Kashi. In response, the Solar Dynasty fought back, expelling the Haihayas from the region of Vatsa. Kartaviryarjuna also defeated the Nagas, a mythical serpent-like race.

After his victories, Kartaviryarjuna established Mahismati (present-day Maheshwar) as the capital of his kingdom. He prevented King Bahu of the Ikshvaku dynasty, who was a descendant of Harischandra, from reclaiming Ayodhya, which was his birthright. However, it was only after Kartaviryarjuna's death that Bahu's son, Sagara, was able to recapture Ayodhya.

The narrative suggests that Kartaviryarjuna's power reached such heights that he was able to defeat and imprison the demon king Ravana at the river Godavari. This event foreshadows the upcoming epic of the

Ramayana, where Ravana plays a significant role as the main antagonist.

Intoxicated by his successes, Kartaviryarjuna subdued all enemies of his status and not satisfied with that he went to the ' sea-shore and challenged the Varuna (ocean) for a fight and began to destroy the animals in the sea by shooting them with his arrows. God Varuna appeared before him and asked him what he wanted and very modestly admitted that he is incapable of meeting the challenge thrown. Kartaviryarjuna asked the god to name a man who had the capacity to fight with him. Varuna answered that that perhaps Jamadagni son, Parasurama might accept the challenge and give him a fight and as per him Jamadagni son Parasurama was the person who satisfied that condition. Kartaviryarjuna accepted the challenge and went in search of Parasurama. **(M.B. Anusasana Parva, Chapter 29).**

Kartaviryarjuna who returned triumphant heard a mysterious voice warning him in the following words: "You fool! Don't you know that a Brahman is superior to a Kshatriya? A Kshatriya governs his subjects in alliance with the Brahman". On hearing this, Kartaviryarjuna became angry. He understood that Vayu, the divine messenger was behind the mysterious voice. He despised Vayu and argued that a Kshatriya was superior to a Brahman. Vayu gave him a warning that a Brahman would curse Kartaviryarjuna. **(M.B. Anusasana Parva, Chapter 152).**

LONG ENMITY WITH BHAGAVAS

There was an old conflict between the Haihaya kings and the Bhargava Brahmins, which is rooted in the broader historical tensions between the Brahmin and Kshatriya varnas (castes) in ancient India. The Haihaya dynasty was considered the most powerful ruling dynasty at that time.

Parasurama, who was a descendant of the sage Bhrigu, is also known as Bhargava due to his lineage. The Bhargavas served as the family preceptors (teachers) of the Haihaya kings for generations. Over time, the Bhargavas took advantage of their influential position within the royal palace and accumulated great wealth, often at the expense of the royal treasury. As the wealth of the Haihayas declined, the prosperity of the Bhargavas grew, leading to an imbalance of power and resources.

During the time of Rucheeka, Parasurama's grandfather, the Haihaya dynasty faced severe financial difficulties. In desperation, they approached Rucheeka for a loan, but he concealed his wealth and refused to assist them. Enraged by this betrayal, the Kshatriya kings, representing the warrior class, killed the Brahmins. The surviving Brahmins fled and settled at the foothills of the Himalayas.

Meanwhile, Rucheeka's pregnant wife kept the child, Aurva, in her womb for twelve years, fearing the consequences of bringing him into a violent world. When Aurva was finally born, he emerged by breaking open his mother's thigh (uru), hence earning the name Aurva. Even at birth, Aurva shone like a brilliant torch and vowed to seek revenge against the Kshatriyas who had harmed his ancestors. The fire emanating from Aurva's face was so intense that it even burnt Devaloka, the abode of the gods. The Kshatriya kings prostrated before him, and the Devas requested him to abandon his anger, which Aurva eventually agreed to. The sparks of fire from Aurva's face were collected by the Devas and deposited in the ocean.

From Aurva was born Jamadagni, and from Jamadagni was born Parasurama. Around the same time, Kartaviryarjuna, a valiant king, was born in the Haihaya dynasty.

KARTAVIRYARJUNA CURSED BY THE SAGE APAVA

Once, Kartaviryarjuna invited Agni for a dinner. Agni began to devour all the mountains and forests in the world. The burning was so indiscriminate that it burnt the ashrama of a sage named Apava also. The sage cursed Kartaviryarjuna saying that the thousand hands of the latter would be cut off by Parasurama born in the family of Bhargavas.

From that day onwards the latent feud in him against the Bhargavas was roused into action, **Chapter 43, Santi Parva** mentions that, Once Sri Krishna on the way to Kurukshetra with Pandavas showed them the Parasuramahradas and narrated to them several stories of Parasurama. Reference to Agni comes when Krishna explains the reason why Parasurama cut off the thousand hands of Kartaviryarjuna. It was at the time when Kartaviryarjuna was ruling the three worlds by his might that Agni went and asked for alms from him.

Kartaviryarjuna gave Agni Mountains and forests for his food which Agni burnt and ate. In one of the forests was the ashrama of sage Apava and that also was burnt. Enraged at this, the sage cursed the King. Kartaviryarjuna was confident that he would kill Parasurama by his thousand hands so the curse was not seriously minded by the King.

RAVANA

In the course of his triumphal march, after conquering the whole world, Ravana once arrived with his forces on the bank of the river Narmada. Enjoying the smooth flow of the crystal-clear stream of the Narmada and the pleasant sandbanks in the river-bed, he spent a night there with his followers.

Early next morning he took his bath in the river and setting up the idol of Siva on the sand bank, began to worship it. Just then Kartaviryarjuna and his wives came to the place and began their water sports, a few yards down the river from the place where Ravana was sitting.

As part of his amusements, Kartaviryarjuna stopped the flow of the river by making a dam with his thousand arms. This caused the level of the water to rise and Ravana with his materials of worship was submerged in the flood. Enraged at this disturbance to his worship, he sent two of his men down the river bank to find out what was happening. They traced the source of the trouble to Kartaviryarjuna and his water-sports and reported the matter to their master.

At once Ravana armed himself with his bow rushed to Kartaviryarjuna and began a fierce fight. At last Ravana fell down under the heavy stroke of Kartaviryarjuna mace and was bound in chains and imprisoned. He lay there for one year. Ravana's father sage Pulastya came to know of this and he went to Kartaviryarjuna palace.

He was received with due respect and at his request, Kartaviryarjuna released Ravana and after that they remained friends for life. (**Uttara Ramayana**). According to **Vayu Purana**, King Kartavirya invaded Lanka and took Ravana as a prisoner, but later, when Kartaviryarjuna was killed by Parasurama and Ravana was rescued. There are multiple stories of different Puranas on how King Kartaviryarjuna was killed, but all the stories mention that it was Lord Parasurama.

PARASURAMA CUT OFF THE THOUSAND HANDS

The Haihaya kingdom, ruled by Kartaviryarjuna, was considered savage and uncivilized. During Kartaviryarjuna visit to the ashram, he abducted the cow Surabhi, which greatly upset Parasurama. When Surabhi companion, Susila, escaped from the king's custody and arrived at the ashram without her calf, Parasurama vowed to bring back the calf and sought revenge.

Accompanied by his disciple Akrtavrana, Parasurama travelled to the city of Mahismati, the capital of Kartaviryarjuna kingdom. There, Parasurama, transformed into the embodiment of revenge, took his stand at the city gates and challenged Kartaviryarjuna to a fight, wielding his axe.

Kartaviryarjuna, being a warrior king, responded to the challenge by sending a formidable army consisting of soldiers, elephants, horses, chariots, and infantry. However, Parasurama single-handedly defeated the entire army, using his prowess and weapons. He skilfully manoeuvred around the battlefield, swiftly dispatching the soldiers and even breaking through the defences of the enemy elephant.

This account emphasizes the intense conflict between Parasurama and Kartaviryarjuna, highlighting Parashurama's remarkable combat skills and his determination to avenge the abduction of the cow and protect the honour of the ashram.

The speed of Parasurama was similar to mind and air. Just, they were going to bite the enemy army. Wherever they attack their days, there were sacks of large and large veins with Sarthi and vehicles, thighs and shoulder cuts were dropped. Sahasarbahu Arjuna saw that the soldiers of his army, their bow, flag and shields have fallen into the battlefield from the bloodstream and the arrow, and then it came in a bigger anger.

He simulates his thousand arms on five hundred bowels and left on Parasurama to arrive. In the terrible fight that followed, **Parasurama** attacked him with his axe (parasu) and cut off Kartaviryarjuna arms just like one cut off the branches of a tree and then brought his axe down on the tyrant's neck and fell down beheaded. When the king fell, his frightened soldiers began to run away for life. This was the end of the pillar of Haihaya dynasty. **(Brahmanda Purana, Chapter 81).**

It was a grim battle and after killing Kartaviryarjuna and many of his followers brought back the calf. On his father's death, his ten thousand boys were scared. He repelled his army by showering arrows on them. The whole country greatly welcomed the destruction of Kartaviryarjuna (Sahasrarjun). The king of Deities, Indra was in possession of Lord Shiva's Vijaya Dhanusha. Indra was so pleased that he presented this most beloved bow named Vijaya to Shri Parashurama on instruction from Lord Shiva.

JAMADAGNI EXPIATE PARASURAMA SIN (ATONEMENT)

In some versions of the legend, after his martial exploits, Parasurama returns to his father ashrama with the calf and tells him about the battles he had to fight. His father was pleased, but seeing the blood stained axe of Parashurama, also concerned. The sage does not congratulate Parashurama but reprimands him stating that a Brahmin should never kill a king. He asks him to expiate his sin by going on pilgrimage. He also cautioned his son he must be aware of wrath and pride.

Jamadagni expressed his disappointment and admonished on his son for committing a great sin by slaughtering the idol of Nardev. As Brahmins, they were expected to embody forgiveness and be revered in the world for their virtuous conduct. Jamadagni reminded Parasurama that forgiveness holds great power, as even their ancestor, Lord Brahma, attained a high position due to the strength of forgiveness. The radiance of the sun itself is enhanced by the shining forgiveness of Brahmins. Furthermore, the Supreme Lord, Shrihari, is pleased and satisfied only with those who possess forgiveness.

Understanding the gravity of his actions and the wisdom in his father's words, Parasurama accepted the reprimand and decided to embark on a pilgrimage to purify himself. He sought to wash away his sins by engaging in acts of penance and visiting holy places. Throughout his year-long pilgrimage, he fervently remembered God and sought spiritual purification.

This account highlights the significance of forgiveness in the Brahmin tradition and emphasizes the importance of atonement and seeking redemption for one's transgressions. It showcases Parashurama's willingness to acknowledge his mistake, learn from his father's teachings, and undertake a journey of self-reflection and purification through penance and pilgrimage.

CHAPTER FOURTEEN

THE STORY VERSION: KARTAVIRYARJUNA EPISODE

At this time Lord Parashurama was sitting on the banks of Saraswati. Shunashep was sitting in front. Two disciples of Vishwamitra, Kavsha and Alab were present nearby. Shakuntala's husband Dushyant, created from the essence of Madhurya, is also present here. The problem could not be solved even after argument, and then everyone kept silence. Nidana Shunhshesh was vocal - "After thinking well, I understand this thing correctly that Bharat should be put on the throne, if there is a delay, then the power of the country will weaken.

Dushyant immediately spoke up - "Bharat has become hysterical, I do not want to be burnt to ashes in the fire of Sudas's anger, he is proud of being victorious, he will definitely attack." Ksh-Ailush also said — "I am telling the truth, people have started saying yes to him. Abhishek should be done on time." Shuna Shep, the officer of Vishwamitra Mantra Vidya, spoke again - "Is there no way to recover? It is also bad to sit like a coward. Is it also forbidden to light a lamp in the dark? Where does the doubting soul get victory? The one who fearlessly walks on the path of fire, success kisses his feet. Lord Parashurama stood up - "I am leaving. If time orders, I will meet again."

Being worried, Dushyant said – "Sit down; you have not given your opinion at all. "What can I say, it will not enter your throats. What is the use of drinking the sip of which you cannot digest? Where there is enthusiasm inspired by devotion, defeat can sometimes peep there? Men shine more when defeated; enemies fill the mind with terror. Victory is a momentary shining flower, it withers the next moment.

The one, whose heart has lost self-confidence, will remain defeated throughout his life. When King Sudas There is so much fear that Sahasrarjun is coming with a storm of fire, who will face it? Do you have to die like mosquitoes? This cannot happen in Aryavarta. One who is self-confident does not have the right to live in Aryavarta. May the virtuous enthusiasm come with me? I will give you victory. What you people are seeing in me, what you are seeing am not me. What you are not seeing am me. I am a unique creature. I am struggling for the impossible. Everyone struggles for the possible.

I am the seer of the unattainable; therefore I am fiercer than Yama. Can't understand the day there is a desire to extinguish, I will extinguish myself. When it is extinguished, along with the smoke, sparks of power will fly and the young men lit by their light will fly the flag of Aryatv. I am immortal; I will continue to shine like the sun even after death." Sparks of bravery were flying in Ram's stream. Everyone was stunned, silent and speechless.

Parashurama " Trahi! Trahi!" Saying all the people fell at the feet of Rama. "Jamdagneya, we are yours, we will remain yours for the rest of our lives. Say what do you want? "I want to remove from the sky the thunderous clouds of attachment and hatred. I want to shed the great source of self-confidence. No peace at this time needed. I want to kindle a bonfire of enthusiasm on the horn of humanity.

I want to measure the earth and sky like Lord Vamana; I want to blow the enemy like grass by blowing the storm of the power of unity. If you all stay with me, then I will put the omnivorous Sahasrarjun on the edge of Parshu. Parasurama, the master of victory, stood firm.

The voices united with the cheers started roaring. "We are one, will sacrifice our lives for Aryavarta." Prashar Muni could not sleep, did not feel like doing meditation in the morning. Kept on thinking- literally like Yamraj, Sahasrarjun is coming to erase even the sign of Aryavarta. Only

Parasurama is capable of stopping this fierce storm. My grandfather is an eternal body, a visionary. He also has so much affection for Ram that he is not ready to hear anything against him.

He believes that only Parasurama can protect Aryavarta and no one else has the guts. He has coroneted Bharata and Shivi in spite of the opposition of Sudas. The ashrams of both Jamadagni and Vishwamitra became one. Not even a straw can move in Aryavarta against his will. He is determined himself to remove this emergency. Maheep Trayyaruna of Asindivat does not know what has happened. Going mad to fight Arjuna alone with the Puruvas, like a paravane on Deepshikha.

Admittedly, the flow of bravery is booming in Asindivat, the atmosphere of bravery is hot, but all that bravery will turn into a blood stream. The edge of the enemy's sword is very sharp. If he had mixed his hunkriti with Bhargavas hunker, he would have become Dharmagopta and would have saved Asindivat as well

Aryatv is the ever-increasing yearning for purification. Where the voice of Aryatv should be raised, where the atmosphere should be sanctified by the sound of mantras, where new creation of knowledge should be done, where experiences gained through knowledge and penance should be exchanged, there people want to shed an ocean of blood. .

This irony of momentary life is so worrying. Today Prashar Muni is limping towards the palace with the help of a stick. There is deep pain in the eyes; the lines on the forehead have contracted. His eyes were filled with tears seeing the bragging people. Whatever be the case, he will try to save Asindivat. Today his silence will be broken.

Survival is the fruit of penance. Seeing Muni going towards the palace, people started saying - "Munivar is going to Mahalaya to bless the king. Move in front, bow down, bow down." One said - "Fill infinite power in our arms, blow Sahasrarjun to pieces." The other said - "A single word from a great man is enough to burn him in to ashes." The third said - "Come, come!" People welcomed. The sage entered the palace limping amid cheers. The guards stood aside with folded hands. Pururaj Trayyaruna came out of his room.

The dust of the sage's feet was put on the forehead, made to sit on deerskin. Worshiped with leaves and flowers and said – "Muninath, you have purified my palace with the dust of your feet. This is the result of my accumulated virtue. Your blessings are greatly needed at this time." The sage said, "Rajan, I have not come to bless you, I have come to warn you." The king was shocked and the royal assembly was stunned! Wiping his eyes, he again said in a trembling voice - "I see Asindivat burning, the streets are soaked in blood. Mahipate, your head is separated from the torso." Hearing the words of the seer Muni, everyone became upset. They started thinking- If he was silent till now, he should remain silent now. He came to curse. People's faith in Muni has decreased. "Munivar, you are unwell, sit comfortably on the hut" said the sad king.

The sage jolted the brain - "I see Parashurama coming, the ocean of violence, leaping and roaring and biting the dust of Aryavarta." King replied "My heroes are standing in his way." "No-no, don't prepare to fight, run away to the forests where the fire doesn't burn." The king said angrily "You have considered me a coward, should I go to the shelter or run away. Munivar you go, your thoughts have defeated you."No "Rajan, the gods have not given me enough power to understand you. I am a seer of the future, seeing everything, but how to show you. Muninath said keeping both hands on his forehead with pain. "Munivar, now you go, what you said to the king in front of everyone is being stitched like a needle.

You had come to make my heroes cowards? Everyone laughed out loud, the commander "Not a coward, I beg you all to avoid the mass hysteria. Wildfires are burning all around. I see Asindivat being consumed. Dev, is there no one to listen to me?" Muni's eyes got wet with tears, Prasar Muni limping on his stick slowly went towards the cottage.

Twenty five days later Asindivat was burning like a huge pyre. The atmosphere was filled with smoke. At times, a desperate cry could be heard. Dead bodies were scattered all around, food for vultures, crows and jackals. Blood was flowing in the streets. The palace had become a mass of ashes. The men were dead; the dogs were dragging the bloodied women by their hair. It was a very horrifying scene, very scary. Muni was standing on the bank of Yamuna. His eyes were swollen from crying. Tears were falling from him equally.

Suddenly herons started rising from the sand of the river, Sahasrarjun with a hundred warriors. Prachanda was seen coming on a horse. The music of their humming river had stopped. Trembling with fear, Prasar Muni went forward and took hold of the reins of Arjuna's horse.

That hungry Arjuna looked at Muni with a violent look. His companions drew their swords. "What do the joggers want?" asked Arjuna angrily. "Hey King, I have come to request you, you control your anger like a skilled charioteer and return. Violence has never borne fruit, and will never bear fruit. Sowing the seeds of violence will only grow forests of poison. Hatred till date No one is a star.

In the fire of hatred, the hater himself gets burnt to ashes. Stop for a moment and think and return. Sahasrarjun, thinking the sage to be mad, listened contemptuously, then laughed cruelly and attacked him on the face. The warriors with him laughed gleefully. A stream of blood gushed out of the sage's mouth. They fainted and returned to the earth. When the news of Sahasrarjun attack started coming in the ashrams, then the ashram residents got scared. The meditation of the ascetics stopped.

Vibrations started coming in the chanting together. It was not possible to stop his army like the flood-ocean. Exasperated Jamadagni said to his disciples - "Call my Rama." Muni Vashisht sent a message all around that everyone should hide in the thickets of bushes, in the caves, but keep practicing penance and learning.

No one should waste his strength without meeting Bhargava on the banks of the Sindhu. Everyone ran away. The ashrams became deserted. The music of Vihangas and the jumping of antelopes went on. Fear prevailed in the atmosphere. Jamadagni and Vashisht stayed with some old ascetics in their hermitage. An unforgettable event was about to happen. Arjuna's army reached Vashisht ashram passing through the banks of Saraswati. Out of fear, many died by jumping into the river. Arjuna entered Vashisht hermitage, dragging captive men and women tied in ropes behind carts, raping Aryan girls. Sahasrarjun moved forward, but no one came forward to resist.

He set fire to the wealth of forests, burnt thousands of villages, looted the cows, sent what he got to Yama's door, but no one could dare to come before me. Yes, then the power to stop me has not arisen at all. What will that son of Jamadagni do to me?" He hurled his heavy mace in the sky and took the world.

On the one hand, Vashisht Muni was offering oblations along with five old men. Sahasrarjun moved forward twitching his moustache. 'O Vashisht.' he called rudely. "You know me who I am, the king of Aryavarta." "I have known you since childhood that you have always been rebellious. Looting Doing, setting fire, breaking the modesty of women and many other bad things.'- said Muni. "I will burn everything belong to you then only you will know." "It is not in your power to destroy what I have sown by the grace of the gods.

As it is lit, new buds will emerge." "Tell all these miracles to your disciples, stop making things up, get up, respect me as your guest." "The terrorist guest is not honored here." - Strictly Vashisht said. Sahasrarjun got angry, snatched the sacrificial liquid with his kick and came forward with a sword.

He extended his hand to hold Muni's beard. The sage rolled down where he was. The desire to humiliate Vashisht remained unfulfilled. Tapo bhoomi was burnt into ashes. Sahasrarjun army now started moving towards Bhrigu Ashram. His footsteps were heard like the rumbling of a flood.

In a short while, the soldiers shouted and entered the Bhrigu Ashram and took possession of the hut. Arjuna's whole anger was on this ashram. He wanted to take revenge from Bhargava, but there was no sign of Bhargava there. He did not like such desolation. Laughing proudly, he went ahead, stood in front of him and looked at Renuka

"Who, Maharishi Jamadagni? I bow down to you Sahasrarjun." "You are cursed, you have corrupted this ashram." "I have come to you to get the same removed." "It has come in vain, the curse of Bhrugukul would have bitten like a Sahasrafan snake."At this time I have come as your death. Where did your son Ram go, where have your disciples gone?" 'When the hour of your death comes, then all will meet together.' "Obey me. You are my traditional guru, become my priest, Haihayas will get peace and my prestige will increase.

I will give a lot of money." Who would be the teacher for the one whose salvation is not possible? "So won't you listen to me? Isn't it? Then I will take your life." Maharishi replied. "Life can be taken even by lions, wolves and snakes." "I will set fire to your ashram. I will loot and kill the disciples and cows after scarching." "If you don't do all this then how can you be called a vampire? I know you are reeling from the curse of my father.

I should remove the curse; but it is not in my control. Sahasrarjun got angry. "Taljung, tie him to the tree." Maharishi himself stood near the tree. This calm resistance made Sahasrarjun furious. Taljung tied him to the tree. "Speak, will the curse be removed or not?" Jamadagni remained silent. He took out an arrow from the quiver and shot it.

He sunk into Maharishi's shoulder. "O old woman, keep watching this, lest the night gets stuck." and laughed profusely. Crying Renuka wiped the blood flowing from the wound, gave water and sat down to cry. Ram my son, when will you come? Bhargava had a stop on the banks of the Indus. Bharat Shivi and Harit etc

Chakravarti stood determined to fight the enemy with his warriors. Don't know where the enthusiasm was raising among the Bhrigu heroes. Footsteps, chariots and air-talking horses were flocking all around. Parshu, Khadga, Gada and a group of bows were waiting for the drivers. The old men and women who had fled from all sides were being taken to safe places. Noise all around happened Bhargava stood alone on the mound, stunned in his own calm ferocity.

His arched brows hung over his menacing eyes, his vision flashed here and there like lightning, his silence was fiercer than his speech, and an aura of intolerable radiance emanated around him. Even for those who used to see him regularly, today it was becoming difficult to see and bear.

Even Brahminishtha Mahatmas like Munivar Vashisht used to respect him as the savior of Aryavarta. Shunashep used to consider him as a deity. As the ashram and the highway became safe, women and men used to bow down in worship on hearing his name. As his power increased, people were drawn towards him with reverence.

Impressed by the sky-high limitless effect, people started considering him as an incarnation of God. Encouraging gaiety with pure humor, mesmerizing everyone with the Prasad of sweet sarcasm, trembling hearts with fierce frown, he used to attract everyone's devotion towards him by staying at an insurmountable distance.

Bhagwati Lomaharshani became the source of power by bearing the Prasad of his heart; she used to mesmerize everyone by drinking somersault of blessings. Parashurama said. The joy of victory was dissolved in his voice. "Harit, you move along the banks of the Indus. Bharata, you take hold of the foothills of the mountains and move cautiously, taking care of the safety of sages, women and children, making the path safe and the places impregnable. I will meet you on fifteenth Day at Bhrigu Ashram. A remnant of the one who has reduced Aryavarta to ashes will not go back. Take your authority over all and spread the news around that Bhargava is coming

Strong horses of one color, fierce Bhargava warriors, Prachanda Parshu, Durdharsha Dhanusha, all these became impregnable by the inspiration and devotion of Parashurama, rich in wonderful personality, came down on Aryavarta like a thunder storm with lightning. "Ram is coming" the boys said running to their Amba. 'Aa rahe Ram' chanted the rishi's hiding in the caves. "Aa Rahe Ram"(Ram is Coming) distressed, injured, oppressed convinced. "Aa Rahe Ram" Jamadagni-Renuka both have tears in their eyes together. Agye. "Ram is coming"

The land of ashrams danced with joy. The news of "Ram is coming" went from house to house in Panghat. As soon as the sound of "Ram is coming" reached Sahasrarjun ears, he was shocked. But, Ram is coming from Kivar, where will he come, no one had the answer. That he would come riding on the wind and shower thunderbolt on all of us. Then Gurudev Ram's Jai-sound started thundering in all the directions.

Sahasrarjun started pacing here and there with his soldiers, the soldiers were trembling. The companion of Kaal Guru Daddnath Aghori of cursed Haihaya caste, successor of great gurus, and lord of the power of Mahadevi Siddheshwari is coming towards him. The echo of Ram's name was echoing everywhere, but no one knew where Ram was. First of all Harit's army reached the banks of Saraswati, Sahasrarjun broke down on him.

Harit was surrounded by the Haihayas. Harit lost his life in that religious war along with thousands of soldiers. The ecstasy of victory had not yet settled down, and then Bharat clashed with Ram's shouts of terror filling the atmosphere with the arrows to all directions. Bharat had learned the art of war from Ram only. With great patience and skill, they were playing the game of war with the mad Haihayas. Till noon the soldiers from both the sides did not budge. The decision of victory and defeat was swinging on the carousel, and then together thousands of lightning flashed.

Bharat soldiers announced Gurudev team with joy. Sahasrarjun looked at it, the drunken horses were swaying. A black horse was coming, breathing like fire, on it the same body, the same face, the same black hair, thick beard, the same parasu, the same eyes piercing him. As if Yamraj himself is coming with Yamdoots. As Parasurama tears apart the forest, so the Bhrigu warriors disintegrate the Haihaya party.

The Haihaya army was horrified by the unrequited semen and the fierce collision started running away from the field. Thousands were beheaded by the blows of the axes. Horses crushed the enemies, overturned the chariots. The horses of the Bhrigu's joined together like a roaring flood and kept moving forward. Bharat was mad with bravery. Cutting off the heads of thousands, they started performing Tandav dance. Haihayas also took their bravery to the limit. Sahasrarjun had gone mad. Swinging his heavy mace, he broke the heads of hundreds of horses.

Countless heads were cut off and laid on the ground. Wherever he went, there used to be a pile of dead people. The Haihaya party retreated and fled to Bhrigu's hermitage. Bhargava and Bharata followed him. Bhargava and Sahasrarjun came face to face in this carnage. Bhargava raised the sword,

Arjuna the mace.

Two fierce weapons collided, sparks started flying. Arjuna's mace broke. Bhargava missed the target in a struggle with his mace, but cut the neck of Arjuna's horse. Arjuna jumped from the falling horse, took out his sword and attacked Bhargava. Hundreds of birds started hovering over his head. Bhargava dissuaded everyone by raising his hand.

Everyone retreated. Bhargava stood in his place, healthy and calm, his eyes challenging the enraged Arjuna. Arjuna's fierce red-red eyes filled with blood. His face became distorted and fearful due to immense hatred. Jumped to the beat, wanted to strangle Bhargava, but got stuck in the middle. He saw with his bloodshot eyes that Bhargava had grown huge, his head wanted to touch the sky, Parshu was burning like the fierce Sun of Nidagh and streams of fire had burst from his eyes.

"Will Ram kill me with his shining parasu?" Wow, gathering all his strength, he attacked Bhargava. His trembling hands started groping Bhargavas throat, Bhargava went back and clung to the whole body and pressed it in such a way that all his bones came out after trembling and started vomiting blood there. He returned to the ground breathless, Ram sat on his chest and started punching him in the face. He started screaming like a dying animal.

Bhargava stood up leaving Sahasrarjun half-dead. As soon as he stood up, his eyes fell on his father. Maharishi Jamadagni, who was tied to a tree, was watching the duel with taktaki. His body was riddled with arrows flowing with the flow of blood. The sage was near death.

Bhargava roared fiercely - "Father, father," ran to him screaming. Arjuna had recovered somewhat. Picked up two arrows lying nearby, threw both arrows with the same hand. One sunk into Jamadagni chest. Renuka started crying. The second arrow shot at Bhargava fell on the earth with a thud. Suddenly the hoarse cry of a jackal rang out.

There bang a sound no one had ever heard before. No one could understand what all this is happening. All distressed, all speechless. As soon as that arrow flying, everyone saw that God started flying in the sky, kept flying. Fierce laughter erupted from his mouth, everyone's heart stopped beating. Bhargava hanged in limbo. Ram's sharp nails sank into Arjuna's throat. Shonit's stream burst, Arjuna's head fell apart from the torso.

The eagle flew away with him; the impudent jackals dragged the torso and ran away. Haihaya army ran away by putting his feet on his head. Flowers started raining on Bhargava from the sky, shouts of victory started emanating from all directions. Yogi-Yati, Sadhus-Sanyasi all blessed - "Jai Ho, Jai Ho." The fire of malice was extinguished, Kalagni itself burnt to ashes due to the storm of fire. Gods started getting Arghya, the rhythmic sound of Veda-recitation from ashrams started advancing the supremacy of Arya-Sankar. Waves of joy resounded in everyone's heart. "Jai Ho, Jai Ho."

CHAPTER FIFTEEN

JAMADAGNI HEAD

To atone for the sin of this massacre Jamadagni advised his son to go and perform penance in Mahendragiri. From that day onwards the sons of Kartaviryarjuna were waiting for an opportunity to take revenge. Taking advantage of the absence of Parasurama from the ashrama, Surasena and two other sons of Kartaviryarjuna, with their followers went to the ashrama of Jamadagni In revenge, they travelled to the hermitage and murdered Jamadagni, surrounding the Rishi and shooting him to death with arrows like a stag.

Afterwards, they decapitated his body and took his head with them because he was the father of Parashurama who had killed their father that felt them the proper revenge of eye-for-an-eye. They first stabbed

Jamadagni twenty-one times and then chopped off his head.

When Parasurama returned home, he found his mother next to the body of his father, crying hysterically as she beat her chest twenty-one times in a row. At the sight, his father lying dead on the floor, Parasurama cried a loud. Parasurama again picks up his axe and killed three sons of Kartaviryarjuna and also kills many warriors in retaliation. He retrieved the head of his father for cremation.

While cremating, Renuka wept beating her breast twenty-one times. Renuka jumped into the funeral pyre and abandoned her life. Seeing this, Parasurama took a solemn vow that he would go round the world twenty-one times and extirpate the Kshatriya Kings, once for each time the hand of his mother hit her chest and the number of times his father was stabbed to death. Parasurama then vowed to enact genocide on the war-mongering Kshatriya twenty-one times over, Parasurama then travelled throughout the Indian subcontinent, killing all men of the Kshatriya caste, guilty or innocent.

In the interval between the Treta and Dwapara Yugas, Parashurama, great among all who have borne arms, urged by impatience of wrongs, repeatedly smote the noble race of Kshatriya and when that fiery meteor, by his own valour, annihilated the entire tribe of the Kshatriya, he formed at Samanta-Panchaka five lakes of blood.

There is another legend that the Nairs, Bunts and Nagas of Kerala and Tulunadu, receiving word as Parasurama approached, took the sacred threads that marked them twice-born, hid them in the forest and travelled south. Parasurama then gave their land to the Nambuthiri Brahmins, and the Nambuthiri then denied the Nairs and Bunts their status as royalty when
Parasurama left.

After he had finally rid the world of Kshatriyas, Parasurama conducted the aswamedha sacrifice, done only by sovereign kings. The Ashvamedha demanded that the remaining Kshatriya kings either submit to Parasurama, or stop the sacrifice by defeating him in battle. They were unable to do either, and so perished.

THE NARRATIVE OF BHĀRGAVA PARAŚURĀMA
Section 3 - Upodghāta-pāda
Vasiṣṭha said:—

1. Then once Śūra (i.c. Kārttavīrya's sons) who had escaped to the

Himalayan forests—went to the forest for hunting along with Śūrasena and others and accompanied by the armies of four different units.

2. After entering the great forest, they killed different kinds of animals. Overwhelmed by thirst at midday, they went to the river Narmadā.

3. Taking their bath there and drinking the waters of the river, they got rid of their fatigue. While going away they saw the hermitage of Jamadagni on the way.

4. On seeing the charming hermitage, they asked sages coming that way—"whose hermitage is this?" In that they were urged by the inevitable future result of their actions.

5. They replied: "Jamadagni of great penance lives in this hermitage. He is a sage of quiescent soul and his son Rama is the most excellent one among the wielders of weapons."

6. On hearing it and because Rama name was mentioned, they were overcome with fear at the outset. Remembering their previous ruthless enmity, they were exceedingly enraged.

7. Then they conferred with one another—"Since our father has been killed by Parasurama, why we should not take revenge by killing the father of the slayer of our father? Direct us now."

8. After saying this, they entered the hermitage with swords in their hands, as the heroic sages had gone to different places. They killed Jamadagni.

9. After killing him, they took away his head like the ruthless Nisadas (hunters). Those wicked ones then returned to their capital along with their armies.

10. On seeing their father killed, the sons of that noble-souled sage lamented, O great king. Afflicted by grief they stood surrounding him,

11. On seeing her husband fallen on the ground after being killed, Reṇukā immediately fell down senseless like a creeper struck down by the thunderbolt.

12. After falling unconscious, she was burnt by the fire of grief in her mind. Like one whose consciousness is lost, she became separated from her vital airs. She died instantaneously.

13. The sons who had regained consciousness saw that she did not utter any word. They became immersed in the ocean of grief and fell down senseless on the ground.

14. Other sages who were living in that penance-grove came there. They too were equally grieved but they consoled the sons of the sage.

15. After being consoled by the groups of sages the sons of Jamadagni duly cremated the bodies of their parents at their instance.

16. They performed all the obsequies that should be performed later on after the death of parents. They were afflicted day and night by the sorrow, due to the death of their parents.

17. In due course of time, at the end of the period of twelve years, Rāma returned from his penance. Accompanied by his friend, he went to the hermitage of his father.

CHAPTER SIXTEEN

KSATRIYAS

The most important event of Parasurama life was the total extermination of the Ksatriyas race. The Purana belief is that he went round the world eighteen times to massacre the Ksatriyas. In many places in the Puranas it is stated that Parasurama fought against the Ksatriyas eighteen times. But in chapter 29 of Ashvamedha Parva it is stated that Parasurama fought against the Ksatriyas twenty one times. So it is to be surmised that Parasurama fought eighteen big battles and three minor ones.

REVENGEFUL ENMITY AFTER JAGDAMBI KILLING

Puranas mention Parasurama killing the Kings of Cola, Cera, and Paundra, and his destruction of the embryos in the wombs of Kshatriya women, the specific details of these events may vary across different Puranic texts.

Parasurama, an avatar of Lord Vishnu, is known for his role as a warrior who eradicated the Kshatriya (warrior) caste multiple times. The Puranas generally depict him as a fierce and relentless warrior, driven by a divine mission to cleanse the earth of the corrupt and oppressive Kshatriya rulers.

Regarding the blood of the slain kings flowing into a holy bath called Syamantapancakam, I couldn't find any specific reference to such a bath in the available sources. It's possible that this particular detail may come from regional or local folklore or variations of the story.

Kartaviryarjuna had one hundred sons. All of them were killed in the battle by Parasurama. However as per Brahmanda Purana, , vrsa the prince one of the sons of Kartaviryarjuna escaped from the Ksatriyas extermination of Parasurama. Those who killed , their names, as given in **Chapter 76 of Brahmanda Purana**, are given below :Nirmada, Rocana, Sanku, Ugrada, Dundubhi, Dhruva,Suparsi, Satrujit, Kraunca, Santa, Nirdaya, Antaka, Akrti, Vimala, Dhlra, Niroga, Bahuti, Dama, Adhari,Vidhura, Saumya, Manasvl, Puskala, Busa, Taruna,Rsabha, Rksa, Satyaka, Subala, Bali, Ugresta,Ugrakarma, Satyasena, Durasada, Viradhanva, Dlrghabahu, Akampana, Subahu, Dirghaksa, Vartulaksa,Carudamstra, Gotravan, Manojava, Urdhvabahu,Krodha, Satyakirti, Duspradharsana, Satyasandha, Mahasena, Sulocana, Raktanetra, Vakradarhstra, Sudarhstra, Ksatravarma, Manonuga, Dhumrakeisa,
Pingalocana, Avyanga, Jatila, Venuman, Sanu, Pasapani, Anuddhata, Duranta, Kapila, Sambhu, Ananta,Visvaga, Udara, Krti, Ksatrajit, Dharmi, Vyaghra,
Ghosa, Adbhuta, Puranjaya, Carana. Vagmi, VIra,Rathi, Govihvala, Sangramajit, Suparva, Narada,Satyaketu, Satanlka, Drdhayudha, Citradhanva,Jayatsena, Virupaksa, Bhimakarma, Satrutapana,Citrasena, Duradharsa Viduratha, Sura, Surasena,Dhisana, Madhu, and Jayadhvaja.

Sloka 78, Chapter 49, Santi Parva mentions that Parsurama killed Gopati III, A son of the celebrated emperor, Sibi. When Parasurama killed and made extinct all Ksatriyakings it was a herd of cows that brought up this child. **As per Vayu Purana, 68. 19** Parasurama killed Harakalpa, One of the sons born to Vipracitti by Simhika. As per **Brahmanda Purana, 3.6. 13-12** Parasurama killed Supunjika son of Vipracitti by Simhika. **Mahabharata, Sand Parva, Chapter 49, Stanza 8** mentions thatDadhivahana, a son of an ancient king of Bharata was saved by the hermit Gautama from the attack of Parasurama .As per **M.B., Drona Parva, Chapter 7, Stanza 12,** Parasurama had defeated the Ahgas once.

As per Mahabharata, with his bow Parasurama slew 64 times 10,000 Kshatriyas. In that slaughter were included 14,000 Brahman hating Kshatriya of the Dantakura country of the IIaihayas, he slew a 1000 with his short club, a 1000 with his sword, and a 1000 by hanging. Rama slew 10,000 Kshatriyas with his axe.

He could not quietly bear the furious speeches uttered by those foes of his and when many foremost of Brahmans uttered exclamations, mentioning the name of Rama of Bhrigu's race, he proceeding against the Kashmiras, the Daradas, the Kuntis, the Kshudrakas, the Malavas, the Angas, the Vangas, the Kalingas, the Videhas, the Tamraliptakas, the Rakshovahas, the Vitahotras, the Trigartas, the Martikavatas, counting by thousand, slew them all by means of his whetted shafts. Proceeding from province to province, he thus slew thousands of scores of Haihaya-Kshatriyas. Creating a deluge of blood and filling many lakes also with blood and bringing all the 18 islands under his subjection, he performed 100 sacrifices.

MANES

Then the Bhargava ancestors like Rucheeka and others came to the sky and requested Parasurama to stop this slaughter. They said: "Oh son, Rama, stop this slaughter. What good do you get by killing innocent Ksatriyas?" By that time Parasurama had made twenty one rounds around Bharata killing the Ksatriyas. **(Chapter 64, Adi Parva ; Chapter 38, Sabha Parva; Chapter 116, Vana Parva; Chapter 49, Santi Parva and 10 chapters from chapter 83 of Brahmanda Purana) .** Then Parasurama was carrying on the annihilation of Ksatriyas, Bhumidevi induced the sage Kashyapa to entreat Parasurama to stop his massacre of Bhopal's.(Protectors of Bhumi = Ksatriyas). **(M.B. Santi Parva, Chapter 79, Verse 44).**

Parshuram conquered the entire world from Kshatriyas 21 times. He is supposed to be immortal and will guide the Kalki Avatar in Kaliyuga to undergo a penance to get all the celestial and magical weapons to save the mankind.

CHAPTER SEVENTEEN

SAMANTA PANCHAKA

Parasurama legends are notable for their discussion of violence, the cycles of retaliations, the impulse of krodha (anger), the inappropriateness of krodha, and repentance. Parasurama killed Kshatriya that their blood accumulated to fill up five lakes, which collectively came to be known as the Samanta Panchaka, the area which in the later days would come to be known as the Kurukshetra. He was so repentant for his sins of murder that he was filled with extreme remorse and prayed to the gods. The ancestors met the Parasurama to stop the blood bath and asked him to seek a boon. In return, Parasurama wanted such a boon which would make the area around the five lakes very holy and blood be transforming into water. His boon was granted, and even now, Kurukshetra is considered to be an important place on the Hindu cultural map.

OFFIRING BLOOD TO MANES

Parasurama made here five rivers (Lakes) through which blood flowed. There, with hands dipped in blood, he offered oblations to the manes. **(M.B.**

Adi Parva, Chapter 2, Verse 4). He stored the blood of the Ksatriyas he killed in the twenty one rounds of killing in five lakes in Samanta Panchaka. By the blessings of the ancestors of Parasurama this place became a holy bath. **(M.B. Adi Parva, Chapter 2, Verse 8)**

He offered blood to the Manes in those lakes. The Manes led by Rucheeka appeared before him and asked him to name any boon he wanted. Then Parasurama said, "Revered Manes, if you are pleased with me, you must absolve me from the sin of this mass massacre of the Ksatriyas and declare the five lakes where I have stored their blood as holy." The Manes declared, "Let it be so." From then onwards the place became holy under the name Samanta Panchaka.

At the end of the Dvapara yuga and the beginning of Kaliyuga a great battle lasting for eighteen days took place at this holy place between the Pandavas and the Kauravas. **(Chapter 2, Adi Parva)** Duryodhana was killed at Samanta Panchaka. **(Salya Parva, Chapter 89, Verse 40).** After killing 21 generations of Kshatriyas, he filled their blood in five pools collectively known as the Samantha Panchaka (Sanskrit: समंतपञ्चक). He later atoned for his sin by severe penance. The five pools are considered to be holy **(Sangraha Parva)** Samantha Panchaka is located somewhere around Kurukshetra. It also mentions that the Pandavas performed a few religious rites near the Samantha Panchaka before the Mahabharata War at Kurukshetra. **(Anukramanika Parva)**

The complete destruction of Haihaya Kshatriyas by Parashurama at a place near to Kurukshetra - literally 'the place of Kuru'. This is because according to the Vamana Purana, King Kuru offered his body parts to Vishnu as seeds in order to cultivate the land and make it fertile. In Rigveda, this place is called 'Saryanvat'. It is also called the Northern Vedi of Brahma ('Uttaravedi' - the holiest part of the yadnavedi or altar), and considered holy ('Dharmakshetre Kurukshetre') since the beginning of time, even before the events of the Mahabharata War.

Today, the region lies mostly in the state of Haryana in modern India, and is still considered a holy ground, with the Brahma tank (lake) and a Shiva temple, and almost two dozen places of worship, and what is presumed to be Abhimanyu's fort near the modern twin-town of Kurukshetra and Thanesar.

Lord Parashurama, after having exhausted all Kshatriya clans twenty one times and seeing the entire massacre and the blood, finally dug up five tanks in the ground with his axe to fill the blood of all his enemies. This is why the place is called a 'Panchaka'. Parashurama's revenge on Kshatriyas, there was a history of genocide and torture of the Brahmins (those in the Bhrigu clan to which Rama belonged) before the actual events of Kartavirya Arjuna stealing Jamadagni cow

CHAPTER EIGHTEEN

KASHYAPA

To atone for the sin of slaughtering eveninnocent Ksatriyas, Parasurama gave away all his riches as gifts to Brahmins. He invited all the Brahmins to Samanta Panchaka and conducted a great Yajna there. Kashyapa is a revered Vedic sage. He was one of the seven ancient Rishis considered as Saptarishees in Rig-Veda, numerous Sanskrit texts and Indian mythologies. He is the most ancient Rishi listed in the colophon verse in the Brihadaranyaka Upanishad, and called a self-made scholar in the Atharvaveda. He was based in the northwestern part of the Indian subcontinent, and legends attribute the region of Kashmir to be derived from his name. The name Kashmir, states may be a shortened form of "Kashyapa Mir" or the "lake of the sage Kashyapa", or alternatively derived from "Kashyapa Meru" or the sacred mountains of Kashyapa. His name appears in Patanjali's ancient bhasya on verse 1.2.64 of Pāṇini. His name is very common in the Epic and Purana literature.

KAŚYAPA, MEANS "TURTLE" IN SANSKRIT

Kashyapa is one of Saptarishees, the seven famed Rishis considered to be author of many hymns and verses of the Rig-Veda (1500-1200 BCE). He and his family of students are, for example, the author of the second verse of 10.137, and numerous hymns in the eighth and ninth mandal of the Rig-Veda. He is mentioned in verse 2.2.4 of the Brihadaranyaka Upanishad,with Atri, Vashistha, Vishvamitra, Jamadagni, Bharadwaja and Gautama. Kashyapa is also mentioned as the earliest Rishi in colophon verse 6.5.3 of Brihadaranyaka Upanishad, one of the oldest Upanishad scriptures. Kashyapa is mentioned in other Vedas and numerous other Vedic texts. For example, in one of several cosmology-related hymns of Atharvaveda (~1000 BCE), Kashyapa is mentioned in the allegory-filled Book XIX:

४९५६. कालो दविमजनयत् काल इमाः पृथ्वीरुत
काले है भूत भव्य चेषति हवतिष्ठत ॥५ ॥
४९५७. कालो भूतमिसृजत काले तपति सूर्यः काले
ह वश्विा भूतानि काले चक्षरूव पश्यति॥६ ॥
४९५८ काले मनः काले प्राणः काले नाम समाहतिम्।
कालेन सर्वा नन्दन्त्यागतेन प्रजा इमाः॥७॥
४९५९. काले तपः काले ज्येष्ठ काले ब्रह्म समाहतिम्
कालो ह सर्वस्येश्वरो यः पतिासीत् प्रजापतेः ॥८॥
४९६०तनेषति तेन जात तद् तस्मनि् प्रतष्ठितिम्कालो
ह ब्रह्म भूत्वा वभिर्त परमष्ठेनिम् ॥९ ॥
४९६१. कालः प्रजा असृजत कालो अग्रे प्रजापतमि् ।
स्वयम्भूः **कश्यपः** कालात् तपः कालादजायत ॥१०॥ ***अथर्ववदे, XIX L51-53***

काल स्वरूप अश्व वश्विरूपी रथ का वाहक हैवह सात करिणो और सहस्र आँखो वाला है। वह जरारहति

और प्रचुर पराक्रम सम्पन्न हैसमस्त लोक उसके चक्र हैं उस (अश्व या रथ) पर बुद्धमिान् ही आरोहण करते हैं॥१ ॥

गतशिीलता अस का पर्याय हैकाल सबको अपने साथ घसीटता हुआ चलता हैबुद्धमिान व्यक्ति ही काल-समय पर आरू होकर करते हैंजैसे अवा व्यक्ति अथ को नति कर लेता हैवैसे ही

बद्धिमान लोग अपने समय को सुनयोजित करके उसे सत्प्रयोजनो में नियोजित कर लेते हैं शेष लोग समय के साथ घसिटते हुए किसी प्रकार अपना समय बिताते हैं] वह काल सात चक्रों का वाहक हौ (उन चक्रों की) सात नाभियाँ हैं तथा वह अक्ष (धुरा) अमृत-अनश्वर है वह प्रथम देव 'काल' सभी भुवनों को प्रकट करता हुआ सतत गतिशील है॥२॥

[वि] वहाण्ड की परधियों कही गयी , काल उन सभी को संचालित किये हुये हौ समय विभाजन में दिन मुख्य आधार हैं सात के बाद यही वह पुर दोहराया जाता हौ कालचक्र विभाग में सात ऋतुओं का भी उल्लेख मिलता है] विश्व ब्रह्माण्डरूप भरा हुआ कुम्भ काल के ऊपर स्थापित हैं सत ज्ञानीजन उस काल को (दिवस-रात्र आदि) विभिन्न रूपों में देखते हैं वह काल इन दृश्यमान प्राणियों के सामने प्रकट होकर उन्हें अपने में समाहित कर लेता है मुनीषीगण उस काल को विकारों से रहित आकाश के समान (निर्लेप) बताते हैं॥३॥

वह काल समस्त भुवनों का पोषण करने वाला तथा सभी में श्रेष्ठ रीति से संव्याप्त हौ वही भूतकाल में इन

प्राणियों का पिता और अगले जन्म में इनका पुत्र हो जाता हौ इस काल से उत्तम कोई भी तेज नहीं है॥४॥

काल ने ही इस दिव्यलोक को उत्पन्न किया और इसी ने सभी प्राणियों की आश्रयभूता भूमि को उत्पन्न किया भूत, भविष्य और वर्तमान सभी इस अविनाशी काल के आश्रित रहते हैं॥५॥

काल ने ही इस सृष्टि का सृजन किया हौ काल की प्रेरणा से ही सूर्यदेव इस संसार को प्रकाशित करते हैं इसी काल के आश्रित समस्त प्राणी हैं नेत्र भी इसी काल के आश्रित होकर विविध पदार्थों को देखते हैं॥६॥

काल में ही मन बाल में ही काल में सभी नाम समाहित है जो समयानुसार प्रकट होते रहते हैं काल की अनुकूलता से ही समस्त प्रजननन्दित होते हैं॥७॥

शक्तिमान तथा बधाइ काल में सहित] है काल हो सभी स्थावर-जम बाका ईश्वर, समस्त प्रजा का पालकताका पिता है॥८॥

हारकालद्वारा प्रेरित उसी के द्वारा उत्पन्न हुआ उसके में प्रति भी हौ कालही अपनी चेतनाको वस्तित करके को करता है॥९॥

काल ने सजीव वस्तुओं की रचना की और सबसे पहले प्रजापति की। काल स्व-निर्मित **कश्यप** से, काल से पवित्र अग्नि का जन्म हुआ।॥१० *अथर्ववेद, पुस्तक XIX L51-53*

The horse in the form of time is the carrier of the chariot of the world, it has seven rays and thousands of eyes. he is toothless And he is full of prowess, all the worlds are his wheels, only the wise ride on him (horse or chariot) ॥

Dragging everyone along with him, only wise people do it from time to time. After doing this, they employ it in good purposes, the rest of the people spend their time somehow dragging with time. ॥1॥

That time is the bearer of the seven cycles. There are seven centers (of those chakras) and that axis (axle) is nectar-immortal. That first god 'Kaal' manifesting all the worlds is continuously moving. ॥2॥ [V] The fringes of Vahand were said, Kaal is operating them all. Days are the main basis in time division, after seven this Pur is repeated. Seven seasons are also mentioned in the Kalachakra section. ॥2॥

Kumbh filled with the world universe is established over Kaal. Saints and wise people see that Kaal in different forms (day-night etc.) that Kaal appears in front of these visible beings and absorbs them into itself. (Nirlep) tells ॥3॥

That Time is the nurturer of all the worlds and pervades all in the best manner. Whereas in the past, he becomes the father of living beings and their son in the next birth. No one is faster than this period. Time itself created this divine world and it created the shelter land of all beings. Past, future and present all are dependent on this imperishable time. ॥4॥

Kaal has created this universe. It is due to the inspiration of Kaal that the sun illuminates this world; All living beings are dependent on this Kaal; the eyes are also dependent on this Kaal; they see various things ॥5॥

Kāla created land; the Sun in Kāla hath his light and heat. In Kāla rest all things that be: in Kāla doth the eye discern. ॥6॥

In Kāla mind, in Kāla breath, in Kāla name are fixt and joined. These living creatures, one and all, rejoice when Kāla hath approached. ॥7॥

Kāla embraces Holy Fire, the Highest, Brahma in himself. Yea, Kāla, who was father of Prajāpati, is Lord of All. ॥8॥

He made, he stirred this universe to motion, and on him it rests. He, Kāla, having now become Brahma, holds Parameshthin up. ॥9॥

10 Kāla created living things and, first of all, Prajāpati. From Kāla self-made **Kasyapa,** from Kāla Holy Fire was born. ॥10॥

— *Atharvaveda, Book XIX, Hymns L51-53*

KASHYAPA- PRIEST OF PARASURAMA

Kashyapa was a known Vedic sage to whom many hymns are attributed. According to the Mahabharata, the Ramayana, and the Puranas, he was the son of Marlchi, the son of Brahma, and he was father of Vivaswat, the father of Maim, the progenitor of mankind.

The **atapatha Brahmawa** gives a different and not very intelligible account of his origin thus:—" Having assumed the form of a tortoise, Prajapati created off spring. That which he created he made (akarot) ; hence the word Mrma (tortoise). Kashyapa means tortoise; hence men say, ' All creatures are descendants of Kashyapa.' This tortoise is the same as Aditya." The Atharva-vedasays, "The self-born Kashyapa sprang from Time," and Time is often identical with Vishnu Kashyapa married Aditi and twelve other daughters of Daksha. "Upon Aditi he begat the Aditya, headed by Indra, and also Vivaswat, and "to Yivaswatwas born the wise and mighty Manu."

The Ramayana and Vishnu Purana also state that "Vishwu was born as a dwarf, the son of Aditi and Kashyapa." By his other twelve wives he had a numerous and much diversified off spring: demons, Nagas, reptiles, birds, and all kinds of living things. He was thus the father of all, and as such is sometimes called Prajapati. He is one of the seven great rishis, and he appears as the priest of Parasurama.

GIFT OF LAND TO KASHYAPA

In the continuation of the legend of Parasurama, after gifting all the conquered lands to the sage Kashyapa, a significant event takes place. A grand Yajna (sacrificial ritual) is organized, and the chief priest for this auspicious occasion is none other than Sage Kashyapa himself. As the officiating priest, Kashyapa is honored and revered by the people in attendance.

To express his gratitude and devotion to Kashyapa, Parasurama ensures that the sage is seated on a magnificent platform made entirely of gold. This platform is ten yards long and nine yards wide, a testament to its grandeur. Kashyapa is respectfully placed upon it and worshipped with great reverence and devotion.

Once the worship and rituals are completed, Kashyapa shares his instructions with Parasurama and the gathered assembly. Following his guidance, the gold platform is then ceremoniously cut into multiple pieces.

These pieces of gold are generously offered to Brahmins, the priestly class, as a token of gratitude and a significant donation.

Upon receiving all the conquered lands and the gold pieces, Kashyapa addresses Parasurama with deep gratitude. He acknowledges the immense generosity shown by Parasurama and expresses his heartfelt appreciation. However, Kashyapa believes that it is now inappropriate for Parasurama to continue residing in the land that rightfully belongs to him.

With utmost respect and compassion, Kashyapa advises Parasurama to seek a new dwelling place in the southern region, particularly along the shores of the ocean. He suggests that Parasurama's path lies in the south, where he can establish his abode and continue his spiritual pursuits.

Following Kashyapa's guidance, Parasurama embarks on a journey to the southern lands. Filled with determination and a sense of purpose, he travels through forests, mountains, and valleys until he reaches the expansive coastline of the southern region. Standing before the mighty ocean, Parasurama humbly seeks a piece of land where he can establish his hermitage.

In response to his plea, Varuna, the deity associated with the ocean, manifests before Parasurama. Varuna recognizes Parasurama's divine nature and the significance of his mission. He advises Parasurama to throw a winnow or, in some versions of the legend, his own sacred Parasu (axe) into the vast expanse of the ocean.

With faith and devotion, Parasurama follows Varuna's guidance and hurls the winnow or axe into the deep waters. In a miraculous display of divine intervention, the ocean responds to his call. The waters part, creating a landmass that emerges from the depths, right at the spot where the winnow or axe had fallen. This newly formed land becomes the sacred dwelling place of Parasurama, his chosen abode on the southern shores of the ocean.

Parasurama, grateful for the benevolence of Varuna and the ocean, embraces his new home with humility and reverence. From there, he continues his spiritual practices, deepening his connection with the divine and preparing himself for his future role in the grand tapestry of Hindu mythology.

The legend of Parasurama, with its episodes of sacrifice, gratitude, divine guidance, and divine intervention, showcases the timeless themes of devotion, righteousness, and the interplay between humans and celestial beings. It serves as a source of inspiration, imparting moral and spiritual lessons to generations of believers.

This is the place Surparaka now known as Kerala. (Surpa = Winnowing basket). After giving this land also to the Brahmins, Parasurama went and started
doing penance at Mahendragiri. **(Chapter 130, Adi Parva; Chapter 117. Vana Parva and Chapter 49, Santi Parva)** . Parasurama gifted lands to Kashyapa. Parasurama performed a Yagna after exterminating all Ksatriyas Kings. At that Yajna he gifted all the lands he had conquered till then to Kashyapa. **(Mahabharata, Aranya Parva, Chapter 117**

KHANDAVAYANAS

Parasurama gave all the countries conquered by him to Kashyapa. Along with the lands he gave a golden dais also. The group of hermits called Khandavayanas cut the dais into pieces and shared them with the permission of Kashyapa. **(M.B. Vana Parva, Chapter 117, Stanza 13)**

KASHYAPI

Parasurama gifted the whole earth to the sage Kashyapa. From that time Bhumidevi has been called "Kasyapi" (daughter of Kasyapa). **(M.B. Anusasana Parva, Chapter 154, Verse 7).**

KASHMIR (KASMIRAKAM).

Kashmir was famous during the Mahabharata period also. Once Arjuna conquered this state **(Sabha Parva, Chapter 27)** . People from the state had attended Yudhisthira's Rajasuya with many articles of presentation. Sri Krsna once defeated its ruler. **(Drona Parva, Chapter 11, Verse 16).** Parasurama also once defeated its ruler. **(Drona Parva, Chapter 70, Verse 11)**

KERALA

After that, Kashyapa drove away Parasurama from the north to the south. Taking pity on Parasurama, the ocean gave him the region known as "Surparaka". Kashyapa seized Surparaka also from Parasurama and gave it to Brahmans. Parasurama went to the forests after it. Later on, intermixture of castes took place in this region and anarchy prevailed there. At one time, Surparaka sank down into Patala (lower world). Kashyapa who saw this held the earth up, brought Ksatriyas from the north and made them rulers of the country. **(M.B. Santi Parva, Chapter 49).** This "Surparaka" is believed to be Kerala.

KASHYAPA TEXTS

Kashyapa is revered in the Hindu tradition, and numerous legends and texts composed in the medieval era are reverentially attributed to him in various Hindu traditions. Some treatises named after him or attributed to him include:

- *Kashyapa Samhita,* also called *Vriddajivakiya Tantra* or *Jivakiya Tantra,* is a classical reference book on Ayurvedic pediatrics, gynecology and obstetrics. It was revised by Vatsya. The treatise is written as a tutorial between the medical sage Kashyapa and his student named Vriddhajivaka, and mostly related to caring for babies and diseases of children.

- *Kashyapa Jnanakandah,* or Kashyapa's book of wisdom, is a 9th century text of the Vaishnavism tradition.

- *Kasyapa dharmasutra,* likely an ancient text, but now believed to be lost. The text's existence is inferred from quotes and citations by medieval Indian scholars

- *Kasyapa sangita,* likely another ancient text, but now believed to be lost. A treatise on music, it is quoted by Shaivism and Advaita scholar Abhinavagupta, wherein he cites sage Kasyapa explanation on *viniyoga* of each *rasa* and *bhava.* Another Hindu music scholar named Hrdanyangama mentions Kashyapa's contributions to the theory of *alankara* (musical note decorations).

- *Kasyapasilpa,* also called *Amsumad agama, Kasypiya* or *Silpasastra of Kasyapa,* is a Sanskrit treatise on architecture, iconography and the decorative arts, probably completed in the 11th century.

CHAPTER NINETEEN

SHIVA

Parasurama had even from the beginning shown an interest in learning Dhanurvidya (archery). For obtaining proficiency in archery, he went to the Himalayas and did penance to please Siva for many years. Pleased at his penance Siva on several occasions extolled the virtues of Parasurama.

RAMA WITH AXE

As Rama grew older, he was sincere in his piety, and pleased Lord Shiva with the perforation of excruciating tapas As blessing, he was granted the parasu of Shiva, after which he was known as Parasurama, or 'Rama with axe'.

Shri Parasurama left home to do devout austerities to please Lord Shiva. Considering his extreme devotion, intense desire and unmoved and perpetual meditation, Lord Shiva was pleased with Shri Parasurama.

At that time the Asuras (demons) acquired strength and attacked the Devas. The Devas approached Lord Siva. Siva called Parasurama and asked him to fight with the Asuras. Parasurama was without weapons and he asked Siva how he could go and fight the demons without weapons. Siva said: "Go with my blessings, in the end you will kill your foes." Parasurama did not wait for a moment. When Siva thus assured him of success, he went straight to fight with the demons. He defeated the Asuras and came back to Siva when the latter gave him many boons and divine weapons.

He presented Rama with Divine weapons. Included was his unconquerable and indestructible axe shaped weapon, Parshu. Lord Shiva advised him to go and liberate the Mother Earth from felons, ill-behaved people, extremists, demons and those blind with pride.

Once, Lord Shiva challenged Shri Parasurama to a battle to test his skills in warfare. The spiritual master Lord Shiva and the disciple Shri Parasurama were locked in a fierce battle. This dreadful duel lasted for twenty one days. While ducking to avoid being hit by the Trident (Trishūl) of Lord Shiva, Shri Parasurama vigorously attacked him with his Parasu. It struck Lord Shiva on the forehead creating a wound. Lord Shiva was very pleased to see the amazing warfare skills of his disciple.

MRGAVYADHA

The disguise Siva took when he went to test the devotion of Parasurama. Parasurama once went to the forests and did penance e to please Siva to learn archery from him. Siva in the form of a Mrgavyadha (forest hunter) appeared before Parasurama and tested his sincerity in his penance in several ways. Siva was pleased to find Parasurama devotion to Siva unwavering and blessed him. He gave instructions in archery and also permitted him to go round the earth. **(Chapter 65, Brahmanda Purana)**

RAMA BECAME PARSURAMA

According to the legend, prior to being known as Parasurama, the name of the great warrior was Rama. However, after receiving a divine weapon named Parasu (axe) from Lord Shiva, he earned the epithet "Parasurama."

The story behind the weapon Parasu dates back to an incident involving Lord Shiva and a Yajna organized by Daksha, where Lord Shiva was not invited. In his anger and disappointment, Lord Shiva threw his divine spike, which struck the sacrificial hall (Yagasala), causing chaos and destruction. The spike then wandered aimlessly for a while before heading towards the hermitage of Badaryasrama, where the divine sages Nara and Narayana were engaged in deep penance.

The spike flew directly towards Sage Narayana's heart, but in response, Sage Narayana emitted a defiant sound, "hum" (hurhkara), signifying his divine power and resistance. The spike, upon encountering this resistance, turned away. Lord Shiva, feeling disrespected by this act, attacked Sage Narayana in his anger.

In that critical moment, Sage Nara swiftly plucked a blade of grass and, reciting a powerful mantra, threw it towards Lord Shiva. Miraculously, the blade of grass transformed into the divine weapon Parasu, taking the form of an axe, and fiercely attacked Lord Shiva. However, Lord Shiva, being the supreme deity, effortlessly shattered the axe into two pieces.

This encounter between Lord Shiva, Sage Narayana (an incarnation of Lord Vishnu), and the transformation of the grass into the Parasu axe highlights the divine powers and interplay between the gods. The Parasu axe became an integral part of Parasurama's arsenal, symbolizing his connection to Lord Shiva and his formidable prowess as a warrior.

By possessing the Parasu axe, Parasurama became renowned as the wielder of this divine weapon, and his name transitioned from Rama to Parasurama. This incident further adds to the mystical and divine aura surrounding Parasurama, solidifying his place in Hindu mythology and showcasing his divine lineage and extraordinary abilities as an avatar of Lord Vishnu.

Then Nara-Narayana bowed before him and worshipped him. Thereafter the two pieces of the Parasu remained with Siva. It was one of these that Siva gave to Parasurama. When Parasurama was returning happy and glorious with boons and weapons he got on his way a disciple named Akrtavrana. Guru and disciple lived in an ashrama and Parasurama became a noted Guru in Dhanurvidya (archery). **(Chapter 34, Karna Parva; Chapter 49, Santi Parva and Chapter 18, Anusasana Parva).**

Indeed, while Rama, the birth name of Parasurama, carried simplicity and beauty, his association with the divine weapon Parasu (axe) bestowed upon him by his guru Shiva led to him being commonly referred to as

Parasurama. The axe became an inseparable part of his identity, accompanying him wherever he went, even to the river when he bathed. This association became so prominent that it became his colloquial name.

As a Brahmin, having a name that emphasized his Kshatriya lineage was not considered appropriate in the traditional societal framework. However, Parasurama chose not to object or resist this designation. He understood that individuals who came to be known by their distinctive characteristics often gained fame effortlessly. It was a natural consequence of their inherent qualities and actions.

Furthermore, Parasurama recognized that he inherited more of his Kshatriya traits from his mother, rather than his Brahmin father. This distinction was the reason why his guru, Shiva, had bestowed the axe upon him. Shiva, the Destroyer and a deity associated with the warrior class, acknowledged Parasurama's inherent nature and potential, which aligned more with the Kshatriya lineage.

While the name Parasurama might have deviated from the conventional nomenclature of a Brahmin, Parasurama accepted it as a testament to his unique identity and divine connection. He embraced his Kshatriya attributes, channeling them through his martial skills and valiant acts. Ultimately, the name Parasurama became synonymous with his legendary exploits and righteous mission, solidifying his place in the annals of Hindu mythology.

VIJAYA DHANUSHA

Parasurama clipped the thousand arms of Kartaviryarjuna (Sahasrarjun), one by one, with his Parshu and killed him. He repelled his army by showering arrows on them. The whole country greatly welcomed the destruction of Kartaviryarjuna (Sahasrarjun). The king of Deities, Indra was in possession of Lord Shiva's Vijaya Dhanusha. Indra was so pleased that he presented this most beloved bow named Vijaya to Shri Parasurama on instruction from Lord Shiva.

BOOMS GRANTED BY SIVA

The Puranas refer to various persons, who had earned boons from him and others who attained heaven on account of their devotion for him. The following are important among such persons.

(i) Sirhhavaktra (Skanda Purana, Asura Kanda).

(ii) Rukml (Bhagavata, 10th Skandha) .

(iii) Bana (Bhagavata, 10th Skandha).

(iv) Sudaksina (Bhagavata, 10th Skandha).

(v) Salva (Bhagavata 10th Skandha).

(vi) Vrkasura (Bhagavata, 10th Skandha) .

(vii) RatidevI (Kathasaritsagara, Lavanakalambaka, Taranga 1) .

(viii) Indrajit (Uttara Ramayana).

(ix) Bhrgu (Padma Purana, Adi Khanda, Chapter 2) .

(x) Gandhari (M.B. Adi Parva, Chapter 109, Verse 107).

(xi) A rsi girl (M.B. Adi Parva, Chapter 168, Verse 6).

(xii) Prabhanjana (M.B. Adi Parva, Chapter 214,Verse 20).

(xiii) Svetaki (M.B. Adi Parva, Chapter 222, Verse 41).

(xiv) Jarasandha (M.B. Sabha Parva, Chapter 14, Verse 64) .

(xv) Banasura (M.B. Sabha Pirva, Chapter 33, Southern text).

(xvi) Mankana (Vana Parva, Chapter 83, Verse 132).

(xvii Sagara (Vana Parva, Chapter 106, Verse 15).

(xviii) Bhaglratha (Vana Parva, Chapter 103, Verse 1).

(xix) Jayadratha (Vana Parva, Chapter 272, Verse 28).

(xx) Amba (Udyoga Parva, Chapter 187, Verse 12).

(xxi) Somadatta (Drona Parva, Chapter 143, Verse 16).

(xxii) Visnu (Drona Parva, Chapter 201, Verse 56).

(xxiii) Parasurama (Kama Parva, Chapter 34, Verse 116; Santi Parva, Chapter 49, Verse 33) .

(xxiv) Skanda (Salya Parva, Chapter 46, Verse 46).

(xxv) ArundhatI (Salya Parva, Chapter 48, Verse 38).

(xxvi) A Brahmin boy (Sana Parva, Chapter 153, Verse 114),

(xxvii) Tandimuni (Anusasana Parva, Chapter 16, Verse 69)

CHAPTER TWENTY

GANESHA

Ganesha is the god of wisdom and remover of obstacles; hence he is invariably propitiated at the beginning of any important undertaking, and is invoked at the commencement of books. He is said to have written down the Mahabharata from the dictation of Vyasa. He is represented as a short fat man of a yellow colour, with a protuberant belly, four hands, and the head of an elephant, which has only one tusk. In one hand he holds a shell, in another a discus, in the third a club or goad, and in the fourth a water-lily. Sometimes he is depicted riding upon a rat or attended by one; hence his appellation Akhuratha. His temples are very numerous in the Dakhin. There is a variety of legends accounting for his elephant head. One is that his mother Parvati, proud of her offspring, asked Shani (Saturn) to look at him, forgetful of the effects of Shani's glance. Shani looked and the child's head was burnt to ashes. Brahma told Parvati in her distress to replace the head with the first she could find, and that was an elephant's.

THE EKADANTA

Another story is that Parvati went to her bath and told her son to keep the door. Shiva wished to enter and was opposed, so he cut off Ganesha's head. To pacify Parvati he replaced it with an elephant's, the first that came to hand. Another version is that his mother formed him so to suit her own fancy, and a further explanation is that Aditya the sun restored him to life again. For this violence Kashyapa doomed Siva's son to lose his head; and when he did lose it, the head of Indra's elephant was used to replace.

LORD GANESHA'S BROKEN TUSK

There are two different versions of how Lord Ganesha, also known as Ganpati, came to have only one tusk. In both versions, Parasurama, an incarnation of Lord Vishnu, is involved in the incident.

In the first version, Parasurama visits Lord Shiva, who is resting. Ganpati, acting as Shiva's gatekeeper, informs Parasurama that Shiva is not available to meet him. However, Parasurama insists on seeing Shiva and tries to enter forcefully. A struggle ensues between Ganpati and Parasurama, during which Ganpati uses his trunk to fling Parasurama away. Enraged, Parasurama throws his axe at Ganpati. In an act of devotion and respect for his father Shiva, Ganpati chooses not to evade the blow and instead allows the axe to strike him, resulting in the loss of one of his tusks.

In the second version, after Parasurama defeats King Kartaviryarjuna and assists Ravana, he desires to meet Lord Shiva on Mount Kailash. However, Ganpati obstructs his path. Parasurama, being known for his temper, becomes enraged and starts fighting Ganpati. In the midst of the battle, Parasurama throws his axe at Ganpati. Ganpati, aware that the axe is a gift from his father Shiva, decides not to defend himself and lets the axe strike him, resulting in the breaking of one of his tusks.

In both versions, the loss of Lord Ganesha's tusk is depicted as an act of devotion, respect, and acceptance of the divine will. It highlights Ganpati's unwavering dedication to his father, Shiva, and his readiness to endure physical sacrifice for the sake of honouring Shiva's gift.

These stories are part of Hindu mythology and are often narrated to convey moral and spiritual lessons, emphasizing virtues such as devotion, respect, and selflessness. The different versions of the stories reflect regional and cultural variations in the retelling of ancient myths.

The loss of one tusk is accounted for by a legend which represents Parasurama coming to Kailash on a visit to Siva. The god was asleep and

Ganesha opposed the entrance of the visitor to the inner apartments. A wrangle ensued, which ended in a fight. "Ganesha had at first the advantage, seizing Parasurama with his trunk and giving him a twirl that lofts him sick and senseless. On recovering, Parasurama threw his axe at Ganesha, who, recognising it as his father's weapon (Siva having given it to Parasurama), received it with all humility on one of his tusks, which it immediately severed ; hence Ganesha but one tusk, and is known by the name of Ekadanta or Kkadanshfra (the single-tusked). **(Brahma Vaivartta Purana)**

Further, the story involving Parasurama, Ganesha, and the loss of Ganesha's tusk as mentioned in the Puranas. This version adds further details to the narrative and involves the intervention of Parvati (Ganesha's mother) and Lord Shiva.

According to this version, as Parasurama was travelling to the Himalayas to pay his respects to his teacher, Lord Shiva, his path was obstructed by Ganesha. In his anger and frustration, Parasurama throws his axe at Ganesha, who recognizes the weapon as the one given to Parasurama by his father, Shiva. As an act of devotion and respect towards his father, Ganesha allows the axe to sever his left tusk.

Upon witnessing this incident, Parvati becomes infuriated and threatens to cut off Parashurama's arms in retaliation for her son's injury. She takes on the form of Durga, becoming all-powerful and ready to punish Parasurama. However, Lord Shiva intervenes and manages to calm Parvati by making her see that Parasurama is an incarnation of Vishnu and should be treated as her own son.

Parasurama, realizing the gravity of his actions, seeks forgiveness from Parvati, expressing his remorse. Ganesha also speaks on behalf of Parasurama, advocating for forgiveness and understanding. Eventually, Parvati relents and forgives Parasurama.

In this version, Parasurama, realizing the significance of his encounter with Ganesha and acknowledging the divine nature of the elephant-headed deity, gives his divine axe to Ganesha as a gesture of respect and blessing. As a result of this encounter, Ganesha is bestowed with the name "Ekadanta," meaning "One Tusk."

The whole incident of Parasurama & Ganesha narrated in religious books. Parasurama was a great devotee of Shiva and was also very proud of the fact that he was free to approach Shiva at any time he wished. When he reached the gate of Shiva's abode, he was stopped by Ganesha as he used to check everybody there. He had made it a rule.

Ganesha said, "You cannot enter inside at this moment."

Parasurama said, "Why?"

Parasurama, being very short-tempered by nature and always ready to quarrel, said, "Get aside. I am Parasurama. I have to see him immediately. I have no time

Ganesha said, "If you have no time to wait, I shall make you wait as I wait for persons like you at this gate!" Then Ganesha lifted Parasurama in his arms.

Ganesha was not impressed and did not budge an inch.

He said, "O respected saint! Calm down. It is not possible. Come some other time." Parasurama had no patience. He got ready to fight with Ganesha. They came to blows. Ganesha entangled Parasurama in his trunk and twisted him around. Parasurama started feeling giddy and ultimately was unconscious.

Ganesha put Parasurama on the ground. When, Parasurama came out of swoon, he found he lying on the ground. He was furious. He was not in the habit of putting up with an insult. How could he tolerate that humiliation?

He raised his battle-axe and threw it towards Ganesha. When Ganesha saw that weapon, he was immobile. He was helpless. He could not catch hold of or throw that away because that axe had been gifted as a present to Parasurama by Shiva when he had worshipped and pleased him. Ganesha recognised the axe and accepted the blow of the weapon respectfully.

CHAPTER TWENTY-ONE

SRI RAMA

Dazzling like myriads of sun, flashing like lightning appearing a luminous mass of energy and power, of form majestic and like the cloud of azure hue with tangled locks, a bow in one hand and the axe in other, stood Parasurama, the slayer of Kartaviryarjuna And the destroyer of the fiery Kshatriya race, even like the king of terrors, before Dashratha, and thus was seen by the valiant Rama Chandra.

-Adhyatma Ramayna

Lord Rama is considered the seventh incarnation of Lord Vishnu and is revered as an embodiment of righteousness, virtue, and moral conduct. His story is extensively narrated in the Ramayana, an ancient epic poem composed by the sage Valmiki.

King Dasharatha, of the Suryavanshi dynasty, ruled over the kingdom of Ayodhya. He was childless and performed a great ritual called the Ashwamedha sacrifice with the hope of obtaining offspring. Pleased with Dasharatha's devotion, the gods granted him a boon of four sons. However, at the same time, the gods were troubled by the demon king Ravana of Lanka, who had acquired immense power through his austerities.

To counter the menace of Ravana, Lord Vishnu decided to incarnate as Rama and put an end to his tyranny. Vishnu appeared before Dasharatha in a glorious form during the sacrificial ritual and handed him a divine pot of nectar. Dasharatha distributed the nectar to his three wives: Kausalya, Kaikeyi, and Sumitra.

Kausalya gave birth to Rama, who possessed half of the divine essence. Kaikeyi's son was Bharata, who received a quarter of the divine essence, and Sumitra gave birth to twins, Lakshmana and Shatrughna, who each had an eighth part of the divine essence. The four brothers shared a deep bond, but Lakshmana was particularly devoted to Rama and played a significant role in supporting him throughout his life.

The Ramayana narrates the journey of Lord Rama, his exile to the forest, his adventures, and his ultimate triumph over Ravana, rescuing his wife Sita with the assistance of Hanuman and an army of monkeys. Rama's story is revered for its moral teachings, illustrating the virtues of righteousness, loyalty, and devotion.

The significant events from Lord Rama's life as depicted in the Ramayana. Here are the key points:

- When Rama and his brothers were still young, the sage Vishwamitra sought their help to protect him from the Raksasas (demons). Despite Dasharatha's initial reluctance, he consented to Vishwamitra request, and Rama and Lakshmana accompanied the sage to his hermitage.
- At Vishwamitra hermitage, Rama successfully killed the female demon Taraka. However, it took some persuasion from the sage as Rama hesitated to harm a female. As a reward for his bravery, Vishwamitra bestowed celestial weapons upon Rama and exerted a significant influence over his actions.
- Vishwamitra then took Rama and his brothers to the kingdom of Mithila, ruled by King Janaka. King Janaka had a daughter named Sita, and he announced that he would offer her hand in marriage to anyone who could string and break the divine bow of Lord Shiva.
- Rama, displaying his extraordinary strength, not only succeeded in stringing the bow but also broke it, thus winning the hand of Sita. Sita is described as a virtuous and devoted wife.
- However, Parasurama, another incarnation of Lord Vishnu, became offended by the breaking of Lord Shiva's bow. Despite both Rama and Parasurama being incarnations of Vishnu, Parasurama challenged Rama

to a trial of strength. Rama emerged victorious, but he spared Parashurama's life due to the latter's Brahman identity and high status.

ARGUMENT WITH LUXMAN, SCOLD JANAK

In the Ramayana, there is a notable encounter between Laksmana, the younger brother of Lord Rama, and Parasurama, the warrior-saint and another incarnation of Lord Vishnu. This encounter takes place when Lord Rama and Laksmana are in exile in the forest.

According to the epic, Parasurama encountered Rama and Laksmana during their exile and engaged in a conversation with them. It is said that Parasurama initially did not recognize Rama as an incarnation of Vishnu and engaged in a conversation with him. During their conversation, Laksmana, who was fiercely protective of his brother, became increasingly agitated as Parasurama questioned Rama's identity and abilities.

Laksmana, being devoted to Rama, grew impatient and intervened in the conversation, defending his brother's honour and asserting his divine nature. This led to a heated argument between Laksmana and Parasurama, with both engaging in a verbal exchange.

However, Lord Rama, the embodiment of calmness and wisdom, intervened and pacified the situation. Rama revealed his true identity to Parasurama, who then recognized Rama as his supreme divine counterpart. Parasurama, satisfied with this realization, acknowledged Rama's divine nature and retreated from the confrontation.

The argument between Laksmana and Parasurama highlights Lakshmana's unwavering devotion and protective nature towards Rama. It also serves as a testament to the intense loyalty and love that Laksmana held for his elder brother. The incident ultimately ends on a peaceful note with Parasurama recognizing Rama's true identity and the divine purpose behind their meeting.

When Parasurama arrived on the scene and saw the mighty bow of Shiva lying in pieces, he was furious. He spoke harshly to King Janaka "Show me the man who has done this sacrilege or I will turn your kingdom upside down, you idiot," and got into a heated argument with the quick-tempered Luxman.

Ram intervened and gently tried to calm Muni Parasurama. "Though you are very angry Muniji, my mistake is really a small one. I hardly touched the bow. It broke by itself. I really cannot take credit for breaking it,"

Parasurama, naturally, did not believe him. He asked Ram to do the same with his bow. Parasurama was amazed when he saw his bow leaving his shoulder and going to Ram's hand.

Ram therefore thought it necessary to show Muni Parshuram that the person who had broken the bow of Shiva was none other than an incarnation of Lord Vishnu. Though he dealt with the Muni gently, it was necessary for Ram to use his divya Shakti on this occasion. At this evidence of Ram's divyashakti, Muni Parasurama was convinced and apologized to Ram and offered him his own "Vishnu Dhanusha'. In this way he did samarpan to Ram and attained the Almighty, recognized Ram's greatness and his happiness knew no bounds. He prayed to Ram with folded hands.

SDRANG – THE BOW OF VISHNU

This is the name of the bow of Visnu. This is called Vaisnava capa (the bow of Vishnu) also. A description is given in **Valmlki Ramayana, Bala- kanda, Sarga 25**, as to how this bow was obtained.

Once, the Devas made Vishnu and Siva quarrel with each other, to test their might. The fight between the two began. Vishvakarma gave each of them a bow. The bow of Vishnu was called Vaishnava capa; the bow of Siva was called Shiva capa. This Vaishnava capa is Sarriga. Due to the power of Sarnga, Shiva was defeated in the fight. Getting angry Siva gave his bow to the King Devarata of Videha. It was this bow that Sri Rama broke at the time of the marriage of Sita. After the fight, Vishnu gave his bow to Rucheeka, grandfather of Parasurama . That bow changed hands from Rcika to Jamadagni and from him to Parasurama, who presented this bow to Sri Rama on his return after the marriage with Sita.

PARASURAMA THREAT: ANOTHER VERSION

Dashratha and others on their way back to Ayodhya passed the Videha kingdom and reached the suburbs of Bhargava ashrama. All of a sudden a shining form of a Brahmin with Ksatriyas effulgence appeared in front of the procession. Vashisht understood that it was Parasurama and Dashratha and others were alarmed. Parasurama approached Sri Rama who was viewing the former with quiet serenity. Parasurama was very angry that Rama broke the bow of Siva who was his (Parasurama) preceptor. All Rama's conciliatory talk failed to pacify Parasurama, who spoke thus to

Rama: "You, impudent fellow! You insulted me and my preceptor. All right, let me see your power. Take this my bow, and shoot with it."

Sri Rama took hold of the bow and bent it easily and fixing an arrow on it asked Parasurama to point out the target for it. As Parasurama feared that if the arrow was sent, it might crush the whole universe, he asked Rama so choose the result of his (Parashurama's) tapas as target for the arrow. Both the bow and the arrow were of Vishnu's power. That power as well as his own Vaishnava power, Parasurama transferred to Sri Rama and having thus fulfilled the object of his incarnation Parasurama went to ashrama for permanent tapas.

UPSET WITH RAJA RAM

According to Ramayana, Lord Parshuram was upset with Lord Rama, who broke the bow that belonged to his Guru, Lord Shiva. Angry warrior sage gave Sharanga *(Bow passed by Lord Vishnu)* to Rama and challenged him to string and shoots him. Rama took the bow and arrow from Parasurama, easily fit the arrow in the bow, drew it to its fullest extent, and asked the sage,"*Where shall I discharge this deadly arrow? As you are my superior, I cannot aim it at you.* Impressed and astonished, *Parasurama* immediately realized that this was no ordinary Kshatriya standing there in front of him. *You surely must be Lord Vishnu himself. I accept defeat, but I am not ashamed as you are indeed the lord of all the worlds. You have already divested me of all my power and my pride. Please release this arrow on my desires for heavenly pleasures and burn them to ashes. The only thing that I now desire is to become your eternal servant.*

Saying so, Parasurama bowed down before Rama, who released the arrow. The sage immediately vanished along with the arrow. Varuna, the god of the water, then appeared before Rama and gave him the celestial bow to keep on behalf of all the gods. Parashurama had given the bow of Shiva to the father of princess Sita for her Svayamvara. As a test of worthiness, suitors were asked to lift and string the mystic weapon. None were successful until Rama, but in the process of being strung, the bow snapped in half. This produced a tremendous noise that reached the ears of Parashurama as he meditated atop the Mahendra Mountains.(**Tulsidas Ramayana)**

Parashurama stops the journey of Sri Rama and his family after his marriage to Sita. He threatens to kill Sri Rama and his father, King Dashratha, begs him to forgive his son and punish him instead. Parashurama neglects Dashratha and invokes Sri Rama for a challenge. Sri Rama meets his challenge and tells him that he does not want to kill him because he is a Brahmin and related to his guru, Vishwamitra Maharshi.(**Valmlki Ramayana**)

Angered Parasurama blocked the way of Sri Rama and challenged him to string and take aim with the mighty Vaishnava bow he (Parasurama) was carrying with him then. Sri Rama with perfect ease took the bow, strungit, and taking the missile asked Parasurama to show the target. Parasurama was astonished and was in a fix. The missile could destroy even the entire Universe. So Parasurama asked Rama to aim at the accumulated tapobala (power accrued by penance) of his self and Rama did so. Then Parasurama surrendered to Sri Ram the Vaishnava bow and arrow and the Vaishnava tejas (divine brilliance) in him. Parasurama after having carried out the purpose of his incarnation gave instructions to Sri Rama to continue the purpose of his incarnation and then after blessing Sri Rama went again to do penance at his holy ashrama (**Kamba Ramayana**)

When the fame that Sri Rama was the best of Kings spread farand wide Parasurama once went to see Sri Rama.Giving him the bow and arrow with which he had done the mass massacre of the Ksatriyas he challenged him to string it and take aim. With a smile Sri Rama did so and then Parasurama said Rama should draw the string up to his ears. Sri Rama got angry and then on the face, which became fierce, by his anger, Parasurama saw besides himself, Aditya-Vasu-Rudras, Sadhyas, Balakhilyas, Devarsis, oceans, mountains, the Vedas and all such things of this universe. Sri Rama sent out his missile from the bow.

The whole universe was thrown into chaos. Thunder and lightning rocked the world. Heavy rains flooded the whole land space.Burning stars and meteors fell to the ground. Parasurama then knew that Sri Rama was the incarnation of Mahavishnu and he stood bowing before him. Ashamed of his defeat he took leave of Sri Rama and went to Mahendragiri. When he reached there he found he had lost all his brilliance. Then the manes appeared and advised him to go and bathe in the river Vadhusara. Accordingly Parasurama went and bathed in the river and regained his lost brilliance. **(Chapter 99, Vana Parva).**

This same story is told by the sage Lomasa to the Pandavas during their exile in the forests. This story is much different from the previous ones: Parashurama arrived to the scene deeply angry. The Kshatriyas were advised by Brahmarishi Vashishtha not to confront the sage, but Sita still approached. Parashurama blessed her, saying "Dheergha Sumangalibhavah," or "You will have your husband alive for your lifetime." When he then turned to confront Rama, Parashurama was unable to lift his axe. He was held back by his own word and pacified by the brilliance of Rama. When the warrior-sage realized he was looking at his own subsequent reincarnation, his bow flew into the hands of Rama, and thus the essence of Vishnu was fully realized in the seventh avatar. **(Played in Ramlilas)**

THE STORY VERSION

Parshuram took a vow not to take up arms in front of Indra. He did not desire to rule by conquering the whole earth with his incomparable prowess and impenetrable soul-power; instead donated it. By removing the ocean, he made a new earth for his abode and there he meditated. Peace all around, religious discussion all around. part Gush gross Brahman got absorbed in Ram-Ram gross Dashratha nandan Ram, who had brought disgrace to the form of Kamadeva, was returning from Mithila to Ayodhya after marrying the immortal beauty Janakandini Sita, who tarnished the beauty of Rati, protected from the mighty soldiers under the protection of his pious father Dashratha and Brahminishtha sages.

Suddenly the inauspicious birds began to speak fearfully and the Trinachari deer started circling all around. Frightened king Dashratha said to Vashishtha Ji, "Gurudev, my heart is trembling after listening to the fierce speech of these sinful birds and the circumambulation of deer. Who knows what is going to happen." Vashishtha laughed and said, 'Rajan, there is nothing to panic, the tigress will come and will go away immediately. You are afraid even after being famously mighty. Open the doors of your mind, the infinite and bottomless ocean of power is flowing within you, at least make a connection with it.

Why fear when the Almighty God is with you. Suddenly clouds of dust started rising, a huge storm came, pebbles of the earth started flying, trees were uprooted and fell away from the wind, the earth shook, the mountains trembled, lightning flashed, the solar system was drowned in a cloud of dust, smoke. It got dark. As Anshumali appears after ripping the darkness of the cube, in the same way Lord Parshuram, the one who pacifies the Kshatriya Chakra-Vartis wearing Jatamandal, appeared burning with Brahmatejas.

He was as invincible as Kailasa, as sorrowful as Kalagni, and was creating glare in the eyes with his brilliance. The bow hanging from his shoulder was shining like lightning and a fiery arrow was present in his hand. Everyone started trembling after seeing Parshuram, who was bright like a blazing fire. The rishis worshiped him, fearing King Dashratha threw his four sons at his feet, "Shatanjiv" - Parashurama's loving voice resounded in the atmosphere

Bhargava looked at Rama - of supernatural beauty and superpower (electric current and cool rays of peace were bursting together. The majestic blood of Ikshavaku clan was flowing in the veins, Kaal in the brow and Brahmatejas in the big eyes. Parshuram was mesmerized. Said - "Pradeep Ram of Ikshavaku clan, I have heard about your unimaginable prowess, you broke Shiva's bow while playing, now put an arrow on this fierce Vaishnava bow of mine and show your strength.

Show it. If you shoot an arrow at it, I will challenge you for a duel war. Hearing about the war, King Dashratha begged, touched his feet again and again, said with folded hands - "Lord, you are a Brahminist Brahmin; you have calmed the anger of killing your father. Give my children fearlessness. I have vowed before you to renounce weapons and live a religious life, then why take up arms? Rama is the soul of all, if one Rama dies, we will all die.' "Lord. Saying, "Mam Pahi", he returned at the feet. Turning his hand on the king's head,

Parashurama said - "Rajan, Ram is loved by all, Videha Raj is the vermilion of Janak's daughter. May it be safe, I also have the same desire, just want to see its strength? If he will shoot an arrow then he is invincible, even death cannot come in front of him. Get up; see the praise of your son. Here Ram increased the arrow on Parashurama's Vaishnava bow.

Seeing this surprise, Parashurama's eyes filled with joy. Said - Thank you, you are blessed, you are the god of gods too. The policy says don't trust anyone. Trust only a little of the one who is very trustworthy. Because of this policy, I teased you, now my confusion has been cleared. Leave your arrow on my sins. I have committed many sins by killing Kshatriyas. Take my invincible Parashu, take my fearlessness and take my knowledge and art. You are able the flag of religion, work and culture should not be bowed down. May the wind of the tradition of sage Vashishtha continue to blow? Everyone knows that I am doing penance somewhere, no! No!! I am merging in you, Glory be to you.

CHAPTER TWENTY-TWO

SRI KRISHNA

Till marriage Sri Krishna spent his childhood in Ariibadi and Balrama (Balabhadrarama), in Mathura. Once the sage Garga went to the house of Vasudeva and it was he

who then told the story behind the births of Balrama and Krishna. Hearing this Vasudeva went to Mathura and brought Balabhadrarama also to Ariibadi. Garga-muni then performed all those sacred rites which were usually done to boys of that age and both of them then remained in Ariibadi.

Several important events happened during their stay here, notable among which are : Putanamoksam (killing of the demoness Putana and giving her salvation). Sakafasuravadha (killing theasura, Saka(a), Trnavarttavadha (killing the asura, Trnavartta) , Vatsasuravadha (killing the asura,Vatsa) , Bakavadha (killing the demon bird, Baka) ,Aghasuravadha (killing the asura, Agha) , Dhenuka suravadha (killing the asura, Dhenuka), Kaliamardana(beating the snake, Kalia) and Pralambavadha (killing Pralamba).

FIRST MEETING

There two important occasions when Parasurama, the warrior-saint, met Lord Krishna.

1. The Meeting at the Mountain of Gomanta: During their journey to the beautiful mountain of Gomanta, Lord Krishna and Lord Balarama encountered Parasurama, who was engaged in penance there. They greeted each other and engaged in conversation. Parasurama requested Lord Krishna to kill King Srgalavasudeva of Karavira, who ruled at the base of the mountain. Lord Krishna promised to fulfill his request and departed, receiving the blessings of the sage.

2. The Meeting during the Pandavas' Travels: On their way to the mountain of Gomanta, the Pandavas and Lord Balarama encountered Parasurama. At that time, the Yadavas, including Lord Krishna, were facing financial difficulties due to their ongoing war with Jarasandha. Parasurama advised Lord Krishna and Lord Balarama to kill King Srgalavasudeva of Karavira and collect wealth and gems from his kingdom to replenish their treasury. Following Parasurama's advice, Lord Krishna and Lord Balarama successfully carried out the task, obtaining money and gems. They returned to the city of the Pandavas with their newly acquired wealth. Additionally, during this time, Garuda, the divine bird, returned Lord Krishna's stolen crown, which had been taken by Banasura.

These encounters with Parasurama played a role in shaping Lord Krishna's actions and decisions. The advice and guidance received from Parasurama influenced the course of events, including the eventual decision for Lord Krishna and the Yadavas to leave Mathura and establish the kingdom of Dvaraka on an island in the western sea.

It's worth noting that these events are mentioned in the Bhagavata Purana (Srimad Bhagavatam), one of the eighteen major Puranas in Hinduism that contains narratives about the life and teachings of Lord Krishna.

SECOND MEETING

The second meeting was when Krishna was going to the court of the Kauravas as a messenger of the Pandavas. On his way Sri Krishna saw a company of sages coming and, alighting from his chariot Krishna talked with them. Parasurama, who was in that company then embraced Krishna and said that he should give a true picture of the situation to the Kauravas when he was conducting his mission? The sages blessed Krishna and wished Krishna all success in his mission. **(Chapter 83, Udyoga Parva; 10th Skandha, Bhagavata).**

There are the sequence of events involving Lord Krishna and Lord Balarama in their interactions with Kansa, Sandipani Maharshi, Jarasandha, and their subsequent settlement in Dvaraka. Here is a summary of the events:

1. Kansa's Capa Puja and Defeat: Kansa, who sought to kill Lord Krishna, organized a grand worship of the bow (Capa Puja) in Mathura. Lord Krishna and Lord Balarama attended the event. During the puja, they confronted and defeated Kansa, putting an end to his tyranny.
2. Education under Sandipani Maharshi: After their victory over Kansa, Lord Krishna and Lord Balarama went to the ashrama of Sandipani Maharshi to receive education and training. They stayed there and completed their studies under the guidance of Sandipani Maharshi.
3. Gurudaksina: As a gesture of gratitude and payment for their education, Lord Krishna and Lord Balarama, at the request of Sandipani Maharshi, offered their Gurudaksina (a fee or gift to the guru) by rescuing and returning his lost child.
4. Events in Mathura: Lord Krishna and Lord Balarama returned to Mathura after completing their education. Several significant events took place there, including the fight between Lord Krishna and Jarasandha, a powerful king who repeatedly attacked Mathura. Lord Krishna, with his divine prowess, defeated Jarasandha.
5. Journey to the Diamond-infested Mountain of Gomanta: Due to financial difficulties faced by the Yadavas, Lord Krishna and Lord Balarama decided to go to the mountain of Gomanta, known for its abundant diamonds. Along the way, they encountered Parasurama, who was engaged in penance under a Banyan tree. Parasurama advised them to

kill King Srgalavasudeva and acquire immense wealth. Following his advice, Lord Krishna and Lord Balarama obtained great riches.

6. Settlement in Dvaraka: Upon their return from Gomanta, Lord Krishna, Lord Balarama, and many Yadavas settled in the island city of Dvaraka, located in the western ocean. Dvaraka became their new kingdom and served as a prosperous and harmonious abode for them.

These events are described in the Dasama Skandha (tenth canto) of the Bhagavata Purana (Srimad Bhagavatam), which narrates the divine pastimes and teachings of Lord Krishna.

SUDARSHANA

According to the folklore, Parasurama gave the Sudarshana chakra to Lord Krishna. It is believed that the main motto of Vishnu's sixth incarnation was to free the earth's burden by assassinating the sinful and irreligious kings who neglected their duties.

GOMANTA

A famous mountain near Dvaraka. This mountain is known as Goma and Raivataka also. Once Sri Krishna went to see Gomanta and on the way met Parasurama. **(Skandha 10, Bhagavata).** Parasurama and Sri Krishna went together and saw this beautiful mountain. Vyasa has devoted Chapter 40 of Vishnu Parva entirely for the description of this mountain of Gomanta. Once Balabhadrarama caught hold of Jarasandha on this mountain but let him off.

KARAVĪRA

There was once a country named Karavira on the base of the mountain Gomanta. That country was being ruled by a King called Srgalavasudeva. He was killed by Sri Krishna and Balrama together as per instructions from Parasurama. **(10ᵗʰ Skandha, Bhagavata)**

CHAPTER TWENTY-THREE

BHISMA

Indeed, the conflict between Parashurama and Bhisma stems from the story of Princess Amba in the Mahabharata. Here is a continuation of the narrative:

Amba, devastated by her rejection and unable to find a suitable husband, sought the assistance of Parashurama, who was renowned for his martial prowess and sense of justice. She approached him with a request to avenge her honor and kill Bhisma, who had refused to marry her despite winning her in the svayamvara.

Parashurama, known for his fiery temper, agreed to help Amba and confronted Bhisma. A fierce battle ensued between the two warriors. Parashurama, a master of weapons, unleashed his skills against Bhisma, who was a formidable warrior in his own right. However, despite Parashurama's prowess, Bhisma displayed extraordinary valor and skill, withstanding his guru's attacks.

Witnessing Bhisma's unwavering determination and prowess, Parashurama recognized his exceptional abilities and acknowledged him as his equal. He then ceased the battle and blessed Bhisma, acknowledging him as the greatest warrior of his time.

Parashurama realized that Bhisma's actions were driven by his steadfast adherence to his oath of celibacy and loyalty to the kingdom of Hastinapur. Understanding the depth of Bhisma's commitment, Parashurama granted him forgiveness and withdrew his desire for vengeance.

Although Parashurama and Bhisma had clashed briefly, their encounter ultimately revealed Bhisma's extraordinary skills and the unyielding nature of his vows. This event further cemented Bhisma's reputation as an exceptional warrior and a man of great integrity.

The story of Parashurama and Bhisma serves as a testament to their remarkable martial abilities and unwavering principles. Despite the conflict, their encounter ultimately resulted in mutual respect and admiration between two legendary figures in the epic narratives of ancient India.

SUITABLE MARRIAGE PROPOSAL FOR VICITRAVIRYA

Amba had two younger sisters named Ambika and Ambalika. Bhisma, who had taken a vow to remain a bachelor for life, had once taken Amba, Ambika and Ambalika, the three daughters of the King of Kashi, to Hastinapur. The circumstances in which this happened, are described in Devi Bhagavata, Prathama Skandha that Santanu, a King of the Chandra Vansha, had two wives, Ganga and Satyavati. Bhisma was the elder son of Ganga, while Citrangada and Vicitravlrya were the sons of Satyavati.

Soon after Bhisma birth, Ganga vanished. After a long period of reign, Santanu also died. Satyavati and the three sons were left behind in the palace. According to a vow he had taken long ago, Bhisma, instead of succeeding to his father's throne, left it to his brother Citrangada. Once, Citrangada went for hunting in the forest. There he came across a Gandharvas named Citrangada. The Gandharvas did not like another man with his own name to be living in this world. So he killed the king. Alter that Vicitravlrya became king. Bhisma had to take up the task of arranging a suitable marriage for Vicitravlrya.

THE SVAYAMVARA

It was at this time that Bhisma came to know that the King of Kasi was arranging the Svayamvara of his three daughters, Amba, Ambika and

Ambalika. Bhisma went there and in the presence of all the kings who had assembled there, took the three princesses with him to Hastinapur. King Salva tried to stop Bhisma way but got defeated. At Hastinapur, Bhisma made all preparations for the marriage. But as the time for the ceremony approached, the eldest and most beautiful of the princesses, Amba went to Bhisma and said

"I had already made up my mind long ago to marry Salva, the King. Besides, we are deeply in love with each other. Therefore, please consider whether it is proper on the part of a great man like you to force me into another marriage."

On hearing this, Bhisma allowed her to do as she liked .Amba then went to King Salva and made an appeal to him to accept her as his wife since they were mutually in love.

SALVA S REJECTION

To her words Salva replied, "What you have said about our mutual love is true. But it is not right for a man to accept a woman who has been accepted by another. I saw Bhisma taking you by hand and helping you into his chariot. Therefore go at once to Bhisma himself and ask him to accept you." Amba who was allowed by Bhisma to marry her lover, King Salva, was rejected by him and returned to Bhisma again stunned by his words, she turned away, to go to the forest to do penance.

Amba had cherished a secret desire to wreak vengeance on Bhisma. She went to the Asrama of Saikhavatya Muni in the forest and stayed there for the night. Her wish to do penance was approved by the Muni Sranjya; the royal hermit was the father of the mother of Amba, the princess of Kasi, and a friend of Parasurama. At the request of Amba who had been forsaken by Salva, Srnjaya first approached Parasurama and then saw Bhisma and persuaded him to marry Amba. **(M.B. Udyoga Parva, Chapter 175, Stanzas 15 to 27)** Hotravahana (Sanjaya) was very upset about her misfortunes. He advised her to inform Parasurama of all her grievances. Just at that moment Akrtavrana, a follower of Parasurama happened to come there. Hotravahana introduced Amba to Akrtavrana. Both Akrtavrana and Sanjay explained all her affairs to Parasurama.**(Mahabharata, Udyoga Parva, Chapter 17)**

BHISMA REJECTED AMBA-PARASURAM PERSUADED

Amba sought refuge with Parasurama. Parasurama undertook to persuade

Bhisma to accept Amba (as his wife). But Parasurama proposal was turned down by Bhisma. Although Parasurama pleaded with him on behalf of Amba, Bhisma did not marry her. **(Udyoga Parva, Chapter178, Verse 32).**

Parasurama ordered Bhisma to marry Amba, telling Bhisma it was his duty. Bhisma politely refused saying that he was ready to give up his life at the command of his teacher but not the promise that he had made. Taking pity on her plight, the avatar agreed to fight his former student on her behalf. The battle lasted twenty-three days, by the end of which, both warriors were bloodied and filled with arrows.

FIERCE BATTLE

The battle between Parashurama and Bhisma is an epic encounter described in various versions of the Mahabharata. Here is a depiction of the battle:

Filled with rage and seeking vengeance for Princess Amba, Parashurama, the fierce warrior sage, confronted Bhisma on the battlefield. Both warriors were renowned for their martial prowess, and their clash promised to be a remarkable display of skill and valour.

Parashurama armed with his divine axe and wielding his formidable powers, attacked Bhisma relentlessly. He unleashed a barrage of powerful strikes and unleashed his divine weapons, aiming to defeat his student and seek justice for Amba.

However, Bhisma, armed with his celestial bow Gandiva and blessed with extraordinary skills, stood his ground and skilfully defended himself against Parashurama's onslaught. He showcased his mastery of archery, deflecting the divine weapons and countering with his own lethal arrows.

The battle between the two warriors raged on for an extended period, with each displaying their exceptional combat abilities and showcasing their knowledge of various weapons and combat techniques. The battlefield was filled with the clash of weapons and the display of divine powers.

As the battle continued, Parashurama, who was renowned for his invincibility, gradually realized that Bhishma's skills and valour were unmatched. He recognized Bhisma's unwavering dedication and adherence to his principles, including his vow of celibacy and loyalty to Hastinapur.

Moved by Bhishma's unyielding resolve and impressed by his remarkable display of martial prowess, Parashurama ultimately decided to end the battle. He acknowledged Bhisma as the greatest warrior of his time and blessed him, acknowledging his exceptional abilities and his unwavering commitment to his duties.

The battle between Parashurama and Bhisma remains an iconic moment in Indian mythology, symbolizing the clash of two extraordinary warriors. It highlights the extent of Bhisma's skills and his unwavering loyalty, earning him a place among the most revered figures in the epic Mahabharata.

On seeing the state of battle Vasus approached Bhisma to give him a lethal weapon known as Praswapa from the eight gods which was unknown to Parasurama. They presented to Bhisma, the Praswapa arrow as Bhisma had to fight against his guru, Parasurama. The knowledge of Praswapa weapon was unknown to all the beings including Parasurama. Praswapa was a deadly missile and its remedy was **Samvohana (Slokas 11 to 13, Chapter183, Udyoga Parva, M.B.)**

Bhisma had knowledge of the divine deadly weapon Praswapa, which had the power to put a foe to sleep, and of which Parasurama was unaware. Bhisma decided to invoke the weapon to defeat Parasurama. When he was about to use the celestial weaponry, all Gods rushed to Bhisma and asked him to hold his hand, as it would humiliate his guru. Out of respect, Bhisma acquiesced. Bhisma withdrew his Praswapa weapon as per Nerada's request. Parasurama considered himself to be defeated since he had no answer to Bhishma's Praswapa weapon. When the fight reached a critical stage, Narada and the gods induced Parasurama to withdraw from the duel. Parasurama was approached by his ancestors who manifested from heaven in the battlefield. Parasurama decided to withdraw from the fight on being requested by his ancestors. Bhisma was able to prevail over Parasurama in the battle with the power of Praswapa weapon. Thus the fight ended with equal victory to both. At the request of the gods, pitrs and Gangadevi, Bhisma stopped the fight and prostrated at the feet of Parasurama. **(Udyoga Parva, Chapters 178-185).**

Bhisma did not, nor was he capable of defeating Lord Parasurama. In fact, when the battle between them reached its height, Lord Parasurama hurled his Parshu towards him, which is a weapon that cannot fail. It is similar to the Rambann gifted by Him to Shree Ram. But Bhisma responded with the Brahmastra to stop it, thus Bhisma was able to prevail over Parasurama in the battle. Pitaras then appeared and obstructed the chariot of Parasurama, forbidding him from fighting any longer. The spirit of Parashurama's father, Jamadagni and his grandfather, Rucheeka, spoke to him:

O son, never again engage in battle with Bhisma or any other Kshatriya. Heroism and courage in battle are the qualities of a Kshatriya, and study of the Vedas and the practice of austerities are the wealth of the Brahmans. Previously you took up weapons to protect the Brahmans, but this is not the case now. Let this battle with Bhisma be your last. O son of the Bhrigu race, it is not possible to defeat Bhisma.

Mahadev Lord Shiva also intervened on Goddess Ganga's request. If the two weapons would have collided, entire universe would have been destroyed. Lord Shiva asked both of them to withdraw their weapons. But princess Amba objected, and said to Lord Shiva that she wished nothing less than Bhisma death.

In the end, the Gods showered praise on Bhisma, and he sought the blessing of Parasurama as his guru. The avatar then acknowledged that his former student was truly invincible, telling Amba:

Using even the very best of weapons I have not been able to obtain any advantage over Bhisma, that foremost of all wielders of weapons! I have exerted now to the best of my power and might. Seek the protection of Bhisma himself; thou hast no other refuge now.

Actually no one won. The fight between Parasurama and Bhisma lasted for 23 days. No one lost. It resulted in a draw and Parasurama gave up. He said that if the fight continued then there would be heavy destruction on Earth due to use of celestial weapons. Parasurama couldn't risk it. Both Parasurama and Bhisma couldn't defeat each other by shastras. And they didn't want to use Astra's. Bhisma once offered puja to Parasurama. **(Udyoga Parva, Chapter 123, Verse 27).**

THE MAHABHARTA BOOK 5

The Mahabharata has described the duel between Parasurama and Bhisma through the following Parva.

[1] UDYOGA PARVA: ULUKA DUTAGAMANA PARVA: SECTION CLXXXVI SECTION CLXXXVI

"Bhisma said, 'Then, O great king, during the night, having bowed unto the Brahmans, the Rishi's, the gods, and all those creatures that wander during the dark, and also all the kings of the earth, I laid myself down on my bed, and in the solitude of my room, I began to reflect in the following way.--For many days hath this fierce combat of terrible consequence lasted between myself and Jamadagni. I am unable, however, to vanquish on the field of battle that Rama of mighty energy. If indeed, I am competent to vanquish in battle that Brahman of mighty strength, viz., Jamadagni son of great prowess, then let the gods kindly show themselves to me this night!--Mangled with arrows as I lay asleep, O great king, that night on my right side, towards the morning, those foremost of Brahmans who had raised me when I had fallen down from my car and held me up and said unto me--Do not fear--and who had comforted me, showed themselves to me, O king, in a dream! And they stood surrounding me and said these words. Listen to them as I repeat them to thee, O perpetuator of Kuru's race! Rise, O Ganga's son, thou needs' have no fear! We will protect thee, for thou art our own body! Rama, the son of Jamadagni, will never be able to vanquish thee in battle! Thou, O bull of Bharata race will be the conqueror of Rama in combat! This beloved weapon, O Bharata, called Praswapa, appertaining to the lord of all creatures, and forged by the divine artificer, will come to thy knowledge, for it was known to thee in thy former life! Neither Rama, nor any person on earth is acquainted with it. Recollect it, therefore, O thou of mighty arms, and apply it with strength! O king of kings, O sinless one, it will come to thee of itself! With it, O Kauravas, thou wilt be able to check all persons endued with mighty energy! O king, Rama will not be slain outright by it, thou shall not, therefore, O giver of honours, incur any sin by using it! Afflicted by the force of this thy weapon, the son of Jamadagni, will fall asleep! Vanquishing him thus, thou wilt again awaken him in battle, O Bhisma, with that dear weapon called Samvohana! Do what we have told thee, O Kauravas, in the morning, stationed on thy car. Asleep or dead we reckon it as the same, O king, Rama will not surely die! Apply, therefore, this Praswapa weapon so happily thought of!--Having said this, O king, those foremost of Brahmans, eight in number and resembling one another in form, and possessed of effulgent bodies, all vanished from my sight!'"

[2] Udyoga Parva: Uluka Dutagamana Parva: section CLXXXVIII SECTION CLXXXVIII

"Bhisma said, 'When I had formed this resolution, O king, a din of tumultuous voices arose in the sky. And it said,--O son of Kuru's race, do not let off the Praswapa weapon!--Notwithstanding this, I still aimed that weapon at Bhrigu's descendant. When I had aimed it, Narada addressed me, saying, 'Yonder, O Kauravas stay the gods in the sky! Even they are forbidding thee today! Do not aim the Praswapa weapon! Rama is an ascetic possessed of Brahma merit, and he is, again, thy preceptor! Never, Kauravas, humiliate him.' While Narada was telling me this, I beheld those eight utterers of Brahma stationed in the sky. Smilingly, O king, they said unto me slowly,--O chief of the Bharata, do even what Narada sayeth. Even that, O best of Bharata's race, is highly beneficial to the world!' I then withdrew that great weapon called Praswapa and invoked according to the ordinance the weapon called Brahma in the combat. Beholding the Praswapa weapon withdrawn, O lion among kings, Rama was in great huff, and suddenly exclaimed, 'Wretch that I am, I am vanquished, O Bhisma!' Then Jamadagni son behold before him his venerable father and his father's fathers. They stood surrounding him there, and addressed him in these words of consolation, 'O sire, never display such 'rashness again, the rashness, viz., of engaging in battle with Bhisma, or especially with any Kshatriya, O descendant of Bhrigu's race, to fight is the duty of a Kshatriya! Study (of the Vedas) and practice of vows are the highest wealth of Brahmans! For some reason, before 'this, thou hadst been ordered by us to take up weapons. Thou hadst then perpetrated that terrible and unbecoming feat. Let this battle with Bhisma be thy very last, for enough of it thou hadst already. O thou of mighty arms, leave the combat. Blessed be thou, let this be the very last instance of thy taking up the bow! O invincible one, throw thy bow aside, and practice ascetic austerities, O thou of Bhrigu's race! Behold, Bhisma, the son of Santanu, is forbidden by all the gods! They are endeavouring to pacify him, repeatedly saying,--Desist from this battle! Do not light with Rama who is thy preceptor. It is not proper for thee, O perpetuator of Kuru's race, to vanquish Rama in battle! O son of Ganga, show this Brahman every honour on the field of battle! As regards thee, we are thy superiors and therefore forbid thee! Bhisma is one of the foremost of Vasus! O son, it is fortunate, that thou art still alive! Santanu's son by Ganga--a celebrated Vasu as he is,--how can he be defeated by thee? Desist, therefore, O Bhargava! That foremost of the Pandavas, Arjuna, the mighty son of Indra, hath been ordained by the Self-create to be the slayer of Bhisma!'

"Bhisma continued, 'Thus addressed by his own ancestors, Rama answered them, saying, 'I cannot give up the combat. Even this is the solemn vow I have made. Before this, I never left the field, giving up battle! Ye grandsires, if you please, cause Ganga's son to desist from the fight! As regards myself, I can, by no means, desist from the combat!' Hearing these words of his, O king, those ascetics with Rucheeka at their head, coming to me with Narada in their company, told me, 'O sire, desist from battle! Honour that foremost of Brahmans!' For the sake of Kshatriya morality, I replied unto them, saying. Even this is the vow I have taken in this world, viz., that I would never desist from battle turning my back, or suffer my back to be wounded with arrows! I cannot, from temptation or distress, or fear, or for the sake of wealth, abandon my eternal duty! Even this is my fixed resolution! Then all those ascetics with Narada at their head, O king, and my mother Bhagirathi, occupied the field of battle (before me). I, however, stayed quietly with arrows and bow as before, resolved to fight. They then once more turned towards Rama and addressed him, saying. 'The hearts of Brahmans are made of butter. Be pacified, therefore, O son of Bhrigu's race! O Rama, O Rama, desist from this battle, O best of Brahmans! Bhisma is incapable of being slain by thee, as indeed, thou, O Bhargava, art incapable of being slain by him!' Saying these words while they stood obstructing the field, the Pitrs caused that descendant of Bhrigu's race to place aside his weapons. Just at this time I once more beheld those eight utterers of Brahma, blazing with effulgence and resembling bright stars raised on the firmament. Stationed for battle as I was, they said these words unto me with great affection, 'O thou of mighty arms, go unto Rama who is thy preceptor! Do what is beneficial to all the worlds. Beholding then that Rama had desisted owing to the words of his well-wishers; I also, for the good of the worlds, accepted the words of my well-wishers. Though mangled exceedingly, I still approached Rama and worshipped him. The great ascetic Rama then, smilingly, and with great affection, said unto me, 'There is no Kshatriya equal to thee on the earth! Go now, O Bhisma, for in this combat thou hast pleased me highly'! Summoning then in my presence that maiden (the daughter of Kasi), Bhargava sorrowfully said unto her these words in the midst of all those high-souled persons.'"

CHAPTER TWENTY-FOUR

AMBA

Amba was the eldest daughter of King of Kashi in the Hindu epic of the Mahabharata. Amba, along with her sisters Ambika and Ambalika, was taken by force by Bhisma from their Svayamvara, where suitors competed for their hand in marriage. Bhisma defeated all the other kings and princes and presented the sisters to Satyavati, the mother of Vicitravlrya, the king of Hastinapur.

However, Vicitravlrya married only Ambika and Ambalika, rejecting Amba because she had already given her heart to another man. Amba sought out her beloved, but he rejected her due to his shame of losing the combat against Bhisma. Feeling rejected and distraught, Amba returned to Bhisma and demanded that he marry her. However, Bhisma declined her request, as he had taken a vow of lifelong celibacy.

Frustrated and desperate, Amba sought help from Parasurama, who fought a 23-day battle with Bhisma on her behalf. However, the battle did not yield any result, and Amba realized that she would remain unmarried and dishonored. Enraged by her plight, she swore to kill Bhisma, at least in her next life, and died.

Amba was then reborn as Sikhandi, the son of King Dhrupad. In the battle of Kurukshetra, Sikhandi played a crucial role in the death of Bhisma. Bhisma, bound by his vow not to raise weapons against a woman, refused to fight against Sikhandi, who was born in a female body but later became a male. Taking advantage of this, Sikhandi fought alongside the Pandavas, ultimately leading to Bhishma's downfall.

AMBA'S REVENGE ON BHISMA

Finding that it was not possible to achieve her object through Parasurama mediation, Amba renounced food, sleep etc. and went to the Yamuna valley to do penance for six years. **(M.B., Udyoga Parva, Chapter 188).**

After that for one year she went on a fast, lying under the water in the river Yamuna. Again for another year she did penance, standing on the tip of the toes and eating only dry leaves. Next, she reduced the sky and earth to flames by doing penance. The goddess Gariga appeared to her and when she understood her plight, she told Amba that it was not possible to kill Bhisma. In her agony and despair, without even drinking water, she wandered about here and there. The goddess Gariga cursed her to become a river in the Vatsa country. As a result of the curse, a part of her was turned into the river known as Amba. The remaining part of her engaged itself in penance and told her that in the next birth she would attain masculinity.

Amba going on a fast under the water in the river Yamuna, doing penance standing on her toes and eating dry leaves, and reducing the sky and earth to flames through penance does not align with the traditional story of Amba as described in the Mahabharata. There might be variations or alternate versions of the story in different sources or folklore. However, the transformation of Amba into a river and the prophecy of attaining masculinity in the next birth are not part of the commonly known narrative.

In the Mahabharata, Amba's story primarily revolves around her rejection by Bhisma, seeking revenge against him, and her subsequent rebirth as Sikhandi.

LORD SHIVA BLESSINGS

At last Lord Shiva, the Great God, appeared before her, drawn by the power of her prayers and penances, and standing over her with the trident in his hand, he questioned her as to the boon she sought. "The defeat of Bhisma!" answered Amba, bowing joyfully at his feet, for she knew that this was the end of the first stage in the execution of her purpose. "Thou shalt slay him," said the Great God. Then Amba, filled with joy, and yet overcome with amazement, said: "But how, being a woman, can I achieve victory in battle? It is true that my woman s heart is entirely stilled. Yet I beg of thee, O thou who hast the bull for thy cognizance, to give me the promise that I myself shall be able to slay Bhisma in battle! "

Shiva replied to her plead: "My words can never be false. You will take a new birth and some time afterwards you will obtain manhood. Then you shall become a fierce warrior, well skilled in battle, and remembering the whole of thy present life, thou thyself, with thine own hands, shall be the slayer of Bhisma." And having so said, the form of Shiva disappeared from before the eyes of the assembled ascetics and the Lady Amba there in the midst of the forest ashrama. Lord Shiva foretold her about the instance in Mahabharata when Nar (Arjun) would be facing the Vasu (Bhisma), and that time she can have her revenge.

He added that she would be born in the Dhrupad dynasty as a great archer under the name of Citrayodhi and kill Bhisma. But Amba proceeded to gather wood with her own hands, and made a great funeral pyre on the banks of the Yamuna, and then, setting a light to it, she herself entered into it, and as she took her place upon the throne of flame she said over and over again : " I do this for the destruction of Bhisma ! To obtain a new body for the destruction of Bhisma do I enter this fire! "And was reborn as the daughter of the king of Panchal, dhrupad.

AMBA REBIRTH

King Dhrupad's queen had been in great distress for a long time because she had no children. Dhrupad propitiated Siva by worshipping him for an issue. Siva blessed him and said that a girl would be born to him, but she would be transformed into a boy. In due course, the queen gave birth to a girl, but it was announced that it was a boy. Therefore the child had to be brought up, dressed like a boy. The child became famous under the name of Sikhandi. When Sikhandi attained youth, Dhrupad decided to look for a wife for him (her). Still he was greatly perplexed as to how to find a wife for Sikhandi who was already a female! But his wife assured Dhrupad that Sikhandi would become a man, according to Siva's blessing. So, Dhrupad made a proposal for Sikhandi marriage with the daughter of the King of Dasharna.

SIKHANDI'S MARRIAGE

Hiranyavarna, the King of Dasharna, gave his daughter in marriage to Sikhandi. The couple arrived at Kambalyapura. By this time the wife came to know that the "husband" was a woman. She disclosed the secret to her Ladies-in-waiting. They in turn communicated it to the king. Enraged at this, Hiranyavarna sent a messenger to King Dhrupad to ascertain the truth of the matter. He even began to make preparations for waging a war against Dhrupad, King of Panchal. Dhrupad and his queen were in a fix. At this stage the distressed Sikhandi proceeded to the forest, determined to commit suicide. People were afraid of entering that forest because a Yaksa named Sthunakarna lived there. Sikhandi went to the premises of the Yaksa and performed certain rites for a number of days. The Yaksa appeared to her. Sikhandi explained the whole matter to him. They entered into a contract. According to it, they exchanged their sexes Sikhandi receiving the male sex of die Yaksa and the Yaksa receiving the female sex of Sikhandi. Sikhandi returned home as a man. Dhrupad repeated with greater force his old plea that his child was a man. Hiranyavarna made at thorough examination of Sikhandi and convinced himself of the truth.

KUBERA'S ARRIVAL

At that time, in the course of his world tour Kubera arrived at the residence of Sthunakarna. The Yaksa, who was in female form, did not come out to receive Kubera. In his anger, Kubera pronounced a curse that the female sex of Sthunakarna and the male sex of Sikhandi would continue forever.

The Yaksa prayed for the lifting of the curse. Kubera released him from the curse by saying that after the death of Sikhandi, the Yaksa would be restored to his own male sex. According to the previous agreement, Sikhandi went to Sthunakarna place after the death of Hiranyavarna. But coming to know of all that had happened, he returned home. Thus Sikhandi became a man permanently. Sikhandi had received his training in arms under Dronacarya. In the great Kaurava-Pandava battle, he became a charioteer.

SIKHANDI'S (AMBA'S) REVENGE FULFILLED

The Mahabharata, Bhisma Parva, Chapter 108, describes Bhishma's encounter with Sikhandi during the Kaurava-Pandava battle. The Pandavas started the day's battle by keeping Sikhandi in the vanguard. Bhīma, Arjuna, Abhimanyu's and other warriors were giving him support. It was Bhisma who led the Kauravas forces. Arrows began to fly from both sides. It was the tenth day of the battle and Sikhandi shot three arrows aimed at Bhishma's chest. Bhisma with a smile of contempt said to Sikhandi, "Sikhandi! Brahma created you as a woman. You may do as you like". Hearing this taunt, Sikhandi became more infuriated. Arjuna inspired him with greater courage. After that, keeping Sikhandi in front, Arjuna began to fight with Bhisma. Sikhandi also showered his arrows on him. Ten of these arrows of Sikhandi hit Bhisma's chest. Bhisma disregarded even those arrows. At last he said: "I cannot kill the Pandavas because they are in vulnerable (avadhyah). I cannot kill Sikhandi because he is really a woman and not man. Earlier, Bhisma narrated to Duryodhana the story of Amba who was re-born as Sikhandi. **(Udyoga parva, Chapters188-192).**

Bhisma adhered that he is also invulnerable and cannot be killed in battle, yet today I have to die; the time has come for me to die."Meanwhile Sikhandi and Arjuna were discharging a continuous and heavy shower of arrows at Bhisma. At last Bhisma fell down. **(M.B., Udyoga Parva, Chapter173).**

Bhisma was a Trikalgyani, and knew about this instance, and personally agreed that she should have her revenge, and so deliberately put down his arms while facing her.

CHAPTER TWENTY-FIVE

DRONA

Drona was indeed a famous disciple of Parasurama. In the later Vedic period, when Parasurama decided to renounce his possessions and embrace the life of a renouncing, Drona, who was a poor Brahmin, approached him seeking alms.

Having already given away his gold to Brahmins and his land to Kashyapa, Parasurama had only his body and weapons left. When Drona asked for alms, Parasurama presented him with a choice: he could either have his body or his weapons and the knowledge of using them. Drona, being a wise and ambitious warrior, chose the latter option. He requested all of Parashurama's weapons and the secrets of their use.

Impressed by Drona's request and his ambition to master the science of arms, Parasurama bestowed upon him all his weapons, making Drona an unparalleled expert in warfare and the use of weapons. This event played a significant role in shaping Drona's future as a renowned teacher and military strategist, eventually leading to his role as the guru (teacher) of the Kuru princes, including the Pandavas and the Kauravas, in the Mahabharata.

DRONA SECURED DHANURVEDA

After travelling throughout the world exterminating the Ksatriyas race Parasurama gave all his wealth to Kashyapa. On hearing that Parasurama was giving away all his riches as gifts to Brahmins Drona rushed to Mahendra parvata to see Parasurama. By then Parasurama had distributed all his wealth excepting Dhanurvidya. Parasurama called Drona to his side and said that only two things remained with him, his body and Dhanurvidya. Drona, he added, could take anyone of the two and then Drona took Dhanurvidya from him. After that Parasurama went to Maharanya for the sake of penance. **(Chapter 130, Adi Parva).**

Hearing that Paras urama was giving Brahmans free gift of wealth and property, Drona reached there. Drona's desire was to get Dhanurvidya (the art of archery) . Drona with his disciples went to Mahendragiri and saw Parasurama, who was about to enter forest giving away everything he had. Parasurama said, "I have given away to the Brahmans gold and everything had. The land I had conquered is given to Kashyapa. Now there remains only my body and some weapons. You can have one of them." Drona preferred the weapons. Thus Drona got the entire armoury of Parasurama. **(M. B. Adi Parva, Chapter 13).**

At that time Drona got new lessons from Parasurama and they were also imparted to Drona's disciples. When Drona became the preceptor of the Kauravas and Pandavas Asvatthama also went with him. **(Slokas 52 to 64, Chapter 130, Adi Parva, M.B.)**

THE BIRTH OF DRONA

Drona was the son of Bharadwaja who had his hermitage erected on the bank of the Ganges. Once, Bharadwaja went to bathe in the river. When he got into the river he saw the celestial maid. The celestial maid ran away as soon as she saw the hermit. But her cloth was caught in grass and slipped off her body. When the hermit saw the complete form 'of her body which was bright and beautiful, he had seminal discharge. The discharged semen was kept in a Drona (trough). A child was born from that and he was named

Drona, who was brought up in the hermitage. **(M. B.Adi Parva, Chapter 13).**

EDUCATION AND MARRIAGE

Drona learned the art of using weapons from his father and the hermit Agnivesa. Dhrupad the prince of Panchal was the fellow student of Drona. They became great friends. On completion of education Dhrupad returned to Panchal. Drona married Krpi the daughter of Saradvan. A son was born to them. At his birth the child neighed like the horse Uccaihsravas; so his parents named him Asvatthama.

THE TEACHER IN ARCHERY

He became the teacher of the Pandavas and the Kauravas. After receiving Dhanurvidya from Parasurama, Drona went to Panchal. Dhrupad who had been a fellow student of Drona was the King of Uttarapanchala then. Though Drona had become proficient in archery, he was very poor. He had no money even to buy milk for his child. Once, the playmates of Asvatthama made him drink a mixture of water and flour saying that it was milk. So Drona approached Dhrupad for financial help. But Dhrupad shunned his fellow student, scolded him and sent him away without giving any help. Drona vowed that he would, somehow or other, take revenge upon Dhrupad and departed from Panchala.

The aim of Drona was to get some capable disciples. He reached Hastinapur and stayed in disguise with Gautama for a while. Once, the Pandavas and the Kauravas who were boys were engaged in the game of outside the palace premises. The ball fell in a well by chance. The princes stood round the well and began to ponder how to get the 'ball' out of the well. They tried all means but in vain. At that time a Brahman of dark complexion, short and aged, came by that way. It was Drona. The boys gathered round the old man. Drona threw his ring also into the well and said: "Your kingly qualities are very poor.Your education in using weapons is not complete. If you give me a meal I will get both the ring and the ball together" The boys agreed to the conditions.Drona took a grass and evoked arrow into it by mantra (spell) and shot it at the 'Kara'. The next grass was shot at the first grass. It struck the first grass. Thus he shot grasses one after another till the grass reached the brink of the well and by pulling the grass he took the ball out. In the same way he took the ring also out of the well. When they got the 'Kara' the boys stood round Drona and asked him what he would like as the reward for his deed. Drona said that they need only tell Bhisma how a short man of dark complexion took the ball out of the well. Accordingly the boys went to Bhisma and told him everything. Bhisma understood that it was Drona. Bhisma thought that Drona was the best person to teach the princes. So Drona was brought to the palace and was engaged as the teacher in archery.(**M.B. Adi Parva, Chapters 130 and 131**).

HIS FAVOURITE DISCIPLE ARJUN

Drona asked the Pandavas and the Kauravas to sit together and then told them. "There is one thing that you should do for me when your education is over". Hearing this they all kept silent. But Arjuna came forward and took the vow that he would achieve that task according to the wish of the teacher.

As Drona loved his brilliant student Arjuna, he taught both his son and Arjuna alike the secrets. Seeing the brilliance of Arjuna Drona ordered the cook not to seat Arjuna in a dark place for meals. Yet it happened once that the light was extinguished by wind while the princes were having their meals. All sat still, without eating, while Arjuna alone ate his food. From this Arjuna discovered that without seeing the object one could hit the target by constant practice. Drona was greatly pleased at this and embracing him promised to try to make him such an expert that there would be none equal to him in archery.The education in archery and the use of weapons was nearing completion. In archery Arjuna was second to none.

As the princes were growing up, Bhisma wanted them to be trained in the art of warfare and in the use of arms. Looking out for the most outstanding teacher, Bhisma chose Drona, the son of Saint Bharadwaja as the tutor for the Pandavas and the Kauravas. Pleased with the reception given to him by Bhisma when he visited the palace on invitation, Drona accepted the assignment. He taught the princes all aspects relating to the use of arms. Both the Kauravas and the Pandavas became proficient in the use of all kinds of arms.

THE STORY

Sage Bharadwaja was living at the source of the river Ganga, observing rigid vows. Once when he went to the river to perform his ablutions, he met Ghritachi, a celestial woman known as an Apsara. Seeing the beautiful woman emerging from the river after taking her bath, the sage was consumed with a burning desire. On seeing her clothes coming off her body, his vital fluid came out. The sage held it in a vessel called Drona. Eventually, Drona, the child, sprang out of the fluid preserved by the sage. The child thus born studied the Vedas and other scriptures. Bharadwaja taught his knowledge of arms to his illustrious disciple Agnivesa, who was born from fire. Agnivesa, in turn, taught the Science of Weapons to Drona.

King Prishata, a great friend of Bharadwaja had a son by name Dhrupad. Dhrupad came to the hermitage of Bharadwaja to study under the sage. He was studying in the company of Drona and was also playing with him. When Prishata was dead, Dhrupad became the king of the northern Panchalas. At about this time, Bharadwaja also ascended to heaven.

Drona continued to reside in his father's hermitage, devoting himself to as ascetic way of life. As per the wishes expressed by his father before his death, Drona married Kripi, the daughter of Saradwat. A son was born to them. When he came into this world, the child neighed like the celestial horse Uccaihsravas. Hearing that cry, a voice from the sky ordained that the child be named Asvatthama, meaning 'the horse-voiced'. Drona, exhilarated by the birth of a son, continued to reside in that hermitage, devoting himself to the study of the science of arms.

Drona came to know that the illustrious Brahmin Parasurama, son of Jamadagni, the foremost among all wielders of weapons, had expressed a desire to give away all his wealth to Brahmins. Having heard of Parashurama's knowledge of arms and of his celestial weapons he possessed, Drona set his heart on getting them as well as the knowledge of ethics and morals that Parasurama possessed.

Drona, accompanied by his disciples set out for the Mahendra mountains, where he met Parasurama. After prostrating before Parasurama and introducing himself as one born in the lineage of Angiras, Drona said, "I have sprung from Bharadwaja. But I have not entered the womb of any woman. I have come to you seeking your wealth."

Parasurama said, "I welcome you. I have gifted all my wealth to Brahmins. I have given the earth conquered by me to Sage Kashyapa. I have only my body and my weapons. I am willing to give you either my body or my weapons. Please indicate your choice."

Drona said, "Please give me all your weapons along with the knowledge of hurling and recalling them."

Parasurama gave all his weapons and the knowledge of using them to Drona. Drona then proceeded to the city of his friend Dhrupad.

CHAPTER TWENTY-SIX

KARNA

Karna is portrayed as the half-brother of the Pandavas and the son of Surya, the sun god, in the Mahabharata. However, there are variations in the different retellings and interpretations of the epic.

According to the Mahabharata, Karna was indeed raised by a low-caste charioteer, but he was not initially aware of his true lineage. He aspired to learn the skills of a warrior and approached the renowned sage Parashurama, who only accepted Brahmins as his students. Karna disguised himself as a Brahmin and received training from Parashurama.

The incident you mentioned about the scorpion bite is also a part of the story. Karna's unwavering silence and endurance impressed Parashurama, but when the truth was revealed, Parashurama cursed Karna that he would forget the knowledge of the powerful Brahmastra weapon at the moment of his greatest need.

During the Kurukshetra war, Karna was a formidable warrior fighting on the side of the Kauravas against the Pandavas. He was aware of his divine heritage but chose to remain loyal to his friend Duryodhana, the leader of the Kauravas. Karna's dream, where he saw his guru Parashurama, was a turning point in his life.

In the dream, Parashurama revealed that he had known Karna's true identity from the beginning and had intentionally cursed him to ensure the balance of power in the world. He instructed Karna to accept his curse and face his fate, urging him to let Arjuna, one of the Pandavas and Karna's rival, be the one to kill him. Parashurama believed that if Karna killed Arjuna, it would lead to chaos and upheaval.

The story of Karna and his tragic fate is one of the most poignant and complex tales in the Mahabharata, exploring themes of loyalty, honor, and destiny.

KARNA'S ARMOUR AND EARRINGS

Karna was born with armour on his body and rings in his ears. Chapter 99 of Adi Parva says thus : *"To Kunti was born of Surya the mighty Karna. Even at his birth he was adorned with an armour over his body and rings in his ears."* Surya had ordained that as long as Karna wore the armour and ear-rings he would be unconquerable. Indra knew this and wanted to get Karna rid of these so that Arjuna, his son, might gain a victory over Karna. Karna was reputed for his charity and Indra under the garb of a Brahmin went to Karna and begged of him his ear-rings and armour. The Sun god had already warned him in a dream that Indra would thus try to deceive him. Still Karna could not bring himself to refuse any gift that was asked of him and so he cut off the ear-rings and armour with which he was born and gave them to the Brahman. The only request that the noble Karna did make was that in separating the ornaments from his body no wound should be made. Indra did it with great skill neither hurting him nor making even a scratch on this body. Indra bade Karna ask for any boon he wanted. The Sun god had also advised him to ask for a good weapon in return in case he gave away his assets and so he requested Indra the best of the weapons he possessed. Indra gave him his weapon, the Shakti, called Vaijayanti also. Karna had to use that weapon to kill the great Ghajotkaca in the Mahabharata battle. Karna lost his clothes during a fight against the king of Virata. **(Chapter 65, Virata Parva).**

KARNA BECAME THE KING OF ANGA.

The Pandavas and Kauravas were studying archery under Dronacarya together and Karna was also among them. When their education was complete a day was fixed to exhibit the skill of the students. The public also was invited to see the skill of the princes. Everybody showed his best and Arjuna displayed super-human skill so that the vast assemblage was lost in wonder and admiration. Then strode Karna to the scene and not only did he duplicate with ease Arjuna's feats but he did show something more. The assemblage was dumb founded. Arjuna turned pale. At this moment Kirpacharya stood up and questioned the right of Karna to compete with those with royal blood in them. Then rose Duryodhana and said : "If the combat is not in order simply because Karna is not a prince it is easily remedied. I crown Karna as the King of Anga". Then there came to the scene the aged Adhiratha, the foster-father of Karna, and as Karna saw him coming he went and bowed before him and Adhiratha embraced him with tears in his eyes. **(Chapters 134 to 136, Adi Parva, M.B.)** .

Karna was rejected by Drona due to his perceived caste. Even while they were studying archery Arjuna and Karna constantly vied with each other. Later, Karna prompted Duryodhana to tease the Pandavas living in the forest. **(Chapter 7, Vana Parva).**Karna swore that he would kill Arjuna. **(Chapter257, Vana Parva)** . Karna once requested Drona to teach him in private the secret of the Brahmashastra to fight against Arjuna. But Drona did not accede to his request. Karna was present at the Svayamvara of Draupadi. **(Slokas 4, Chapter 185, Adi Parva).** Bhīma defeated Karna once in a single combat. **(Slokas 20, Chapter 34. Sabha Parva).** Karna took part in the Rajasuya of Yudhishthira. **(Sloka 7, Chapter 34, Sand Parva)** .Karna defeated Jarasandha once in a single combat. **(Chapter 44, Sabha Parva).** Karna defeated in his victory march many kings like Dhrupad, Bhagadatta and Kerala. **(Chapter 254, Aranya Parva).** Karna conquered the cities of Malini and Campa and annexed them to the country of Anga. **(Chapter 5, Karna Parva).**

KARNA WAS DISCIPLE OF PARSURAMA

Karna approached Parasurama at Mahendragiri and pretended to be a member of the Bhrigu family, not a Kshatriya. In this version of the story, Karna lied about his caste and convinced Parasurama to accept him as his student.

Parasurama, known for his vow to teach only Brahmins, accepted Karna as his disciple and imparted various teachings and techniques in archery. Karna learned extensively from his guru and gained knowledge of the powerful Brahmastra weapon, which was considered one of the most potent and destructive weapons in Hindu mythology.

The story of Karna's education under Parasurama is an important aspect of his character development in the Mahabharata. It showcases his determination, perseverance, and his willingness to overcome obstacles in order to acquire the skills he desired.

KARNA WAS CURSED

Karna then stayed peacefully at Mahendra Hill, the residence of Parashurama. There he began the study of the science of throwing and retracting the brahmastra. There he got the opportunity to meet many demigods, heavenly singers, and other denizens of heaven. Once Karna was wandering in the vicinity of the asrama when he saw a lonely cow grazing there and Karna without knowing that it belonged to a Brahmin killed her. Karna mistook the cow to be a violent animal and chopped off her head with his sword. The Brahmin got furious and cursed Karna thus "Oh, sinner, the wheel of your chariot would go down in the mud when you face the enemy to fight against whom you are now taking training. Then, when you stand perplexed, your opponent would cut off your head." Karna requested for a removal of the curse but the Brahmin refused to show any mercy.

However, this specific incident mentioned here, where Karna mistakenly kills a cow belonging to a Brahmin and receives a curse is not part of the traditional narrative of Karna's story in the Mahabharata.

Karna's life and character in the epic are filled with various challenges, moral dilemmas, and tragic circumstances, but the specific incident described is not a commonly recognized part of his story. It's possible that this variation or addition may exist in certain regional or folklore versions of the Mahabharata or other retellings of the epic.

In the traditional narrative, Karna faces many trials and tribulations but is not associated with accidentally killing a cow and receiving a curse related to his chariot wheel or the cutting off of his head.

THE BEETLE EXPOSED THE KARNA

One day tired after a day's fast and a walk around the ashrama with his disciples Parasurama slept resting his head on the lap of Karna. Then a beetle named Alarka attacked Karna and started sucking blood from his thigh. Blood was oozing from his thighs and it slowly made the body of the Guru also wet and still Karna did not stir from his position lest it should disturb his guru in his nap.

Suddenly Parasurama awoke and stared at the beetle and the beetle killed it with his mere glance. A surprising event then occurred. A fearsome demon became visible in the sky. The demon folded his hands in front of Parasurama, and said, '0 greatest amongst sages! Thank you for relieving me of the hellish situation of life that I was suffering in. Now I will return back to the place that I had come from Parshuram asked the demon, 'Who are you and how did you fall into such a dreadful condition of life?' "The demon replied, '0 Lord! In satya-yuga I was the demon named Damsha. I forcibly tried to kidnap the wife of the sage Bhrigu. I was cursed in turn by him to fall into a hellish condition of life as a carnivorous insect. Upon my begging forgiveness from him, he blessed me by saying that the duration of the condition of being in that insect body would end by the glance of Sri Parshuram, who would be born in his dynasty. Now that I've met you, my punishment is over. Saying this, he left that place after paying obeisance to Sri Parshuram.

ALARKA, THE BEETLE THAT BIT KARNA.

Shanti Parva chapter 3 mentions the story behind Alarka, the beetle that bit Karna. This beetle was in his previous birth a demon named Darhsa. Darhsa once tried to molest the wife of the sage Bhrigu. The Maharshi cursed him and made him into a beetle. On his request for mercy, he said he would get release from the curse by Parasurama. So, the beetle became the Raksasas again and left the place. When the demon disappeared saying so much Parasurama turned to Karna who stood with respect, his dress all covered with blood. Parasurama said: "No Brahmin can bear so much pain with such patience. Surely, you are not a Brahmin. *Parshuram then angrily asked Karna, '0 fool! The pain of the sting of that kind of insect is something that a Brahman can never tolerate. Your tolerance of pain is like that of a Kshatriya.* Let me know the truth." Trembling with fear Karna revealed his identity and then Parasurama cursed him for deceit against his Guru saying that he would never be able to remember the Brahmastra when the time to use it came. Saying this, Karna trembled and fell on the ground while folding his hands. Sri Parshuram laughed sarcastically, and said, *'O fool! By speaking lies to me you have cheated me. Therefore, when your death will be near and you'll most desperately need this Brahmastra, you'll forget all about invoking it. However, in all other times of war you will remain unmatched.'* Saying this, Sri Parshuram left. Parasurama cursed him saying *"You will forget the secret of the Brahmastra at the time when you want to use it against your enemy."* **(Chapters 2 and 3, Santi Parva).** Karna took leave of Parasurama and went to Hastinapur.

DEVINE VIJAYA WEAPON

There was divine bow Vijaya of Karna. This bow was the most deadly of all weapons. This bow which was made by Vishvakarma originally belonged to Indra. At that time Indra had defeated many Asuras with the help of this bow. Indra gave this bow to his loved disciple Parasurama. Karna got it from Parasurama. It is said that this bow was superior to Gandiva.It was with the help of this bow that Parasurama conquered the Ksatriyas twenty-one times. **(M.B. Karna Parva, Chapter 31, Stanza 42)** Kandaprstham is the name of Karna's bow.

KARNA TRAINED BY PARSURAMA

The great battle of Mahabharata lasted for eighteen days. Karna was a warrior and that was a worrisome discussion in Pandavas camp. Before the great war started Kunti , mother of Pandavas went alone to the shores of Ganga and met Karna. She then confessed to him that she was his mother and that the Pandavas were his brothers. She advised Karna to join sides with the Pandavas and the Sun god approved of it. But Karna refused to do so. He said he would never for sake Duryodhana who had brought him up from his childhood at a time when he was in peril. But he promised his mother that he would never kill any of her other four sons but would kill Arjuna in the battle-field. **(Chapter 146, Udyoga Parva).** Karna started his fight against the Pandavas after taking blessings from Bhisma. (Chapter 3, Drona Parva) . Karna fought against the princes of Kekaya, Arjuna, Bhīma, Dhrstadyunma and Satyaki in single combat. **(Chapter 32, Drona Parva).** Abhimanyu's defeated Karna in a single combat.**(Chapter 40, Drona Parva)** . Karna made Bhīma unconscious. **(Chapter 139, Drona Parva).** Karna once withdrew a bit when hit by the arrow of Arjuna. **(Chapter 139, Drona Parva).** Karna insulted Kirpacharya at one time. **(Chapter 158, Drona Parva).** Karna killed Ghatotkaca with the weapon Shakti which Indra had given him in exchange for the armour and earrings which he had given to Indra. **(Chapter 180, Drona Parva).** Karna ran away from the battlefield when he heard that Drona was dead. **(Chapter 193, Karna Parva)** .Karna was made the General of the Kauravas army when Drona died. **(Chapter 10, Karna Parva).** Salya became the charioteer of Karna **(Chapter 86, Karna Parva).**

THE STORY

As stated in chapter six of the Adi Parva, Kunti, before her marriage to Pandu, had conceived a child by the Surya, the sun god. Due to fear of her relatives, she placed the child in a basket and set it afloat on the river Ganges. The child was picked up by Adhiratha, a well known carpenter and chariot driver, and his wife Radha. They were attracted by the beautiful features of the child, especially his kavacha [natural golden armor] and kundala [golden earrings]. He was given the name Karna. They raised the child very carefully for sixteen years.

On Karna's sixteenth birthday, his father offered him a new chariot and horses. Not feeling a desire to drive the chariot, he addressed his mother, Today, father has brought me a chariot and horses, but I do not feel the desire to drive a chariot; I feel the desire to hold a bow and arrow. I cannot think of anything else. Waking or sleeping, my thoughts are ever fixed on this desire. I want to be an archer and fight.

Radha then explained to her foster son Karna all that had happened; how she had found him at the bank of the Ganges wrapped in precious silk and floating in a basket. Hearing about his mysterious past, he was struck with wonder. After consulting with his mother and father, he took permission from them and left for the city of Hastinapur, desiring to find a martial guru.

Karna's goal was to learn archery. He approached the great Drona who was teaching the Pandavas in Hastinapur. After receiving an audience with him, he pleaded, My lord, please accept me as your pupil. I want to learn the science of archery. I am the son of Adhiratha, a carpenter and chariot driver by caste. Drona did not like the idea of teaching archery to the son of a suta (chariot driver) and sent him away.

Karna was determined to learn archery. He decided to approach Parashurama, the chastiser of the Kshatriyas. Previously Parashurama had annihilated the warrior race twenty-one times because of the death of his father. Knowing that the great sage hated warriors and kings, Karna decided to tell him that he was a Brahman, a priest. Actually Karna's foster father was born of a mixed caste, a Brahman and a Kshatriya; therefore he decided to request tutorship from the Rishi despite the fact that he might be cursed or even killed.

With this plan in mind, Karna approached Parashurama's hermitage. When Karna first saw Parashurama, he was seated in meditation. Upon his head were matted locks of hair, and his eyes were burning like fire. Falling at the feet of this awesome personality, Karna requested, I have come to you with a deep longing. Please do not send me away without granting me your mercy.

Karna was weeping and his body was trembling. Parashurama picked up Karna, and asked him, Are you a Kshatriya? Karna replied, No, my lord, I am a Brahman. Parashurama smiled at him and said, I will certainly impart to you the military science. I am pleased with your humility, and because you are a Brahman, I have a natural affection for you.

Karna's education began, and he spent many months in the ashrama of the renowned sage. He forgot the pain in his heart of being a carpenter's son. He even forgot the mystery attached to his birth. Karna was only interested in education--how to become a powerful warrior. He learned all the astras; even the Brahmastra and the very powerful Bhargavastra. He pleased his martial teacher in all respects. When his education was complete, Parashurama advised him, your presence in my ashrama has brightened my life.

I have taught you the complete science of military arts. You are very honest, fond of those who are elder to you, and you are eager to walk the path of righteousness. You must never use the knowledge I have given you for an unrighteous cause.

It was now noontime, and the sun was at its meridian. Feeling tired, Parashurama told Karna to bring him a roll of deerskin to use as a pillow. My lord, Karna replied; please use my lap as a pillow. I can at least do this service for the foremost of men. Parashurama then laid his head in his disciple's lap and fell fast asleep. Karna was meditating on all that had taken place over the past year.

He had lied to the great sage telling him that he was a Brahman. Would the reaction to this ever come upon him? His only desire was to acquire knowledge. The wise declare that the end justifies the means. He had not tried to commit any sin. Surely his small offense would be forgiven.

As Karna was thinking in this way, he felt a pain in his right thigh. The pain became unbearable. He looked down and saw a boar-like insect cutting into his skin. Karna could not stop it from penetrating his flesh. But what could he do? He did not deem it proper to awaken his guru. The insect bored right through his thigh and blood touched the face of Parashurama. The great Brahman awoke, and seeing the blood exclaimed, where did the blood come from?

My lord, It came from my thigh, Karna answered. While you were sleeping, an insect bit me on the leg. It caused me pain for some time but I did not want to awaken you. Parashurama flared up with anger, you say this insect stung you, and you tolerated it? Why did you not awaken me and stop the pain?

My lord, replied Karna, you were asleep, and I did not want to disturb you. For this reason I have tolerated this pain. Parashurama was furious, how could a Brahman bear so much pain? Only a Kshatriya could have done so. Have I, after all this time, taught my astras to a sinful warrior? I will never forgive you for this deception.

Karna fell at the feet of his teacher and tears flowed from his eyes thinking that all he had learned would be futile. He held onto the feet of his guru and pleaded, forgive me, my lord. You have been more of a father to me than my own father. A father should forgive the faults of his son. I am not a Brahman, but neither is I a Kshatriya. I am the son of a carpenter named Adhiratha. I only wanted to learn the science of archery. I told a lie to you, but it was only to become your student. I have been devoted to you, and you are dearer to me than anything else in this world. Please show mercy and forgive me.

Parashurama was furious, and he was not moved by Karna's prayers. The only thought in his mind was that this person had told a lie and a Kshatriya is supposed to be truthful. He then remembered the Kshatriyas who had killed his father and, becoming angry, he cursed Karna, and you have learned the science of archery under false pretenses. I curse you that when you are in desperate need of an Astra (weapon), your memory will fail you. You wanted fame, however, and I say that here after you will be known as one of the greatest archers of all time. Parashurama then left and went back to his ashrama leaving Karna in tears.

Wiping the tears from his eyes, Karna began walking aimlessly. He walked for days thinking of the curse of the great Rishi. Suddenly, what he thought was a lion flashed by him, and out of instinct, he took an arrow from his quiver and shot the animal. However, it was not a lion but a cow. Karna was horrified. He went to the Brahman who owned it and told him that he had shot the cow in ignorance.

Karna tried to appease him, but the Brahman was not to be pacified. He cursed Karna saying, when you are fighting with your worst enemy, the wheel of your chariot will sink into the mud, and just as you killed my poor innocent cow when she was unaware of danger, you will also be killed by your opponent when you are least prepared for it. Karna was stunned that all these things were suddenly happening to him.

Karna then understood that this was his karma. Otherwise how could these events take place without his control? He took it that he was the chosen target of providence and thought how cruel she was. He remembered his mysterious birth and the stigma of his being a sutaputra (son of a chariot driver). He might have overcome it by being the student of the great Parashurama, but his teacher had cursed him and gone away.

Now he had been cursed by another Brahman. This was all his fate. He accepted it as such and went back home to his mother. His mother was proud when she heard that he had learned from the great Parashurama, but he did not tell her of Parashurama's curse, or of the curse of the Brahman. After some time he heard about a tournament of weapons at Hastinapur and decided to go there to enter the competition.

When peace negotiations between the Pandavas and the Kauravas failed, Krishna approached Karna and revealed to him his true identity as the eldest Pandavas. He then asks Karna to join their side. Krishna also assured him that Yudhishthira would most certainly give him the crown of Indraprastha. But Karna refused the offer because he had already sworn fidelity to Duryodhana and had to repay his debt to Duryodhana. He also remarked that as long as Krishna was with the Pandavas, defeat would certainly be awaiting him. Krishna was saddened, but saluting Karna's sense of loyalty, accepted his decision and promised him that his true lineage would remain a secret.

Indra, the King of the Devas and father of Arjuna, knew that Arjuna would be invincible in battle as long as he had his Kavacha and Kundala that he was born with. Indra hence decided to take them away and thereby weaken Karna. He approached Karna as a poor Brahmin during his mid-day prayer. Surya warned Karna of Indra's intentions, asking him not to give away his armor and earrings. But Karna decided that he could not send anyone from his door empty handed, even if it meant his own death.

Karna readily gave away his Kavacha and Kundala to Indra, cutting the armor and earrings off his body, earning the name Vaikartana. Ashamed, Indra reciprocated by giving Karna the boon to use his most powerful weapon, the Vasavi Shakti, only once during battle. As the war approached, a restless Kunti went to meet Karna to reveal his true identity. Mother and son shared a touching moment together. Kunti asked him to call himself Kaunteya instead of Redeye, but Karna gently denied her this desire. He also refused to join the Pandavas, saying that it was too late now to do that, since he was already a close friend of Duryodhana. However, Karna promised Kunti that he would not kill any of the Pandavas except Arjuna.

Karna was well aware that Arjuna would be invincible, as he was blessed with Krishna's divine grace. But this way, he would be able to repay Duryodhana, while also perform the rightful duties of an elder brother. Hence, Karna told Kunti that she could get to keep only five sons, the fifth one being either him or Arjuna. Karna also requested Kunti to keep their true relationship under wraps until his death.

Bhisma, the commander-in-chief of the Kauravas army, did not want Karna's participation in the war under his leadership. Bhisma said that Karna had insulted both Parashurama and Draupadi and such a person should not fight the war. Bhisma, who knew about Karna's true identity, did not want him to fight against his own brothers. Hence, Karna entered the battlefield only on the eleventh day after Bhishma's fall on the tenth day.

The Mahabharata war fought on day 16 and day 17 are jointly referred to as the Karna Parva - when Karna becomes the commander of Kauravas army. Krishna warns Arjuna to be caution in the battlefield, as Karna is his equal and even much superior to him at times. This proves that even Krishna knew that Karna was almost invincible and could easily succeed in destroying Arjuna if he really focused on it.

Krishna hence asks Arjuna to slay the Sutaputra as early as possible, so as to save himself from most certain defeat and destruction. Karna defeated all the Pandavas on the sixteenth day of battle. He first defeated Bhīma, but left him alive, since he was his own younger brother. He did not kill any of the four brothers, since he had given Kunti his word that he would only take Arjuna's life.

Karna then asked his charioteer, Shalya, to take him to Arjuna. He took out his powerful Nagastra and hurled it at Arjuna. This would definitely have killed him, but for the fact that Krishna subtly lowered the chariot into the earth by putting pressure with his feet. Arjuna let off a volley of arrows, which Karna answered almost effortlessly. Finally, Arjuna was left weaponless. But by that time, the sun had set, and so, Karna spared his life, observing the rules of the war.

On the seventeenth day, both the brothers fought again. Karna cut Arjuna's bow strings many times, but Arjuna was also equally quick in tying it again and again. Karna could not but admire his younger brother's tenacity on the battlefield and commented to Shalya that not for nothing was Arjuna termed as the greatest archer of their time. Karna fought long and hard, but just when the battle between the brothers would have reached stalemate, Karna's chariot wheel sank into the ground and got trapped in the loose wet soil, rooting his chariot to the spot.

As the curse of the past took effect, he also forgot the incantations of the divine mantras taught to him by his Gurus. Hence, he could not summon up divine weapons either. Karna descended from his chariot to free the wheel and requested Arjuna to wait till it was set right, according to the rules of the battle. But Krishna asked Arjuna not to stick by the rules this time, as Karna had also committed enough atrocities against the Pandavas.

Though Arjuna objected to Krishna's stand, the latter convinced him that it would be no sin to kill a man who had stood by evil all through his life. Arjuna then shot several arrows at the helpless and weaponless Karna, critically wounding him. But Karna still did not die. Krishna then explained that Karna's acts of generosity were saving him from certain death. Krishna then took the form of an aged Brahmin, went up to Karna and requested alms from him. The ever-generous Karna told him he had nothing to offer anymore, whereupon the Lord asked him to give away the fruits of all the charity he had done all his life. Karna, being the kind-hearted soul he was, acquiesced and offered the Brahmin his blood as a representation of the fruits of his charitable actions.

Krishna was touched by the greatness of this warrior and in return, gave him his Viswaroopa darshan (glimpse of his gigantic cosmic form) and blessed him. Karna was one of the very few characters in the Mahabharata to have had this darshan from Krishna.

If he had remembered his lessons he could have used other means to remove the wheel from mud without getting down and dropping his bow.

Arjuna used this opportunity to kill Karna.

Few texts suggest that Parashurama visited Karna before his death and preached him the righteous course of life.

CHAPTER TWENTY-SEVEN

MAHABHARTA

The praise of Arjuna's skill and valor by various renowned figures like Parasurama is indeed a significant aspect of the Mahabharata. Arjuna is widely recognized as one of the greatest warriors of his time, and his expertise in archery is highly revered.

Arjuna's encounters with formidable opponents like Bhisma and his triumph over them are significant events in the Mahabharata. While Bhisma was a highly skilled warrior and remained undefeated on the battlefield, Arjuna's unique bond with Krishna and his guidance played a crucial role in Bhishma's defeat. It was Krishna who devised a plan to bring an end to Bhishma's invincibility, and Arjuna actively participated in that strategy.

Arjuna's ambidexterity, or the ability to use both hands equally well in archery, is also a prominent aspect of his character. This skill allowed him to unleash a higher level of proficiency and adaptability in battle, making him a formidable opponent.

The acknowledgement of Arjuna's superiority by Parasurama and his recognition as the chosen one by Krishna for the divine purpose aligns with the narrative of the Mahabharata. Arjuna's role as a central figure in the epic and his close association with Krishna are key elements that shape the course of events leading up to the Kurukshetra war.

The Mahabharata is a rich and complex epic with various interpretations and retellings, and the character of Arjuna and his achievements are celebrated throughout the epic.

ROLE IN MAHABHARTA

Parashurama is described in some versions of the Mahabharata as the angry Brahmin who with his axe, killed a huge number of Kshatriya warriors because they were abusing their power. He plays important roles in the Mahabharata serving as mentor to **Bhisma (chapter 5.178), Drona (chapter 1.121) and Karna (chapter 3.286),** teaching weapon arts and helping key warriors in both sides of the war.

Parasurama appears in the Mahabharata and has interactions with various characters, including Arjuna, Bhisma, Dronacharya, and Karna, there are variations and interpretations in different versions of the epic.

Parasurama is indeed depicted as a complex character in the Mahabharata, embodying contradictions and moral dilemmas. His teachings of the art of war to Bhisma and Dronacharya showcase his expertise and influence as a teacher. However, his relationship with Karna is different. According to the mainstream narrative, Karna approaches Parasurama to learn from him but conceals his true identity as a Kshatriya. Karna pretends to be a Brahmin, and Parasurama teaches him various skills, including the knowledge of the Brahmastra. When Karna's true identity is eventually revealed, Parasurama curses him, causing him to forget the knowledge of the Brahmastra when he needs it most.

The reference of Parashurama appears in the epic Mahabharata a few times. The Mahabharata includes legends about both Arjuna. Parasurama is a fusion of contradictions, possibly to emphasize the ease with which those with military power tend to abuse it, and the moral issues in circumstances and one's actions, particularly violent ones.Parshuram also had to fight a small war with Bhisma, his disciple, over the controversy of princess Amba, in which Bhisma defeated Parashurama.

HIS PRESENCE AT KARU SABHA

Parasurama along with a few other sages was present at the Sabha pravesa of Dharmaputra. **(Sloka11, Chapter 53, Sabha Parva)** .

Parasurama was present at the court of the Kauravas when Sri Krishna was speaking to Dhritrastra on behalf of the Pandavas. When the Kauravas did not reply the questions put by Sri Krishna, Parasurama rose up to tell a story to illustrate the evils resulting from the arrogance of man. There was once a King called Dambhodbhava who was very arrogant because of his great strength. He wanted to diffuse his energy by fighting and laboured much to get good opponents and roamed about in search of fighters. One day the Brahmins directed him to Nara narayanas and accordingly Dambhodbhava went to their ashrama at Badarika and challenged them for a fight. They refused to fight and yet the King showered arrows on them. Then the sages took a few blades of the isika grass and threw them at him. They filled the sky as great missiles and the King begged to be pardoned and prostrated before the sages. They sent back the befooled King to his palace. **(Chapter 96, Udyoga Parva).** Parasurama sits in the court of Yama. **(Sloka 19,Chapter 8, Sabha Parva).**

Parasurama was the preceptor to three reputed warriors of Dwapara. They are the known figures and great warriors. They were Bhishma, Drona and Karna. Parasurama conquered a place called Kali & Gadatta. **(Sloka 12, Chapter 70, Drona Parva)**

Yudhisthira met and conversed with Parasurama at the mountain Mahendra. **(Chapter 117, Vana Parva).**

CHAPTER TWENTY-EIGHT

SURYA

Parasurama once became annoyed with the sun god Surya for making too much heat. The warrior-sage shot several arrows into the sky, terrifying Surya. When Parasurama ran out of arrows and sent his wife Dharani to bring more, the sun god then focused his rays on her, causing her to collapse. Surya then appeared before Parasurama and gave him two inventions that have since been attributed to the avatar, sandals and an umbrella. However, in some scripts the said story talked about his father and mother as follows.

Once, Rishi Jamadagni was practicing Archery with his bows and arrows. He repetedly used to shot arrows at aim. His wife Renuka assisted him in bringing those arrows back to him every time. Once in the afternoon in the month of Jyesthamula, Jamadagni started his practice again and ordered his wife to fetch the shafts he shot from his bow. At that time the heat of the sun from sun rays was much intense. Renuka hsi wife went to bring back his arrows. But she was forced to sit under a shed of a tree because her head and feet are being scorched by the heat of the sun. She somehow even in pain managed to bring the arrows to Jamadagni bit late.

Seeing this Rishi Jamadagni with wrath asked Renuka about why she was late in the said work of bringing the arrows back. Renuka then told the incidence of her head and feet being affected by the heat of the sun rays and she was oppressed by the heat. Knowing this Rishi Jamadagni said to his wife that if it is so he will destroy the sun with his energy of weapons i.e. arrows. He then aimed at the sun. Seeing this Lord Surya himself taking the form of a Brahman came to Rishi and told him various things about necessity of the sun for the life on the earth . But insisted by Jamadagni about to bring him down, Surya deva came under his protection .Jamadagni Rishi then asked surya for some remedy for his intense rays which affects the people. Surya deva then presented him the umbrellas and pair of Sandals a remedy a . P.173

एतावदुक्त्वा स तदा तूष्णमिासदि् भृगूत्तम : |
अथ सूर्योsददृत तस्मै छत्रो पानहमाश्वै ||13 ||

Bhishma continued, 'So saying, that excellent descendant of Bhrigu remained silent for a while, and Surya forthwith made over to him an umbrella and a pair of sandals.'"

सूर्य उवाच
    अद्यप्रभतृ चैवेह लोके सप्ंरचरष्ियति ||
पुण्यकृषे् च सर्वषे् परमक्षयय्यमवेच ||15 ||

Surya said, 'Do thou, O great Rishi, take this umbrella wherewith the head may be protected and my rays warded off. This pair of sandals is made of leather for the protection of the feet. From this day forth the gift of these articles in all religious rites shall be established as an inflexible usage!'"

Bhisma continued, 'This custom of giving umbrellas and shoes was introduced by Surya! O descendant of Bharata, these gifts are considered meritorious in the three worlds. Do thou, therefore, give away umbrellas and shoes to Brahmans? I have no doubt that thou shalt then acquire great religious merit by the act.

So the story is mentioned in Mahabharata.

CHAPTER TWENTY-NINE

KERALA

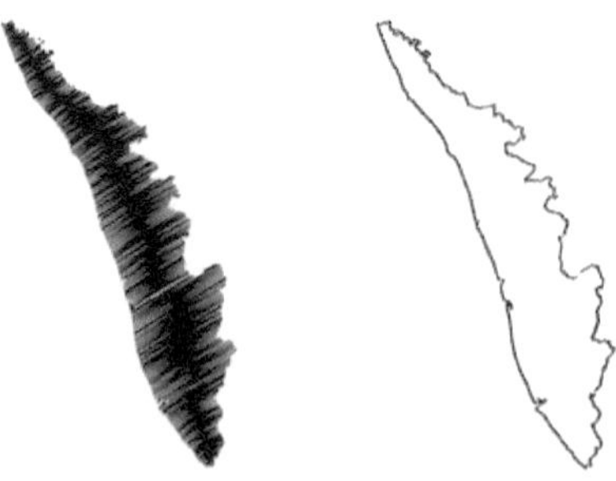

Parasurama cleared the earth of the Kshatriya caste twenty one times, subsequently restoring the sovereignty to the Brahmins, and establishing order and system amongst them. He was, however, told to vacate the land donated by him to Rishi Kashyapa. He decided to spend the rest of his days in peace and meditation. Parasurama accordingly journeyed to the Malabar Coast, where he begged of Varuna, the god of the ocean, to grant him as much space as an arrow would fly over. Fearing, when apprised of the divine nature of Parasurama, that the request contained some trick of Vishnu's, deprive him of his possessions, Varuna appealed to the other Gods for advice. Under their direction it was arranged that, on the night previous, the god of death should in the shape of a white ant almost sever the string of Parashurama's bow, so that the arrow when shot forth would go but a little way. The plan succeeded admirably, and Parasurama was obliged to content himself with a limited plot of land, formed by the receding of the sea on the Malabar Coast, where, according to the legend, he is still living.

GOKARNA AND THE ORIGIN OF KERALA

Brahmanda Purana gives a story associating Gokarna with the origin of Kerala.

By the request of Bhagiratha the river Ganga fell on earth and flowing as different brooks emptied its waters in the ocean. The level of the water in the ocean went up and the temple of Gokarna and the land of Kerala were submerged in waters. The sages who were in the temple somehow escaped and took refuge on the mountain Sahya. Parasurama was doing penance there then and the sages went to him and told him of their plight. Parasurama went and stood in Gokarna and threw an axe to the south. All the land from Gokarna up to the place where the axe fell rose up from the ocean to form a piece of land which was named Kerala. **(Chapter 97 of Brahmanda Purana).**

ORIGIN OF KERALA

There are two statements, slightly different from each other, in the Puranas, about the origin of Kerala.

For performing the funeral ceremony of the sons of Sagara whose ashes were lying in Patala (Nether world), Bhagiratha performed penance and brought the heavenly river Ganga to the earth. The river fell in North India and flowed in torrents to the sea and the surrounding regions were submerged in water. Among the places submerged, there was the important holy place and Bath of Gokarna also, lying on the west coast of India. Those hermits who lived in the vicinity of the temple at Gokarna, escaped from the flood and went to Mahendragiri Mountain and informed Parasurama of the calamity of the flood. Parasurama went with them to the seashore. Varuna did not make his appearance. The angry Parasurama stood in deep meditation for a little while. The weapons came to his hands. Varuna was filled with fear and he instantly appeared before Parasurama, who asked him to release the land

swallowed by the sea. Varuna agreed. Parasurama sent his bow and arrow back to the sky. Then he took a winnowing basket and threw it at the sea. The sea retreated from the place up to the spot where the winnowing basket fell, and the portion of land including Gokarna which had been swallowed by sea was recovered. This land is called Kerala, which is known by the name 'Snrparaka' also. **(Brahmanda Purana, Chapters 98 and 99).**

Parasurama went round the world eighteen times and killed all the Ksatriya Kings. After that he performed the sacrifice of Ashvamedha (horse sacrifice).In the sacrifice he gave all the lands as alms to Brahmins. Kashyapa received all the lands for the Brahmins. After that he requested Parasurama to vacate the land. Accordingly Parasurama created new land by shooting an arrow at the sea, for his own use. "At the words of Kashyapa, he made the sea retreat by shooting an arrow, thereby creating dry land." This land was Kerala. **(M.B. Drona Parva, Chapter 70)‘**

KERALA AND PATALA (NETHER WORLD)

The ancient sages of the Puranas have grouped the worlds into three, the Svarga (heaven), Bhoomi (the earth) and the Patala (the nether world) . The three worlds taken as a whole were divided into fourteen worlds. It doesn't appear that this grouping was merely imaginary. A keen observation of the Puranas would lead one to infer that the Himalayan plateau was considered as Devaloka-Svarga (heaven), the planes between the Himalaya and the Vindhya as Bhuloka (the earth) and the regions to the south of the Vindhya as Patala
(the nether world), by the ancient people of India. The seven worlds of Patala such as Atala, Vitala, Sutala, Talatala, Mahatala, Rasatala and Patala might
have been seven countries in this region. The description which occurs in **Devi Bhagavata, Skandha 8,** would substantiate this inference.

"Patala is below the earth. This Patala is a group of seven worlds one below the other, with names, Atala, Vitala, Sutala, Talatala, Rasatala and Mahatala. In all those worlds, there are several beautiful cities and houses, palaces and castles, parks, gardens, open temples and halls, natural arbours etc. made by Maya. There live the Asuras, the Danavas (a class of Asuras-demons) the nagas (serpents) and others, with their families, with happiness and comfort. Chirping birds, pigeons, parrots, docile parrots etc. always play there with their
inseparable mates. Trees bearing sweet fruits, plants covered with fragrant flowers, arbours with creepers growing thick, beautiful houses floored with white marble, and so many other things giving pleasure and comfort are seen there in plenty. In these things the Patala surpasses heaven. Daityas, Danavas and the Nagas (the Asuras and the serpents) are the dwellers of these worlds. They lead a happy and pleasant life with their families

enjoying all sorts of comfort and luxury."

PATALA

Patala, one of the seven divisions of the world is described as follows: "This is the region of the Nagas (the serpents). At the root-place of this region there is a particular place having an area of thirty thousand yojana's. Vishnu Kala who has the attribute of 'tamasa' (darkness) lives there under the name 'Ananta'. The real Ananta or Adisesa is the radiant embodiment of this Kala. The daughters of the Naga Kings are of fair complexion and very beautiful, with clean body. They use perfumeries such as sandalwood, aloe wood, saffron, etc." In this description, the words Daityas, Nagas, Ananta, Sandalwood, aloe wood etc. and the mention of natural beauty should be paid particular attention to. From the Ramayana we can understand that the Aryans referred to the Dravidas as Asuras, Raksasas (Giants) etc. History says that the Nagas were the early inhabitants of Kerala. The ancient -word 'Ananta' denotes Trivandrum (Tiru-Ananta-puram). The temple of Sri Padmanabha at Trivandrum answers to this description. The perfumeries such as sandalwood, aloe wood (cidar) etc. are the wealth of Kerala. On the whole the description of Patala fits well with that of Kerala. So it is not wrong to infer that the description of Patala in the Puranas is entirely about Kerala in all its aspects.

SURPARAKA

Another name for Kerala. In Brahmanda Purana, Chapter 99, we read that Parasurama threw a "Surpa" winnowing basket from Gokarna southwards and the ocean up to the spot where the Surpa fell, became dry land. Since the land was formed by throwing the Surpa, it came to be called "Surparaka". References to Surparaka in the Mahabharata, are given below: -

In the course of his triumph of the southern lands, Sahadeva conquered "Surparaka". **(M.B. Sabha Parva, Chapter 31, Verse 65).**There is a sacred bath here, known as "Surparaka tirtha". By bathing here, one would obtain golden rasis. **(M.B. Vana Parva, Chapter 85, Verse 43).** In Surparaka Ksetra, there is a sacrificial platform originally used by Jamadagni. Close by, there are two holy places called "Pasana tirtha" and "Candra tirtha". **(M.B. Vana Parva, Chapter 88, Verse 12).** Yudhisthira once happened to visit this sacred place. (M.B. **Vana Parva, Chapter 118, Verse 8).** Surparaka is the land formed by the withdrawal of the ocean. It is also called "Aparantabhumi". **(Santi Parva, Chapter 49, Verse 66)** . By bathing in the water of Surparaka Ksetra and observing a fast for a fortnight, one would be born as a prince in the next birth.**(Mahabharata, Anusasana Parva, Chapter 25, Verse 50)**

APARANTA

On the western border.' A country which is named in the Yislmu Purawain association with countries in the north; and the Yayu Puraraareads the name as Aparita, which Wilson says is a northern nation. The Hari-vansa, how- ever, mentions it as " a country conquered by Parasurama from the ocean," and upon this the translator Langlois observes " Tradition records that Parasurama be sought Varuna, god of the sea, to grant him a land which he might bestow upon the Brahmans in expiation of the blood of the Kshatriya. Yarama withdrew his waves from the heights of Gokarna (near Mangalore) down to Cape Comorin". This agrees with the traditions concerning Parasurama and Malabar.

THE MACKENZIE MANUSCRIPTS

The people of the land addressing Parasu Rama stated that, though the land was fertile, yet that they knew not how to cultivate it. He in consequence is represented as giving them instructions how to proceed.

The first part relates to preparation of the ground, care of oxen, and qualifications of the cultivator, who must not eat flesh, nor use intoxicating liquors, nor allow himself indulgence in sleep ; with various other details.

The second part is put into the mouth of a rishi, as deputed by Parasurama. It relates to choice of seed, and propitious time for sowing, in well ploughed ground, by oxen well fed, near to places where there are many inhabitants and where water can be obtained, as without water the best labours will be fruitless. Other connected details.

The third part relates to manure by decayed skins, ashes, dung and the like. The rainy season when water descends in torrents from the mountains, to be intended to, and the streams collected into reservoirs. The planting and cultivation of rice have been address. The planting of coconut trees, areca, palms, pepper, vines, and other trees, as productive of great advantages. These, and similar matters, are given in detail.

The fourth part refers to the following topics. Times of beginning agricultural activities, labours, reference to astrological configurations etc are there. . Time of harvest; rules as to the choice of horses, bullocks, and other cattle, in the purchasing of them, and modes of managing or taking care of them so as to become most useful for agricultural purposes.

The four parts are in poetical language. They form a kind of brie georgics; not well capable of being abstracted.

CHAPTER THIRTY

COLONIZATION

The Kerala Mahatmya or Keral'olpi (in 104 chapters) pretends to be a Purana which Rishi Garga expounded to the Brahmins during their exile. It is written in a poor sort of Sanskrit; and has hardly any poetical merit. A literal translation of it in Malayalam, and a copious Index; which however in several places seem to be based on another text than the present, helps to recognize the Malayalam appellations in their Sanskrit dress.

THE KERALA MAHATMYA, BY THE REVD. DR. GUNDERT

The three first chapters bear a separate title Kshatriya- nanam. They relate the growth of Carta-Viryarjuna's power who ruled on the shores of the Narmada over eight countries (Avanty-ady-ashta desheshu) and thro' penance received power to subject even Gods and Brahmans to his scepter. The Gods consult: Narada prepares two charmed balls; one filled with Kshatriya glory, the other with Brahma-tejas and gives them to the wives of the Brahman Jamadagni, and of the Kusika king. The balls are interchanged, and the princess gives birth to the sage Vishwamitra, whilst the Brahman's son, the incarnation of Vishnu enters the world with the mace (parasu) in his hand. He is called Parasurama. One day his father, doubting Renuka's fidelity, orders the boy to slay his mother. He does so; and is directed by the Rishis to atone for his sin by destroying Kartavirya Arjuna and the Kshatriya, the enemies of the Brahmans; a task which he effected in twenty-one expeditions.

In the Tretayug a certain Parasurama, who wished to crown his prosperous reign by a perfect donation to Brahmans? He assembled all the Rishi and gave the sixteen gifts in profusion; but Vishwamitra observed, that the most sin destroying gift was a grant of land. Accordingly the king made over to the Rishi's all the earth within the four seas, with all the blood guiltiness attached to it, by making them drink the water of possession (a ceremony still observed in transfers of ground). The Brahmans thought proper to turn him out of the property he had given away, but with Subramanian's assistance he obtained, by penance, from Varuna the grant of some land to dwell on. The throw of his mace was to determine the extent of the ground: it flew from Kanyakumari to Gokarna, and the whole intermediate country of ten yojana's breadth (Malay: version, one yoj), and 100 yojana in length was rescued from the sea. The gods pay a visit to the new country, call it Kerala, the holy land of Parasurama; and Shiva condescends to be henceforth worshipped in Gokarna the metropolis (Sri Miilasthanam).

Brahmans are collected by Parasurama to colonize the land: first a poor Brahman from the shores of the Krishna, whose eight sons receive the title of Yogasharyas the eldest being appointed head of all the Brahmans and settled in Vrishadripura (near Gokarna,—others say in Trishiva- perur: Trichoor). Other Brahmans are introduced, and settled in different localities; until the number of 64 grammas, or colonies, is completed. Of these Brahadvana, Sangamesha- pura and Ganagrama are the three particularly mentioned follows an importation by ship of seeds, and all kinds of animals; with eighteen Lamantas or sons of Kshatriyas widows from Brahmans Vaishyas (Maiversion Chettis) Sudras and low casts. Some of the Brahmans emigrated to obviate which; distinct customs were instituted for the Kerala Brahmans. One Tarana received the hereditary rule over the temples (alayanam tantrani) which now arose in many places.

They are chiefly Ghata puri (Coombla) Maruca (?) Trichamram close to Taliperambu, and to the salubrious seven hills (Saptashailas. Yeli mala M. Mt. Dilli) Caripuri, or Parasuramapuri (a residence of the Colattiri M.

Carippattu) Subrahmanyapuri with a yearly feast to the god of war, and the residence of the only Kshatriya whose life was spared by Parasurama. (He is called a Mushica Kshatriya, and appears to be the Raja of Coombla) Nileshwara with a Samanta prince (Nelisseram) Mukambica, with a Bhagavati temple. Caveri and other jungle temples, with worship of demons, sprung from Shiva, Lacshmishapura (Taliparambu, the glories of which are described in glowing terms its prince is said to belong to the Mushica Kshatria's family, Balashailam (Cherucunnu) Sahay- malaka (Tirunelli in Waynadu, the chief place for offering Shraddham) Vihara puri (Pallicunnu, Saraswati temple) 'Swetaranya puri (Tiruwangadu, near Tellicherry) Trishirah- parvatam (Tricherucunnu) with a yearly feast in May, by the celebration of which alone the independence of the country could be secured.

Curumbipuri (worship of a hunting deity and residence of a Samanta the Curumber Raja) Gopacuda puri (the original residence of the Eradi, or Samorin) Vilvadri (Cuvalam) Vatalayam (Guruvayiir in the Cochin territory whither pilgrims resort to be freed from disease) Sri Cotarapuri (Codungalur with service of Bhadracali, and rich bazars) Tripurna (Tripunattunpura now capital of the Cochin Raja) with a Samanta and rich Concana merchants. Bala puri (Cochi) near the sea. Simpapuri residence of the Samanta Bhanu Vicrama, Anantashayanam (Trevandram or Tiruan-anta-puram) Sri Yardhanapuri [Tiruwitan codu] full of bazars and elephants the residence of four Samanta brothers of whom the first Bhanu Vicrama is to rule over Kerala, whilst his younger brother Rana Vicrama is appointed as Viceroy in Gokarna. Lastly Suchindra [Indra's temple] and Kanya Kumari.

From this journey Parasurama returned to Gokarna, and decided several doubtful cases, which gave rise to the different castes of half Brahmans [Ardhabrahmanas] Ambala vasi [temple servants] Nambidis, singers, dancers, and Brahmans were ordered to live with the women of these castes, as well as with the Sudra wives, in order to multiply Brahmanical descendants throughout the country. Some of the half Brahmans [Nambis] were instructed in the use of arms, to defend temples and Brahmans all over Kerala; which for military purposes is divided into three provinces, each with a head fencing school.

Whilst Parasu Rama was engaged in holy services at Subrahmanyapura, a Demon came with Buddhists, and killed the prince he had placed over the Gokarna province. He went to seek a ruler for the northern parts; and on the seven hills fell in with three princesses whom he gave into the charge of the

Brahman deputies of Lacshmipura, telling the Yogasharya to anoint the first prince born by them. [The intention of the Purana is evidently to describe Kerala as being first under the rule of the united Travancore and Colattiri dynasty, the sway of which being contracted by foreign aggression in the North, paved the way for the independent rule of the Colattiri branch].

Afterwards Parasurama went with the Brahmans of these 64 colonies to his residence near the Vrihannadi (M Peraru, the Ponani river) and ruled the country for 5300 years. He then assembled the Brahmans, and promised to give them rulers, each for 12 years, and brought from the southern shore of the Caverian excellent Samanta, whom the Brahmans crowned king on the shore of the Yrihannadi [probably a viceroy of the Chola king]. On the Mahamakha feast of the 12th year they deposed him, and chose another. Twenty-one kings having thus ruled in succession, the last ran away with the crown jewels. The Brahmans were in consternation, but Parasurama promised again indigenous rulers and located two princesses at Sri Yardhana [Travancore] and Mangalapura. The third one was Subhangi at Lacshmisapura, married to a Brahman. Her son Udaya Varma [head of the Colatiri family] was crowned by the Brahmans as king of the northern half, and presented by Shiva with a ring. He destroyed the Bacshasas [Tulu aborigines] with their families, and furnished a prince Allohala, to whom Parasurama had confided the care of the Subrahmanya temple, for the pride with which he had usurped the Brahminical territory of eight yojanas extent. Parasurama blessed the king, exhorted him to righteousness, and prophesied that one of his successors would prefer wicked Brahmans from the Tunga bhadra to the priests of the country; and thus become the author of a general confusion of castes, which would prove the ruin of the country.

From there Parasurama proceeded to Gopacudapuri (Eranadu) and founded the Samorin's dynasty (M. Tamuttiri) by depositing a Samanta virgin with the Brahman chiefs. Her son ruled in Curupuri, endowed with Parashurama's sword.

Lavaputra, descendant of Ayodhya Kshatrias,was placed at Balapuri (Cochi) his grandson by a daughter married to a Brahman was Rama Yirya, whose dynasty Parashurama's white umbrella (M. Yencotta cuda) is inherited.—But finally Parasurama declared whole Kerala to be the property of the Brahmans of sixty-four Gramas, assembled at Gokarna.

CYCLE OF JUPITER

One of the Rishis took it into his head to undo Parasurama's creation, by preventing the celebration of the yearly feast at Trisiracunnu in order that the fools of Buddha's might enter the country. Soon after a clever Buddhist woman named Mali appeared on the seven hills; fascinated a Rishi; and procured to the son she bore to him, the right to the crown; by secretly exchanging her infant against that born to the Queen of the 11 th Colattiri King. The stolen child was called Marnali (name of the Cannanur Bibi, and of the Laccadives belonging to her) and brought up under Cannan's fostering care. A powerful minister Croda who alone knew of the exchange, abode with the supposed prince, till he was of age, and made him King. But Bhadracali on the coronation day refused to protect a prince, whose mother was a Buddhist, calling him Nasamipa, Nasanga, not permitted to approach, from which he took occasion to build a town and chapel Nasamipapuri (Maday or Payangadi, south of the seven hills) where as the Index says the first Buddhist vihara or palli (chapel, mosketi) was erected.

By the ministry of Croda, this 12th King entirely changed the rules of the state ; and though kind to Brahmans so as to load them with all manner of gifts, he ruled only through Buddhist officers and subjected to them, the whole country from Kanya Kumari to Gokarna (akhitam bhumim akramya Buddheis sakam sthita tatat Rajabhut Kerala'khite) made it abound in pallis and bazars, and during a reign of 35 years set altogether aside the laws of Parasurama. When the latter returned, he extirpated the Buddhists, and lopped off the hands and feet of the King. But he, not dismayed, praying to his father the Rishi, had his members restored by degrees; and with the assistance of thirty-five Bhutas built Vriddhipura (Yalarpat- nam or Billipatam) ruled there also with Buddhas (whom the Index here calls Mapillas) and stole even the holy sword from Taliparambu, so that he reigned securely without an enemy.

But Parasurama by discourse of devotions brought the happiness of the infidel King to a sad end. He was detained in the chase by Shiva in disguise; whilst the Queen fell in love with Croda the minister and made offers to him; the flat refusal of which prompted her to devise a speedy revenge. She acts all the part of Potiphar's wife ; but the faithful servant, when on the point of being executed, is discovered mounted on the heavenly chariot; and parting, advises the King to go to Mecca, and worship there Vishnu incarnate in all shapes (Vishwa rupavatara) in order to go to Vishnu's heaven. The King did so; and left his maid servant Sphulli to rule in Madai, with Buddhist aid, for evermore. Parasurama wished to restore the undiminished sway of the Colattiri princes; but this was rendered impossible by a compromise made in the meanwhile by the rival Queens Sphulli and Subhangi. The taint, brought by this occurrence on the Colattiri family, could only be expiated by the ceremony of Hiranya Garbha; that is, by the creeping of all princes and princesses thro' a golden cow, and by the gift of that, and of a silver bullock to the Brahmans. This holy act is to be repeated every 12th year.

NATIONAL FEAST, MAHA MAKHAM

Description of the national feast, maha makham, celebrated at Navayogipura (M. Tirunavai) on the northern bank of the Vrihannadi, where the Brahmans of the sixty-four colonies, the four kings (S. bhupas Colattiri, Travancore, Sa- morin, Perimpadappu or Cochin] assemble with all the aristocracy, the 1400 lords [vxras, M. idaprabhu] 1000 Nayakas ; and all their vassals. Also the Tulu Raja [Tulasibhus S.] makes his appearance with his Racshasa Nayers. Parasurama crowned again as king of kings, annexes great promises to the repetition of the feast in every 12th year. **[It was celebrated the last time A. D. 1743)**—[An account of the 18 gymnastic and warlike exercises (18 ayudhabhyasa] with the institution of pallestras and headmasters in the four great districts of Kerala. The origin of some caste divisions is explained.

DACSHINA KANDASYA MAHATMYA THE SOUTHERN PROVINCE

Aditya Varma the sister's son of Bhanu Vicrama is made king at Sri Vardhana pura to rule over the land from Kanya Kumari to the Ghoza river comprising 21 Brahman colonies. Parasurama tells him that one of his successors will call for northern Brahmans and honour them above others: from their usurpation, internal commotions will ensue. Brahmans become merchants and until Sakas and Buddhas come and overrun the country. A fourth of the whole country is to be set aside, and dedicated to the serpents or Nagas, the former rulers of the country. Description of the temples at Suchindra, Tiruwanantam and also of Bhutapandya, this is a holy spot on the eastern border, where the aggression of a Pandyas prince was stopped by divine intervention.

COLATTIRI AFFAIRS

An assura Darika attacked the country and encamped on the Sri Mauna Mula Mt. King Kerala Sekhara, the sister's-son of Cula Sekhara was advised by Cali, the guardian of the land, to build a palace in the S.E. corner of the seven hills, when she would come and manifest her glory. The king began the work and staid with his army on the seven hills. Cali appears and is worshipped by the Asuras with great reveling till she arose, slew Darika, and frightened the Asuras into subjection. Several new temples are built, and dedicated to Shiva, Kali, Vishnu.

GENEALOGY OF COLATTIRI AND TRAVANCORE (VAMSA PARAMPARYA.)

Kerala Varma was followed in his just rule over the middle province by his sister's-son Arka Tejasah, he by his famous sister's-son Ravi,he by his nephew Vicramaditya, he by his nephew Sunabha. The succession of Kings in the Southern province: Bhanu Vicrama, then his sister's son Rana Vicrama; whose nephew, being made king, had from a Brahman woman a son Vandhivirya Chaturbahu, that followed him on the throne. His nephew Jayasakhara, followed by his sister's son Vijaya Yikrama who rules now in the beginning of the " Dwapara yuga" and was by Parasurama's order made also king over the northern province (in Mangala-, pura) extending from the Cotishwara to the Cumbha river. This northern province is ruled by Viceroys [ardha simhasana] the first Ardha Chuda Prabhas, then his nephew Mohana Vamsajah; his nephew Sringasura; his nephew Indu Sekhara; his nephew Mana Sekhara, who rules at present for evermore, whilst the Valabhut Bala Sekhara [Colattiri] with 4 mantris and 350000 Nayers is enthroned in Angaviddhi [Valarpattanam]. The latter, at a temple dedication, exhorts once more to the practice of virtue; lest Kerala fall into the hands of Sakas and Bauddhas.

PARASURAMA DEPARTS

A long time having elapsed, the Brahmans assembled at Gokarna proposed to try Parasurama as he had left them word he would reappear whenever they should jointly meditate on him. Having made every effort, they saw at last the god coming: but when asked what they wanted him for, they stood ashamed. So he cursed them to live hence forth without his help;

and to hold no more their united council at Gokarnam. Yet would he visit Kerala annually after the monsoon on the Onam [Shravana] festival: let therefore the Brahmans wait for me! The Rishi concluding this Bhargava Mahatmyam, Keralotbhavam, with the customary praises of its sanctifying powers, received from his hearer's remuneration in the shape of 100,000 cows, 1000 elephants and other royal donations.

CHAPTER THIRTY-ONE

GOA- KONKAN

It is not just Kerala which is believed to be reclaimed from the sea by Parasurama with the help of this axe (Parashu). The entire West Coast of India - to the west of the Western Ghats and spanning Southern Maharashtra, Goa, Karnataka and Kerala - is considered as Parashuramakshetra. Those who do sandhyavandanain those regions do the sankalpa by saying 'parashuramakshetre'. There is a Parashurama temple in Poinguinim village of Canacona, Goa.

There are at least two versions of the story. One is that Parasurama, after cleansing the earth of evil Kshatriyas, gave away the conquered lands to Rishi Kashyapa & Brahmans and then reclaimed the coastal plains to the west of Western Ghats from the sea for his own penance; the reason is that what one gives away should not be used by oneself again; he could not have lived in the lands that he had already given away. The other is that the temple of Gokarna in Karnataka, which has Shiva's Atmalinga, was submerged in the sea and in order to reclaim that temple, Parasurama used his axe.

Legend also has it that Parashurama flung his axe from atop the summit of the Kodachadri Hill in the Western Ghats of Karnataka and retrieved the plains of West Coast from the sea. Legends also hold that he cleansed his blood stained axe in the Malaprabha and Tunga rivers which are also in Karnataka.

According to Hindu tradition, Parasurama reclaimed the land of Konkan after donating the earth to Maharshi Kashyapa. Then he requested different Gods and Goddesses to settle in the newly created land and to take responsibility of various clans. Parasurama, being a devotee of Shiva, requested Shiva to give him audience every day, while he is living in the newly created land. Lord Shiva accepted his request. Lord Parasurama also brought 60 'Vipras' to settle in Kokan.

In the regional literature of Kerala, Parasurama is the founder of the land, the one who brought it out of the sea and settled a Hindu community there. He is also known as Rama Jāmadagnya and Rama Bhargava in some Hindu texts. Parasurama retired in the Mahendra Mountains, according to chapter 2.3.47 of the Bhagavata Purana. He is the only Vishnu avatar who never dies, never returns to abstract Vishnu and lives in meditative retirement. Further, he is the only Vishnu avatar that co-exists with other Vishnu avatars Rama and Krishna in some versions of the Ramayana and Mahabharata, respectively.

CANACONA IN SOUTH GOA

Parasurama surrounded by settlers, commanding Lord Varuna, God of the waters to recede to make land known as Kerala from Kanyakumari to Gokarna for the Brahmins. There are legends dealing with the origins of the western coast geographically and culturally. One such legend is the retrieval of the West Coast from the sea, by Parasurama, a warrior sage. It proclaims that Parasurama, an Avatar of Mahavishnu, threw His battle axe into the sea. As a result, the land of the Western coast arose, and thus was reclaimed from the waters.

The place from which he threw his axe (or shot an arrow) is on Salher fort (the second highest peak and the highest fort in Maharashtra) in the Baglan taluka of Nasik district of Maharashtra. There is a temple on the summit of this fort dedicated to Parasurama and there are footprints in the rock 4 times the size of normal humans. This fort on a lower plateau has a temple of goddess Renuka, Parashurama's mother and also a Yagya Kunda with pits for poles to erect a shamiyana on the banks of a big water tank.

In present-day Goa (or Gomantak), which is a part of the Konkan, there is a temple in Canacona in South Goa district dedicated to Lord Parshuram. The chief interest centres in the stories told of how Parasurama recovered land from the ocean. In the Mahabharata he generally resides on Mt. Mahendra, which is undoubtedly connected with the tradition that his golden altar was on the Vaitarani, and that there he celebrated his asvamedha.

This may be a fairly old Orissan tradition ; but though it has gained entrance into the Great Epic it seems to one decidedly to be of secondary origin. For there is little doubt that, according to traditions which are still flourishing, the land which Parasurama recovered from the sea was Konkan

(Apardnta) ; and his chief residences were Surparaka (Sopara) and Mt. Sahyadri. South Indian traditions also have it that the land recovered was in reality Malabar or even the whole stretch of land below the Ghats from Gokarna to Cape Comorin; but these stories are apparently of later origin.

Already the Mahabharata tells us that Rama Jamadagnya intimidated the ocean by shooting an arrow across it, and this is repeated in later sources. According to another tradition he performed the same feat by hurling his axe from Gokarna to Comorin. Finally a third version tells us that Parasurama in a magical way produced a corn-swing (Surpa), which he threw across the waves or simply shook and thus made the sea into the land thus recovered by the sea, Parasurama according to one tradition led Brahmins from the North. However, other traditions tell us that he turned fishermen into Brahmins, making sacrificial cords from their nets; that he raised ship wrecked corpses to life and turned them into Konkanasth Brahmins; or even that he created the Karhad Brahmins from camel bones. The relative age and value of these various traditions is, unfortunately, not known.

CHAPTER THIRTY-TWO

KALARIPAYATTU (MARTIAL ARTS)

Parashurama and the Agastya are regarded as the founders of kalaripayattu the oldest martial art in the world. Parashurama was a master of shastras vidya, or the art of weaponry, as taught to him by siva . As such, he developed northern kalaripayattu, or vadakkankalari, with more emphasis on weapons than striking and grappling. Southern kalaripayattu was developed by Agastya, and focuses more on weapon less combat. Kalaripayattu is known as the 'mother of all martial arts'

Kalaripayattu is an ancient Indian martial art form that originated in Kerala, a state in South India. It is considered one of the oldest fighting systems in existence and is known for its comprehensive approach to combat, incorporating strikes, kicks, grappling, weaponry, and healing techniques.

The word "Kalaripayattu" is derived from two Malayalam words: "Kalari," meaning battlefield or combat arena, and "Payattu," meaning practice or exercise. Kalaripayattu encompasses various physical techniques, body conditioning exercises, and mental discipline.

Training in Kalaripayattu involves mastering different levels or stages of learning, which are known as "Meipayattu," "Kolthari," "Angathari," and "Verumkai." Meipayattu focuses on body movements, flexibility, and coordination. Kolthari involves practicing the use of wooden weapons like staffs and sticks. Angathari emphasizes unarmed combat techniques, such as strikes, kicks, and grappling. Verumkai is the final stage that involves fighting without any weapons.

In addition to physical training, Kalaripayattu incorporates various other aspects such as breathing exercises, meditation, and healing techniques. These include the use of medicinal oils, massages, and specialized treatments known as "marma chikitsa," which aim to rejuvenate the body and enhance overall well-being.

Kalaripayattu is not only a martial art but also a traditional art form, with practitioners often showcasing their skills through performances and demonstrations. It has gained international recognition for its dynamic movements, acrobatics, and aesthetic appeal.

Today, Kalaripayattu continues to be practiced both as a martial art and as a form of physical exercise, self-defence, and cultural heritage preservation. It is appreciated for its emphasis on discipline, physical fitness, coordination, and mental focus.

KALARI

In Kalaripayattu, the training begins with physical conditioning exercises to develop strength, flexibility, and agility. The practice involves a combination of vigorous movements, stances, and postures to build a strong foundation. Students learn various techniques of striking, kicking, blocking, and grappling, which are taught in a progressive manner.

The techniques of Kalaripayattu are categorized into different modules. The first module, known as "Meipayattu," focuses on body movements, footwork, and coordination. It includes exercises such as jumps, spins, and leaps to enhance agility and balance.

The second module, "Kolthari," introduces the use of wooden weapons like staffs, sticks, and swords. Students learn the correct techniques of handling and wielding these weapons, emphasizing precision, speed, and control.

The third module, "Angathari," is the unarmed combat segment of Kalaripayattu. It involves strikes, kicks, punches, locks, and throws, emphasizing both offensive and defensive techniques. Students learn to effectively engage with opponents using their bare hands and master the art of close-quarter combat.

In addition to physical training, Kalaripayattu also incorporates breathing exercises and meditation techniques. Breathing exercises, known as "Pranayama," help in developing breath control and focus. Meditation cultivates mental discipline, concentration, and self-awareness, enabling practitioners to channel their energy effectively during combat.

Another unique aspect of Kalaripayattu is its emphasis on healing methods and body conditioning. Marma chikitsa, the therapeutic aspect of Kalaripayattu, focuses on the vital points or energy centers in the body known as "marma points." Manipulation of these points through massage, pressure, and herbal treatments promotes healing, relieves pain, and enhances overall well-being.

Kalaripayattu is not just a martial art but also a cultural tradition. It is often performed as a spectacular display, showcasing the artistry, grace, and athleticism of the practitioners. The performances include choreographed sequences, acrobatics, and weaponry demonstrations set to the rhythm of traditional music and drumming.

Today, Kalaripayattu continues to be practiced and preserved in Kerala and other parts of India. It has also gained international recognition and is practiced by martial artists and enthusiasts worldwide. Kalaripayattu serves as a testament to the rich heritage and fighting traditions of India, embodying a holistic approach to physical, mental, and spiritual development.

PARSURAMA CONNECTION TO KALARI

According to legend, Parasurama is believed to have learned Kalaripayattu from Lord Shiva and then taught it to the original settlers of Kerala. It is said that after Parasurama brought Kerala up from the ocean floor, he established the first 108 Kalaris (training schools) throughout Kerala and instructed the first 21 Kalaripayattu gurus in the region.

Historians suggest that the combat techniques of the Sangam period, which existed around 3rd century BCE to 3rd century CE, were early precursors to Kalaripayattu. During this period, warriors received regular military training in various skills such as target practice, horse riding, and elephant riding. They specialized in weapons like the spear, sword, shield, and bow and arrow.

However, with the arrival of European invasions and colonization in Kerala, Kalaripayattu began to lose its prominence. The usage of firearms started to surpass the traditional weapons like swords and spears. As a result, the practice of Kalaripayattu declined during that period.

In the modern era, Kalaripayattu has seen a revival and is practiced by individuals interested in the traditional martial art form. It is also integrated into the training regimens of Keralite dance styles such as Kathakali and Mohiniyattam. The movements, postures, and techniques of Kalaripayattu are incorporated into these dance forms, enhancing the grace, agility, and expression of the dancers.

Kalaripayattu holds cultural significance and continues to be a source of pride for the people of Kerala. Efforts are being made to preserve and promote this ancient martial art form, both within India and internationally, as a valuable part of India's rich cultural heritage.

Parashurama taught it to the original settlers of Kerala shortly after bringing Kerala up from the ocean floor. A song in Malayalam refers to Parashurama's creation of Kerala, and credits him with the establishment of the first 108 kalaris throughout Kerala, along with the instruction of the first 21 Kalaripayattu gurus in Kerala on the destruction of enemies. Certain historians believe that the combat techniques of the Sangam period were the earliest precursors to Kalaripayattu. Each warrior in the Sangam era received regular military training in target practice, horse and elephant riding. They specialized in one or more of the important weapons of the period including the spear (*vel*), sword (*val*), shield (*kedaham*), and bow and arrow (*vilambu*). In the modern era, Kalaripayattu is also used by practitioners of Keralite dance styles, such as Kathakali and Mohiniyattam, as part of their training regimens.

CHAPTER THIRTY-THREE

ATHARVAN ZARATHUSTRA

The Atharva Veda consists of two books, The Bhargava Sanhita and Angiras Sanhita. That is why to the Atharva Veda, the double-barreled name Of Bhrigu-Angiras Sanhita has been given by the Gopath Brahman

(Bloomfield). The Iranian name of The Bhargava Sanhita is Avesta. There are two currents in Atharva Veda- the Bhargava current and the Angiras current. Bhargava Veda and Angiras Veda come into existence after the Indo –Iranian divided on the question of monotheism and iconolatry. Vrigu or Sukra the priest of Asuras(Worshipper of Asura).

The Asuras emphasize the importance of direct monotheism and anionic worship. Angiras or Brihaspati was the priest of the Devas (Worshippers of Devatas). Zend Avesta is the popular name of Bhargava Veda. Zend Avesta in Sanskrit is Chand (Chhandas means Veda) Upastha (Upat Mantra karane Panini 1/3/25) Chand Upastha means books of hymns. Zarathustra has been described in Avesta as "the Atharvan" per excellence (Farvardin Yasta 94), while Rig-Veda describes the Bhrigu's as Atharvan **(Rig Veda 10/14/6)**. 'Asura', the meaning of this word degraded later and became 'Devil' type, but in earlier Varuna had been called Asura in Rig-Veda **(Rig Veda 4/15/12)**. 'Through the grace of Asura, the sages see clearly within themselves the up growing soul. Their sight can scale the depth of the sea. They desire from Vedas, the status of saints **(Rig Veda 10/117/1)**. Chatterji Jatindra Mohan, Atharvan Zarathustra **(Kolkata, The Parshi Zoroastrian Association: 1971)** pp 2-41. 'Asura' means Pragya (supreme) in Nighuntu (3/9). Tantric fire cult and Parshi fire cult is the same in the sense of esoteric worship, both derived from Bhargava Veda. 'Sukra' means water in Nighuntu (1/12).

Therefore, Sukra (Usana Acharya) the son of Bhrigu, the son of Varuna the 'Great Asura', became the worshipper of Asura (Pragya, Chit or Chittam is another synonym of Asura 3/9), the non-personal Oceanic Presence. Varuna is the Lord of Ocean and most important Devata in Rig-Veda. *"Mahat Devanam Asurattvam Ekam,"* is the Injunction of Vedas. Therefore, Bhargava connection with Asura (Ahura in Zend) worship is understandable. Maha Vidya Worship of Parasurama Kalpa Sukta connotes and denotes the inherent Asura worship and asks to become 'Asura' in the previously mentioned sense. Parshu is the Vedic name for Persia. "I would now speak to Rama, the incomparable seer of the world and also about Asura and the Maghavats"**(Rig Veda 10/93/14)**. Ram was an honorable term in Iran (vide Rama Yasht). So if we try, we may find that Tantra and Avesta had a close connection in the matter of esoteric spiritualism.

ATHARVAN ZARATHUSTRA —THE FOREMOST PROPHET

Jatindra Mohan Chatterji, authored a **book ATHARVAN ZARATHUSTRA —The Foremost Prophet.** The book does a Comparative Study of Hinduism, Zoroastrianism and Islam. The aid book was having a forward note by The Hon'ble Chief Justice Mr. S. P. Kotval, High Court, Bombay and a Preface by Mahamahopadhyaya Dr. Gopinath Kaviraj, M. A., D. Litt., Padma-Vibhushan sare published by the Parsi Zoroastrian Association. The cover page carries महद् देवानाम् असुरत्वम् एकम् ~—**Rig-Veda 3-55-1** (All the Devas are concentrated in Mazda). The publisher i.e the Association makes no claim that the conclusions drawn by Sri Chatterji are infallible, and it is quite possible that scholars may differ very strongly with the particular views taken by the author. It must, however, be remembered that these conclusions and views are the result of a life-time of deep and devoted study and we therefore present them to the learned public in all humility.

This can be termed as brilliant work by Jatindra Mohan Chatterji, praised by S. Radhakrishnan, on **The Hymns of Atharvan Zarathushtra (1967).** He argues Zend Avesta = छान्द उपस्था, & known to Panani . We are generally unaware of how Uttara Kuru beyond the Himalayas (it also included Iran) was one of the provinces of the Vedic Age (see the Aitareya Brahmana for details of kings). Atharvan texts were from this region. Dasa of Skt. = Daha of Old Persian <=> people. These facts point to fatal logical flaws in reports on DNA and migrations to India from trans-Himalayan steppes in 2nd millennium BCE: Circular reasoning and leaving out the fact that ancient India was the most densely populated region.

The Hon'ble Chief Justice Mr. S. P. Kotval while forwarding the Chatterji book talks about the Chatterji submissions with full endorsement. He mentioned, in this volume Chatterji has in a more detailed study shown beyond cavil that connection. Drawing inspiration from entirely original sources the learned author not merely uses the facts of history but also philological comparisons with devastating effect. Himself an eminent Sanskrit's, he may be pardoned for drawing deeply from Vedic and Puranic sources, but his comparisons and deductions are so telling, the total effect of his ratiocination so convincing, as to leave one dazed and breathless.

A few examples will suffice.

To prove that the Rigveda itself refers to Zarathustra. he quotes the following passage :—**पुरतद्दूःशीमपेर्थवानेवेनोसहालवोचम्असुरेमघवत्स॥ (Rigveda 10-93-14).**

I would now speak of Rama, the incomparable Seer of Parthia, and also about Asura (Ahura) and the Maghavats. (Magis)]. "Evidently 'Rama' here refers to Parashurama (the Rama of Persia—Zarathustra), for Raghu Rama (the Indian Rama), had very little concern with Ahura or Magians....The original designation of Parasurama had been simply Rama and it is. by this name that he is very often described in the Maha-bharata and the Puranas------That Rama was an honourable term in Iran, is evident from Rama being the name of a Yazata (vide Rama Yasht).-..-. Parsu is the Vedic name for Persia...... Zarathustra was designated Parsu Rama becays[शुनाभ्य belonged to the land of Persia." (0. 22, 23)

"Bhrigu was the preceptor of the Asura-worshippers and Angirasa the preceptor of the Deva-worshippers. The Bhrigu people adopted Mazda Yasna and Angirasa people stuck to Deva Yasna....... Thus there grew up a dissension between the Bhrigu's and the Angiras. The Bhrigu occupied the western regions, the Angiras spread eastward. Indra is called Afina, the greatest patron of the Angiras (Rig-Veda 1-100-4). He predominated in Sapta Sindhu (Rig 8-24-27) i.e. the eastern provinces.

We may trace references to the Angirasas and the Bhrigus even in the Gatha. The Gatha says that the Angiras devised the practice of icon-worship, शुया AAA करपनो तहदखहुल्लौ" Yasna 48-10 The difference between the Bhrigus and the Angirasas resulted in the compilation of a supplementary Veda (the Atharva Veda—the Veda of the Fire Priest)" (pages 43-44).

The author has mentioned Parasurama as the key personnel of that time. The following are his mentions about Parasurama. This famous King Vasu lived in the beginning of the Treta age. Thus he was considerably earlier to Ramachandra who lived at the end of the Treta age.

समन्पुराप्तेत्रेतायांद्वापरस्यच।अहंदांशरथ:रामोभवष्यियामजिगत्पत॑:॥

Mahabharata—Santi Parva 339-84 Prophet Parsu Rama had flourished in the beginning of the Treta age.

तादूरापरयो:सन्धौराम:शाहलस्लाँवर: | weed, पाधविंक्षत्र:जघानामर्षचोदति:॥

Mahabharata-Adiparva (Parva Sangrahadhyapa) 2-3 त Thus Parsu Rama and Vasu were contemporary. This well accords with the fact that Zarathustra and Vistaspa were — contemporary. The traditional Indian pair might be the replica of the historical Iranian pair (the Prophet and a Prince).

ZARATHUSTRA AND PARASHURAMA

Maha Ratu Zarathustra also saw that the people must learn to. defend themselves against the enemy before they think of progress and prosperity. So he spoke in praise of militancy. This has earned for Zarathustra the title of "the warrior prophet" and the Padma Purana went so far 25 to say that. Though Parashurama's an avatar, he does not deserve to be honored like the other avatars, on account of his excessive militancy.

नोपास्यहंभिवेत्तस्यशक्तयवशेान्महात्मन:,

Padma Purana—Uttara Khanda 93-392

It is for us to realise that the view of the Padma Purana is vety erroneous, Mahabharata had rightly appreciated the worth of the Kshatriya,

हय्-सौसिअन: राजाइत्यवेमनतअव्रवीत् 1

Adiparva 41-31 [Manu has said that one Kshatriya is worth ten Brahmins. dea It is through Kshatriyahood thad one can reach the status of the Brahmin. Unless one has the power to retaliate, all talk about forgiveness is only a veil for cowardice ; that does not deceive anybody < We should therefore dismiss the opinion of the Padma = Purana and appreciate the greatness of Parsu Rama and re-instate him with all honour which is due to him as the first prophet of the Aryan race. And to atone for the previous neglect we should take up his gospel (the Gatha) with as much devotion as we entertain towards the gospel of Ramcandra (the Prisni). In any case there was, at the time, a crying need fora gospel like the Gatha. For, over and above teaching the the most correct method of God-realisation, it taught the lesson of national solidarity (as the Aryans were surrounded by enemies on all sides.) The trouble still persists, and so the utility of the Gatha. has not ceased.

For the sake of organisation, Maha Rata Zarathushtra inculcated the lesson of one God

(मज्अदाओसखारेमहरदितो, 29-4),

one prophet (aa He इदावस्तितो 29-8),

and one Scripture (यथाइम्मनेाइचावओचाचा 45-3),

and emphasised the need of militancy (यवेरेज्अनेाइबड्उहीम्दात्फूसस्तीम् 49-7),

and the Iranians became such a powerful nation that the whole of-western Asia and eastern Africa bowed to them, and the expedition of Marathon and Thermopylae caused terror. to the .most advanced of the European nations. It is only when the Sassanians took to paying more attention to the rules of the Vendidad than to the principles of the Gatha, that the downfall started. The reformation of Maha Ratu Zarathushtra brought about change in the social structure of the Indo-Iranians. The Angirasas had adopted the four-fold caste and the four-fold stage. The Bhargavas stick to one stage (viz. that of the house-holder) and to one caste (viz. that of the Kshatriya), Zarathushtra is the pioneer of the prophets who uphold to man the ideal of a caste-less caste.

At the outset, it would be interesting to'note that the complexion of Maha Ratu Zarathustra was very fair. This is the meaning of the epithet Spitama स्पतिम 15 the shortened form of feqaaa, whose Sanskrit equivalent is उवेततम् == ४116 Most.

The fame of his complexion had spread to India and the Harivamsa describes him (or his duplicate in India if one so likes) as very fair

गौरअग्ना-शिखाकार; तेजसाभास्करोपमम्।

भार्गवरामआसीन; मन्दरस्थंयथारवमि॥

Hari Vamsa—Vishnu Parva 82-21

As a matter of fact, the whole family was famous for its white complexion. The popular name of Bhrigu, the champion of the Ahura cult is Sukra. Sukra is a variant of Sukla or white. The family was also known for: its iconoclastic tendencies. The Padma Purana relates how Bhrigu had dealt a kick on the chest of Lord Vishnu. Zamad Agni was a scion of the Bhrigu family and Parashurama was his son, But Parashurama also came to be called Zamad Agni. In that age, the son sometimes inherited the name of his father. "As a father transmits his qualities to his son, his name is also occasionally transferred; something like a modern surname, Thus Viswaroopa, an epithet of Twastar, becomes the proper name of his son. Analogously the name of Vivasvan is applied to his son Manu, in the sense of Patronymic Vaivasvata—(Vala Khilya 41), Similarly Parashurama is sometimes called Bhrigu. "The Bhargavas 'claimed descent from the primeval Rishi Bhrigu, and they ate also called Bhrigu indiscriminately. Thus Chyavana is called Bhrigu (Mahabharata, 18-51), his descendant Rucheeka is equally called Bhrigu (Vayu Purana 65-93), and Rucheeka grandson Rama Zamadagnya is also called Bhrigu (Mahabharata

'7-70-2435)",

Thus we find that Parshurama has indiscriminately been called जमदन्नि (Zamad-Agni), जामद्त्नि (Zamad-Agni) or भय् (Bhrigu). Zamad Agni and Zarat-Ustra express the same idea. The root Zam (जम) means 'to eat'? And Zamad Agni means one who eats up fire. Zarathustra also carries the same meaning. The root ज् means 'to digest? And 3g, which comes from the root वस॑ (=to shine), means sun (as the cognate word उता =dawn, would also attest). Thus Zarathustra means one who digests the sun i.e . Outshines the sun.

PARASURAMA IS THE REPLICA OF ZARATHUSTRA

The Puranas repeatedly describe these two deeds to be the outstanding feats of Parasurama viz. that he extirpated the Kshatriyas and that he killed his mother (at the order of his father), Evidently these two acts of Parashurama are to be understood figuratively, For taken in the literal sense, such heinous crimes are genocide and matricide, would prove — Parashurama to be an abominable rogue, far below the level of an ordinary man, not to speak of his fitness for claiming the dignity of a Prophet. Extirpation of Kshatriya should therefore be understood, as the extirpation of the Kshatriyas as a separate caste. Parasurama 'was himself a militant - prophet, inspired with the Kshatriya ideal, and it is unlikely that the destruction of the people who cherished similar ideals would be his first business. Parasurama established one caste which represented the Kshatriya type, and thus there was no necessity of maintaining the Kshatriya as a separate caste for the protection of the nation. Thus the one caste principle of Parasurama practically amounted to the annihilation of the Kshatriyas, as a separate caste, the meaning of his extirpation of the Kshatriyas. Though the principle of one caste means the abolition of the other three castes as well, the Kshatriyas are singled out in order to indicate the extreme revolutionary character of his reformation, which had scant regard for the Brahmanical hierarchy of the Angiras.

Similarly the murder of his mother is figurative for Parashurama's championing the ancestral Father cult in religion as against the Mother-cult which was an innovation of the Angirasas. The Mother-cult (conception of God as Divine Mother, instead of as Heavenly Father) was subsequently confirmed by Ramachandra, whose untimely evocation (अकाल-बोधन) of the Divine Mother, is remembered in the annual Durga Puja throughout India. Parasurama had opposed the movement at the inception, and therefore

Angirasas ridiculed him as a matricide. The entire world has accepted the Father-cult championed by Parasurama, and they are all matricides according to the Puranas. It would he our misfortune, if we fail to discover Zarathustra behind the picture of Parasurama. It may be noted that according to the Satwata Sanhita, Narada learnt the satwata form of worship (1. €. anciconic worship) from Parshurama himself.

From pre-historical times Aryayana (Arya land=Iran) and Arya Varta (Arya region= India) were very close to each other, knitted together by race, by religion and by culture. After their separation, the Sapta Sindhu area was the common platform where the two people freely intermingled. The area covered by the Indus and its seven branches (i. e. Punjab and Eastern Afghanistan) was known as Sapta Sindhu—the land of seven rivers. Five of its branches, viz. Vitasta (Jhelum), Asikni (Chenab), Parusni (Iravati-Ravi) Bipasa (Beas) and Satadru (Sutlej) flow over the eastern tract, and two branches, Gomati (Gomal) and Kuva (Kabul river) flow over the western tract'. S of Sanskrit changes ` to H in Zend, and Sapta Sindhu becomes Hapta Hindu in Zend. Hapta Hindu is profusely praised in the Upastha as the best of all lands? It was shortened by dropping "Hapta' and gave rise to the name "Hindu" as the designation of the Indians. The area covered the major portions of the Panjab and Afghanistan. This is. How Hertel concludes Afghanistan to be the scene of the Rig-Veda period. Rig-Veda gives to Iranian culture the name of Ira (इरा), the Indian culture the name of Bharati (भारती), and to the joint culture of them both, which prevailed in the Sapta Sindhu area, the name of, Saraswati (सरस्वती). These three Ideals have been honored as angelic (देवी), and have been praised together in numerous. Passages of the Rig-Veda, We may cite here one 3 of them.

आभारतीभाइलौलिः सजोषा, इरादेवेभरि्मनुष्यभरि्अभिः।

सरस्वतीसारस्वतभरि्अर्वाक, लिभौदेवीर्वरि्इदसदन्तु॥

(O Agni, may'these three presiding deities, viz that of India (भारती), Iran (get) and Sapta Sindhu (सरस्वती) take their seats here on the grass, along with divine men thereof).

'Saraswati' is the religious name of the river of which 'Sindhu' is the secular name. Sindhu is the general name श for a river, and the Sindhu (Indus) being the largest river of the area was known as "the river", On account of its seven branches the Saraswati is described as सप्तथी सधि्मरात (Rig-Veda 6-61-10, 7-86-6). Major portion of the Rig-Veda was written on the banks of the branches of the Saraswati (Indus), is and in gratitude for this, people of later ages referred to Saraswati as the goddess of learning—goddess of Veda (knowledge). It is in Saraswata area, that Panini, the greatest grammarian of the world was born. He has been called Salaturiya, for Salatura was the name of his native village . It is now known 25 Latar and lies about seven kilometers from Und? The rules of Panini govern the Zend as much as they do the Sanskrit. For out of the ten Lakaras (tenses and moods) dealt with by Panini the ऊङ् form is the normal past-tense in the Gatha, while it is very rarely met with in the Veda. Panini lived in the sixth Century B.C. when Afganistan had becomes a part of the Achamenian empire, and thus he became familiar with the Upastha (Avesta). If these lines of the Rig-Veda have any historical significance, they certainly refer to Maha Ratu Zarathustra and to nobody else. For we know of no other person to whom all the: three adjectives apply.

Take another passage

पूरतद्दू:शीमपे्रथवानेवेनो ;

सशालवोचम्असुरेमघवत्सु॥ (10-93-14)

[I would now speak of Rama, the incomparable seer of Parthia, and also about Asura (Ahura) and the Maghavats (Magis)] Evidently 'Rama" here refers to Parashurama (the Rama of Persia = Zarathustra) for Raghu Rama (the Indian Rama) had very little concern with Ahura or Magians .The qualification "Parthian (Prithavana) Seer [Vena]" the inference almost certain. The same Rama referred to in Aitareya Brahman (7-2) as 'Rama Margaveya" i. €. Rama of Margu or Merv, who conferred on the Syaparnas, the right to participate in the sacrifice of Viswantara. Both Prithu and Margu lie outside India. The original designation of Parasurama had been simply Rama and it is by this name that he is very often described in the Mahabharata and the Puranas. But when another prophet came up bearing the same name, probably so named in remembrance of the glory of his illustrious predecessor, it became necessary to distinguish the one from the other and the former was called Parasurama, and the latter Raghu Rama. That Rama was an honourable term even in Iran, is evident from Rama

being the name of a Yazata (vide Rama Yasht.)

Parsu is the vedic name for Persia. The Iranians, in the Bihistan inscription, name the country as Parsa (Hodi-vala—Parsis of Ancient India—p. 3). Zarathustra was designated Parsu Rama because he belonged to the land of Persia. Subsequently Parsu (which also means a hatchet) was utilised to express the austere severity of the prophet against polytheism and iconolatry. There is also the tradition that Maha Ratu Zarathustra used to carry in his hands the Asa staff of nine knots,t as symbolic of his strict adherence to the rules of Asa (rectitude). In India the Asa staff was converted into a hatchet. The Skanda Purana relates the story reversely and says that the hatchet was converted into a staff. As the hatchet brings up association of violent wrath, it was changed into staff. This was done at Hatakes- war (Herat ?)

तेषांतद्वचनंश्रुत्वाराम:हालानुलावर: |
चक्ररोहमयीम् ay तंभक्तवासुकटुारकम्॥
Skanda Purana —Nagara Khanda (6,-94-

In the above quoted passage of the Rigveda, the reference to Zarathustra is made not by his Iranian name, but by his Indian designation. Yet the association of Ahura and Maghavat points to the identity. To some people the identification May appear to be a mere conjecture. Let us therefore look up if there is any firmer ground to take our standon. The history of the two words "Deva" and "Asura" seems to provide such a ground, Herein there is unmistakable reference to the Reformation of Maha Ratu Zarathustra, even without a direct mention of his name. When the Aryas (Indo-Iranians) were living together, both the words Deva and Asura were terms of respect. Thus we find that in the older portion of the Rigveda, all the prominent gods, such as Varuna, Rudra, Agni and even Indra, have been described as Asura,* which leaves no doubt that Asura had once been a term of respect even to Vedic people. That Deva had been an honorable term for the Avestic people is evident from हुहूनिलाला (divine—Sukta 48—1), देवाज्ञङ्हा(having divine lustre—Sukta 47-6) and देवाज्ज्ञयति(exalts—

Sukta 44-6

तत:राम:सुरुक्षिायंजगामहरम् अनृतकिी

ज्ञात्वासर्वाणशिास्त्राणतिस्माद् अस्त्रवदिांवर:॥ ` क

Siva Purana, Dharma Samhita 30-34 |

The attempt of Maharshi Swetaswatara to introduce the ideals of Maha Ratu Zarathushtra was, however, more methodical. His totem Ashwatara (mule)? has considerable resemblance

Like his spiritual Successors, Ramachandra and Sri Krishna. Zarathustra also belonged to a royal family, i. €, the Kshatriya caste, The caste system had not, however become So rigid in those days, Only in one verse of Rig-Veda (10-90-12)we find the mention of the four castes, This is how Vishwamitra, though born a Kshatriya, could become a Brahmin, This is not 8. Solitary case. We find that a number of Kshatriyas (like Garga, Maudgalya, Priyamedha) become Brahmins. They were known as "Kshatropeta Brahmanas'—Brahmins who came out of Kshatriya stock. This accounts for the fact that though Zarathustra came out of the Kshatriya Stock (royal family), Parasurama is considered to be a Brahmin in India, it seems that like his maternal uncle Vishwamitra, —Parasurama also Started a Kshatriya and became a Brahmin. The Puranas described the same fact in the reverse way, viz: that Parasurama

started as a Brahmin and became a Kshatriya.

We may remember in: this connection the statement of the Avesta (Farvardin Yasht—88).that Holy Zarathustra was the first priest, the first warrior and the first husbandman. The name of the father of Zarathustra was Paurushaspa and the name of his mother Dugdhaba. Something unusual happened at the birth of the child. All children start weeping on coming out of the mother's womb, but Zarathustra began to smile The tradition was so well known that even the Roman historian Pliny mentions-the fact. The laughter is prognostic of the future greatness of this unique child—prognostic of the fact, that this infant will one day teach the people, how one can be optimistic in spite of the hostility of his immediate cnvironmcnt. At the age of fifteen Zarathustra wore the sacred cord (Junnar). In Indian language this is called Nivita. The cord, is called उपवीत-- यज्ञोपवीत when worn on the left shoulder, प्राचीनावीत when on the right, and निवीत when worn round the neck or waist'.

Serialkh is only four or five hundred kilometres from the'border of India. Thus to a tesident of Peshawar, Bactria is much more familiar than Benaras. And so the religious movement started in Balkh by Maha Ratu Zarathustra, rapidly spread over to India. It did so under the lead of the Bhargavas, The three main provinces of Iran at that time were Persia,
Parthia and Media, All of them are mentioned in the Rigveda.

PERSIAशतम्अहम्तरिन्दरि **acer** परावआदद **Rigveda 8-6-46**

Obtained (as largess) hundred coins in Titindira, and a thousand coins in Parsu.

PARTHIAद्नुशयिम्दक्षणिापार्थवानाम् **Rigveda 6-97-8**

(The largess that the Parthian give, is beyond the capacity of others.)

PARTHIA AND PERSIA (TOGETHER) :पूराचागव्यन्त:पॄथुपर्शवोयय् Rig-Veda 7-83-1

(The Parthian and the Persians proceeded eastward in search of wealth)
Thesé provinces had largely adopted Mezda Yasna, and ar Indra-worshipper feels pained at that.

संमांतपन्त्य्अभति:सपल्लीर्इवपर्शव: —–—-Rigveda 1105-8

[The Persians prick me always, just as a co-wife does a co-wife}.

मूषोनशाहलाव्यदन्तमिाध्य:, स्तोतारतंशालकृषलौRigveda 10-35

{ 0 Satakratu (Indra), the Medians bite your worshipper, | just as a rat bites the weaver's thread.]

Persia,look to the Vedic tradition. It has already been stated that "Kisti" is the vedic word for Avestic "Cisti". The Rig-Veda says that the Bhrigu's were famed as Kistis (Cistis)

द्वतियद्ईम्कीस्तासोअभयिवो,

नमस्यन्तउपवोचन्तभगव: |

Rigveda 1-127-7

{When the illustrious Bhrigu's—Dualists and Cistis as they are—respectfully belaud this (Agni)]

It thus appears that the Bhrigu's were protagonists of (1) Duality (ie.. Bhakti Yoga, implying the Duality of the worshipper and the worshipped, as against the Non-Duality

of the Brahma of the Janan Yogin and of (2) Cisti. Unity through Love, as against Seraoshem or formal worship). It is thus reasonable to hold that Bhrigu (the Prophet of Ahura-worship) promulgated the Cisti cult. And when Zarathustra says that Urvazima or Love is the special featureof the new religion, (Yasna 32-1) we may reasonably conclude — that the Khizir of the Sufi tradition, and the Bhrigu of the — Vedic tradition, are one and the same Prophet, and that both of them are no other than Zarathustra himself. A pum — on the word "Zarat-Vastra" (Zarat—Harit, Skt=greet,—Vastra=garment) may explain the green mantle of Khizir. |It is worthy of note that Khizir is immortal according to — Iranian tradition, and that Parasurama (Bhrigu) is immortal |according to Indian tradition.

CHAPTER THIRTY-FOUR

PERSIA

'Parsu mystery in Rig-Veda; Iranian – Yadava link ' written by London Swaminathan

Of all the avatars of Vishnu, the most violent is the Parasurama Avatara. Other Avataras killed one or two demons but Parasurama exterminated generations of Kshatriyas to revenge his father's death. The history of Persia is also as violent as the life of Parasurama. His name Parasu stands for AXE .He carries it on his shoulder forever. Yesterday I refereed to Kuru of Iran/ Persia whose name was corrupted by the Greeks and English and today we know him as 'Cyrus the Great' 600 BCE.

We also met one Parasu in the Rig-Veda. So the Hindu names such as Kuru and Parasu were used very easily by the Hindus who migrated to Iran.

When did they migrate? Why did they leave India?

Did they migrate to Iran or did they come to India from Iran? Where is the proof?

Fortunately we have unassailable archaeological proof in the form of inscription from Bogazkoi (Turkey- Syria border area) and Dasarathaas letters in Egypt. They are dated 1380 BCE or before that. The way they lined up the Hindu gods in a treaty between two kings of Mitanni and Hittite showed that it was Rig Vedic mantra. Additional proofs came from Kikkuli's horse manual with Sanskrit numbers. Egypt which didn't know horse and other Hindu things suddenly started using them after the Pharaohs married Hindu girls. Dashratha letters also known as Amarna letters have more details about it. Even Eka Nathan (Akhenaten) introduced One God (Sun Worship) in Egypt around 1400 BCE. That is why he was called ONE GOD= Ekanathan (corrupted as Akhenaten in Egypt)

Whatever I have said about Bogazkoi, Dashratha letters, Kikkuli's horse manual etc are available in all encyclopaedias including Wikipedia.

So what is new?

The migration is FROM INDIA to other places is confirmed by the above and the following points .

Who is Zoroaster What is Zend Avesta?

Kanchi Paramacharya (1894-1994) was not only great Saint but also a great linguist. He says,

"All castes have rites to be performed with the sacred fire. During marriage people belonging to all varnas must do Aupasana and the fire in which the rite is performed must be preserved throughout. Today only Parsis seem to keep up such a practice of preserving the fire. Their scripture is called Zend Avesta which name must have been derived from the Vedic Chando-vasta. Their teacher was Zoroaster /Zarathustra. This name must have been derived from Saurashtra. Their homeland is Iran/ Arya. If the fire kept by them is extinguished at any time they spend a good deal of money in expiatory rites

LINK BETWEEN PARASURAMA AND IRAN

A.   Kalyana Raman in his excellent book 'ARYATARANGINI' says,

"The Persians were schismatics, if not avowed heretics. They decried the Vedas, and through their Prophet Zoroaster (circa 800 BCE) , formed their own religious code, popularly called the Vendidad (Sanskrit Vedavat) . The Avesta which corresponds to the Yajur Veda in some respects, exhibits a dualism in which good spirit, god, addressed as Ahura Mazda (Asura Mahatha), later corrupted into Oromazdes by the Greeks, is opposed by an evil spirit Angra Mainyu later identified with Ahriman (Vedic god Aryaman). . All wild beasts and all creeping things on earth are zealously to be destroyed, as the offspring of the Evil One".

Zoroaster made Varuna the chief God to be worshiped;

He made Indra an evil one . He praised Asuras and belittled Devas

He rejected cremation and asked the dead bodies to be thrown to the eagles . Parsis in Mubai still do it.

He abandoned Soma sacrifice, substituting pomegranate twigs for Soma;

He elevated Yama to a higher position and he was called Yima and his dog was honoured.

Hindus considered cow as sacred and Parsis considered dogs as sacred.

Their law book Vendidad says,

"The dog with four eyes is the faithful attendant of Yima, the principal god of the Asuras. Every Parsee corpse is first shown to a white dog with yellow ears— four eyes —- in order to chase away evil spirits from the body . The punishment for man slaughter is in the Vendidad was 200 stripes; for killing a puppy 500: a house dog 700; a shepherd's dog 800; and 1000 for a hedge hog. Hedge hog kills all the creatures in the farm and help us.

USANAS WAS FAMILY PRIEST

The Persian kings had family priests whose surname was Usanasa. This is the name of Sukra, the Asura guru in Hindu Puranas. He clashed with Brihaspati, guru of Devas. Usanas was a great poet and his name became ancient even to Rig Vedic poets . Krishna in the Bhagavad Gita says he is Ushana kavi among the poets. Even Greek Thucydides said that Persian king Xerxes had a chief counsellor called Usanas; in Greek, he corrupted the name as Oosaenes.

So the title Usanas was used for generations of family priests like Hindu priests Vasistha and Visvamitra. The Manu Smrti mentions that the offspring of a Brahmin father and a Sudra wife was called a Paraasava.

Sukra alias Usanava was a Bhargava, and in the Vedas Bhrigus are called fire worshippers. They are closely allied to the Angirasas.

Jamadagni and Parasurama belongs to the Bhrigu clan.

Even the Deva guru Brihaspati came from the same family

Sangam Tamil literature called them TWO BRAHMINS (Iru Anthanar) .

Like Drona taught both Kauravas and Pandavas, two Brahmins from the same Gotras were teachers of Asuras and Suras.

Both of them have been there in all the Hindu scriptures. Asuras and Devas went together along with the humans to get message from the gods and God said 'D"D" D' three times. All the three races interpreted with three different 'D' words. This is in the oldest Upanishad.

And they were used to churn the Milky Ocean to get Amrita. All these shows they have been living together from the beginning. Even today we see both Asuras and Devas amongst us. The beauty of Hinduism is that all the races in the world are recognised as brothers. Manu and Mahabharata give a long list of people and divided them as followers of Vedic dharma and non-followers.

So the Asura kings of Assyria, the pharaohs of Egypt. The Kassites and the Hittites are also part of one big Hindu family.

Aryatarangini and Kanchi Paramacharya give more details to show that the whole world was one family at one time. Kanchi Shnakaracharya explains the Veda followed in Greece and the origin of Yahwe/Jehovah. He amazed the visiting Jewish rabbis at one time by showing the similarities between the Torah and the Veda.

WERE PERSIANS THE MIGRATED KHASTRIYAS?

The Mahabharata also calls the area of Persia as the land of Parsikas, which some people think of as the Parsu (Axe) wielding people, who carried it for defence. However, this can also refer to those who were removed from Bharatavarsa by Lord Parashurama many years ago. The name Persia is a derivative of the Sanskrit name Parasu, which was the battle axe of Parashurama. Lord Parashurama had led 21 expeditions around the world to chastise the Kshatriya warriors who had swayed from the Vedic principles and became cruel and unruly. This was before the time of Lord Ramachandra. Persia was overrun by Lord Parashurama and his troops and succumbed to abide by his administration. According to E. Pococke on page 45 of his book, India in Greece, the land of Persia was known as Parsikas.

One of the first to begin recognizing how the influence of Indian forces spread throughout the Mideast was E. Pococke. He says, "I have glanced at the India settlements in Egypt, which will again be noticed, and I will now resume my observation from the lofty frontier, which is the true boundary of the European and Indian races. The parasoos, the people of Parasurama, those warriors of the axe, have penetrated into and given a name to Persia; they are the people of Bharata; and to the principal stream that pours waters into the Persian Gulf they have given the name of Eu-Bharat-es (Euphrates), the Bharat Chief."

The Persians or Parsikas, having been banished from Bharathvarsha by Parashurama, later changed their religion even more with the appearance of Zarathustra who established Zoroastrianism. However, it is said that the Parsis who have settled in India are accepted as the Parsikas, the ancient people of Persia, and are also related to the Koknastha Brahmins of Maharashtra who worship Parashurama at Chiplun in coastal Konkan. Dr. Poonai is another researcher who describes the ancient migrations out of Bharatavarsa, India. He explains that several Sanskrit speaking Aryan clans emigrated to the west beyond the Aegean area. He says that in the early part of the third millennium BCE that states of Caria, Miletus, Lydia, Troy, and Phrygia and surrounding areas were occupied by people who spoke various Sanskrit dialects.

The Indian fables, legends and literature also made their way to the West and into the Middle East as early as the 6th century BCE and had considerable influence wherever they went. The earliest of these collections included the Buddhist Jatakas, and the Vedic Panchatantra and the Hitopadesha. Also the Shukasaptati was translated several times into Persian under the name of Tutinamah, and through its transmission many Indian stories found their way into Europe. The story of the two jackals, Karkataka and Damanaka is yet another example of an Indian fable which was rendered into Pehlavi in the sixth century, and then in the seventh century into Arabic before being translated into Persian, Syriac, Latin, Hebrew, and then Spanish. Most of these fables and stories, if not all, were woven into the very fabric of European literature, and Indian motifs continued to be utilized in medieval Europe no matter if people recognized them or not.

Mr. Pococke further explains his conclusions. Even during his day of the mid-1800s, he wrote: "Who could have imagined that latitudes so northerly as the line of Oxus and the northern Indus would have sent forth the inhabitants of their frozen domains to colonize the sultry clime of Egypt and Palestine! Yet so it was. These were the Indian tribes that, under the appellation of 'Surya,' or 'the Sun,' gave its enduring name to the vast province of 'Suria,' now Syria. It is in Palestine that this martial race will be found settled in the greatest force."

Here we can see also, as did Pococke, how the names of the countries changed yet still held the seeds of its original influence, and from where that influence was coming from.

However, things changed, and the Vedic influence subsided, which is briefly described by V. Gordon Childe in his book The Aryans: "In Palestine the Aryan [Mitanni] names have totally disappeared by 1000 B.C., and even in the Mitanni region that have scarcely a vestige behind them. Here at least Aryan speech succumbed to Semitic and Asianic dialect, and small Aryan aristocracies were absorbed by the native population."

CHAPTER THIRTY-FIVE

AKSHAYA TRITHIYIA PARASHURAMA JAYANTHI

Akshaya Tritiya is reckoned as Sri Parashurama Jayanthi the sacred day Lord Parashurama Arghya to be given to Parashurama Devaru with the following sloka...

जमदग्नसिुथोवीराक्षत्रयिथंकाराप्रभो!
गृह्राणार्घ्यमंायादत्तमकृपायापरमेश्वर !!

Jamadagnisutho Veera Kshatriaanthakara Prabho!
Gruhaanaarghyam Mayaa Dattam Krupayaa Parameswara!!

Vaisaakha Sukla Trutheeya is celebrated as Akshaya Thrutheeya, one of the most auspicious days in Hindu calendar.

Akshaya means... the one that is not perishable; everlasting; the one that makes everything in life abundant.

Trutheeya is the 3rd day in Hindu Lunar calendar known as Jaya thithi.

Akshaya Thrutheeya is assumed as the day Tretha Yuga had commenced known as Tretha Yugaadi. It is also reckoned as Kalpaadi (Niilalohita). According to sacred scripts, Tretha Yuga had commenced on 3rd day of the bright fortnight (sukla Thrutheeya) in the lunar month Vaisakha Masam; Krutha Yuga on the 9th day of the bright fortnight (sukla Navami) in Kaartheeka Masam; Dwaapara Yuga on the New Moon day (Bahula Amaavaasya) in

Maagha Masam; Kali Yuga on 13th day of the dark fortnight (Trayodasi) in Bhaadrapada Masam; In Maha Bharatha, Lord Sri Krishna enlightened Dharmaraja about the significance of Akshaya Thrutheeya.

Vishnu Purana

Bhavishyottara Purana has also described the prominence of Akshaya Thrutheeya. Astrologically Akshaya Thrutheeya is the day royal planets Sun and Moon will be in their signs of exaltation; Sun in Aries (Mesha Raasi) and

Moon in Vrushabha Raasi (Taurus). If the day coincide with Wednesday and Rohini constellation it is considered to be more meritorious. Special celebrations are held at all Vishnu related temples on this sacred day of Akshaya Thrutheeya; Brundavanas of Sri Raaghavendra Swamy including the Moola Brundavana at Mantralayam will be adorned with Chandana lepana on the day of Akshaya Thrutheeya.

At Simhachalam Sri Varaaha Lakshmi Narasimha Swamy temple, special celebrations are held on this sacred day with a unique ritual called Chandanotsavam. It is only on this particular day in the year, Lord gives darshan in Nija roopa without any decoration which is otherwise always fully covered with Chandana (sandalwood paste) Worshiping Lord Sri Krishna with Chandana (sandalwood paste) on this day is highly meritorious;

य: करोथि तत्तीययाम कृष्णम चंदन भूशथिम!
वैसाखस्य सठि पक्षे सयाच्युता मंदरिम !!

Ya: karothi thruteeyaayaam Krushnam Chandana Bhooshitham!
Vaisaakhasya sithe pakshe sayaachyuta mandiram!!

One who worships Lord Sri Krishna with Chandana on this day
will attain Vishnu Loka. Reading/Listening/sponsoring Sri Venkatesa
Mahaatmya (Srinivasa Kalyaana) Purana for a week-days starting from
this day is highly meritorious. Giving daana on this auspicious day is given
lot of significance; which is highly sacred; celestial that will give multi-
folded
meritorious results.

DAAN ON AKSHAYA TRITHIYIA

Though there are many types of charities that can be given; giving Udaka
Kumbha Dana on this auspicious day is given lot of prominence.

येशा धर्मघाटो धतो: ब्रह्मा वष्णि शविात्मका
अस्य प्रधानाथस्कलम ममसंत मनोरथ;

Yesha DharmaGhato Dhattoh Brahma Vishnu Sivathmaka
Asya Pradhanathsakalam mamasanthu manoratha;

Meaning: Let this water pot called Dharma Ghata signifying the trinal lords
(Brahma, Vishnu and Siva) bring unto me fulfillment of all desires. This can
be given either in memory of fore fathers or to please the Lord;

Apart from Udaka Kumbha Daana; what else can be given as charity on
this day?

• wheat;

• curd rice;

• umbrella;

• paada raksha;

• vasthra (clothes);

• Gho-Daana (cow),

• Bhoodana;

• Hiranya Daana (Gold/silver/Cash)

Giving on this day is sacred, punyadayaka. which will produce multi-fold and everlasting (Akshaya) merits. Vasantha Pooja: giving Paanaka, Kosambari etc. (Palahar Pooja), to Brahmanas; Yava homa, Yava Daana, Yava Bhakshana on this sacred day is meritorious - paapa parihaara;

AKSHAYA TRITHIYIA = SADE THEEN MUHURTHA

In Hindu astrology Akshaya Thrutheeya is an auspicious day when one need not look into the Almanac (Panchaanga) to select an auspicious moment. It is called as Sade Theen Muhurtha.Sade theen means 3½ and muhurtha means auspicious time.

Four such auspicious days in Hindu calendar are...
• Chaithra Sukla Prathama (Paadyami) – Ugaadi day;
• Vaisakha Sukla Thrutheeya (Tadiya) – Akshaya Thrutheeya;
• Aaswayuja Sukla Dasami (Vijaya Dasami) – Dussera;
   • Kaartheeka Sukla Prathama (Paadyami) – Bali Paadyami;

Akshaya Tritiya is one of the most sacred days (Parvadina) in Hindu religious/spiritual calendar. Maxims of sacred texts prescribe that during any Parva-Punya kaala one should perform meritorious activities (punya kaarya)
like Snaana - Daana - Prayer - Pithru tharpana etc.

ESSENCE OF AKSHAYA TRITHIYIA

Akshaya Tritiya is one of the most sacred days (Parvadina) in Hindu religious/spiritual calendar. Giving Dana is one of the essentials of Akshaya Tritiya, but how it should be that pleases the supreme God Sri Hari;

   Lord Sri Krishna says in Bhagawadgita....

'पत्रम पुष्पम फलम तोयम यो मे ंभक्त्य प्रयच्छति
   तद् अहम् भक्ति-उपहृतम् अश्नामि प्रयतात्मान:'

'Patram pushpam phalam toyam yo me bhaktya prayacchati
tad aham bhakty-upahritam ashnami prayatatmanah'
(Bhagawadgita - 9th Canto - sloka # 26)

That means whoever offers me with devotion a leaf, a flower, a fruit, or water, that I accept, offered with pure-mind and devotion. It is not the intricacies of their design, elaborateness of the ritual, nor the splendour of gold and wealth exhibited, nor even the number of devotees attending, that contribute to their essential success. Ultimately it is the sincerity and devotion (Bhakti) that counts in divine worship. The very language and diction of the above stanza clearly sound the note that the material objects that one might offer are of no value to the Lord of the Universe, but it is the devotion and love that prompt the offerings that are accepted by the Deity.Be it "a leaf, a flower, a fruit, or water" it is but an insignificant thing that you offer; be it a golden temple, or be it a dry leaf, *"whosoever with devotion offers" whatever be the offering, Lord Sri Krishna assures "THAT I ACCEPT."*

Perhaps this could be the quintessence of Akshaya Tritiya the meritorious day. For, when lovingly given, it becomes "a devout gift" and when it is offered by a sincere "pure minded" devotee, Lord has to accept it. Therefore, on the whole, it is clear that an offering can be efficient, only when it is accompanied basically by two required conditions;

(a)"offered with devotion" and
(b) "by the pure-minded." (Saattvika)

One should not make a tall claim of giving Dana rather, should be performed selflessly with utmost humility. Publicizing everywhere the Dana given, one will lose its merits. Without Na-Mama.... there is no significance for Dana.

When once Na-Mama & Sri Krishna Arpana is said it is only ignorance to make a claim for Dana. To the extent these features are absent all offerings are mere economic waste and superstition breeding false-beliefs. If properly done, it can serve as a good vehicle to tread the spiritual path of self-development. There are several Puranic references in this context like, offering of Tantalum (beaten rice/avalakki) by Sudhama (Kuchela) etc.

Akshaya Tritiya is believed to be the day Sudhama (Kuchela) went to Lord Sri Krishna and offered Avalakki with utmost humility, sincerity and devotion. In recent times a tradition has cropped up especially in South India wherein, one would have observed people buying Gold on the day of Akshaya Tritiya with a belief that their wealth would get multiplied. We find citizens rushing to Gold shops forming long queues; in turn gold and jewel merchants offering fabulous discounts/schemes attracting customers etc. It is only a myth that has no relevance and sanctity. If at all anything is happening (good or bad), it is happening according to one's own destiny.

But, giving Dana and performing sacred deeds is indeed recommended and prescribed on the day of Akshaya Tritiya that will produce multifold meritorious results if not in this birth, at least in future births. **Chaanakya neethi** says that be content with what you have already got; but don't ever be content with your knowledge, self-improvement and charity. Satisfaction and contentment are the two wheels of life chariot. To have a mind for giving Dana when one is prosperous is a fruit of no ordinary austerity. Maxims of sacred texts prescribe that during any Parva-Punya kaala one should perform meritorious activities (punya kaarya) like Snaana - Daana - Prayer - Pithru tharpana etc.There should be celebrating festivals with understanding the significance and spirit behind them.

GIVING CHARITY

Giving alms is extremely important as means for achieving Punya. Alms always have to be donated when one goes to visit a temple or a place of pilgrimage. The giver must always face the east and the receiver must always face the north when alms are being given. Such donations have to be made after one has had a bath. The best objects for donations are gold, horses, oilseeds, snakes, maids, chariots, trees, houses, daughters and cows. If one promises to give something but later goes back on one's promise, one is sure to be destroyed. It should be remembered that the entire object of donation alms is lost if one expects gratitude or friendship in return. It is better to give something to a brother than to a daughter, it is better to give to a father than to a mother.

The entire concept of donation alms is different in the four different eras. In satya yuga, the giver went out in search of recipient to whom he could give something. In treta yuga, the recipient had to come to the giver's house before he would be given anything. In dvapara yuga, the giver never gave anything without being asked for it by the recipient. And in kali yuga, the giver gives only to those who are servile to him.

न क्ष्यति इति अक्षय

na kshyathi ithi akshaya

The one and the only one Entity in this Universe which is everlasting (Akshaya) not perishable is Hari Sarvottama, Lord Vishnu the Supreme God;

TRADITIONAL FOODS EATEN DURING PARSHURAM JAYANTI

- **Fruits and milk products**: These are considered to be sattvik or pure foods that are suitable for fasting and worshipping Lord Vishnu. They are also offered as bhog or Prasad to the deity.
- **Sweets**: These are also offered to Lord Vishnu and distributed among the devotees as a symbol of joy and gratitude. Some of the common sweets prepared on this day are kheer, halwa, ladoo, barfi, etc.
- **Sabudana khichdi**: This is a popular dish made with soaked tapioca pearls, peanuts, potatoes, and spices. It is easy to digest and provides energy during the fast[45].
- **Singhare ki poori**: This is a deep-fried flatbread made with water chestnut flour, which is allowed during fasting. It is usually served with aloo ki sabzi or potato curry.
- **Makhana kheer**: This is a creamy dessert made with fox nuts, milk, sugar, cardamom, and nuts. It is rich in protein and calcium and has a soothing effect on the stomach.

SIGNIFICANCE OF FASTING DURING PARSHURAM JAYANTI

The significance of fasting during Parshuram Jayanthi is to show devotion and respect to Lord Parshuram, the sixth avatar of Lord Vishnu, who was a warrior. Fasting is also a way of purifying the body and mind, and seeking blessings from the deity for good health, wealth, and success. Fasting on Parshuram Jayanthi is known to be very beneficial for everyone. It is believed that by fasting on this day, one can get rid of sins, diseases, and enemies. Fasting also helps in attaining peace, happiness, and prosperity. Fasting on Parshuram Jayanthi starts a day before and ends after sunset on the day of the festival. Devotees consume only fruits and milk products during the fast, as they are considered to be sattvik or pure foods that are suitable for worshipping Lord Vishnu. They also offer these foods as bhog or Prasad to the deity and distribute them among the devotees.

CHAPTER THIRTY-SIX

EVER LIVING CHIRANJIVI

The Chiranjivi are immortal living beings in Hinduism. There are seven main Chiranjivi, and they represent different attributes (or virtues) found among mankind. As long as they live, these attributes will exist among humanity. If legends are anything to go by then **Parshuram** is still on earth as he is Chiranjeevi and stays in meditative retirement. There are several temples of Lord **Parshuram**, like the famous one in south India at Pajaka near Udupi.

There are many immortals, according to Hindu scriptures and stories. In Sanskrit, Chiranjeevi means a long-lived person, *Chiram* (means long), and *Jivee* (means lived). The word is also known as Amaratva or Immortality.

Parshuram is considered one of the Astha Chiranjeevi (Eight Immortals) who has lived from one Satyayuga to another. They will remain alive through Kali Yuga and wait for the next Satya Yuga. Lord Parshuram appears in Mahabharata and Ramayana stories, events from two different Yugas, Mahabharata in Dwapara and Ramayana in Tetra Yuga. He will reappear in Kali Yuga to instruct Lord Kalki in Astra and Sastra Vidya.

According to Vishnu Purana, he was trained by Lord Shiva himself and was initiated with Rudramsha *(Element of Lord Shiva himself)*. Only Shiva himself can kill those who received Rudramsha. That is why he is immortal, and according to Kalki Purana, he will reappear in Kali Yuga to instruct Lord Kalki in Astra and Sastra Vidya.

Unlike other incarnations of Vishnu, Parashurama is a Chiranjivi, and is said to still be doing penance today in Mahendragiri. The Kalki Purana writes that he will re-emerge at the end of Kali Yuga to be the martial and spiritual guru of Kalki, the tenth and final avatar of Vishnu. It is foretold that he will instruct Kalki to perform a difficult penance to Shiva, and receive the celestial weaponry needed to bring about end time.

Along with sage Vyasa, sage Kripa and sage Ashwatthama, Parashurama is considered to be foremost among the rishis in Kaliyuga. Parasurama will also become one of the Saptarishi in the 8th Manvantara along with sage Vyasa, sage Kripa and sage Ashwatthama.

Another story mentioned in the Kalki Purana believes that Parshuram still resides on the earth. It states that Parshuram will be the martial guru of Shri Kalki, who is going to be the last avatar of Lord Vishnu. He instructs Kalki to perform a long sacrament to please Lord Shiva. After being pleased Lord Shiva will bless Kalki with the celestial weaponry.

STILL DOING PENANCE

It is written in the Puranas that Lord Parshuram is still meditating on Mount Mandaranchal and Lord Parshuram left an indelible impression of his superiority, there is a wonderful mention in Shaivism. There are ashrams of Lord Parshuram's father Jamadagniji at many places in India, and so are the temples of Renuka. Lord Parashurama reached Janakpur quickly from Mount Mandaranchal after Shri Ram disbanded Shiva's bow in Sita Swayamvar.

OTHERS CHIRANJEEVEES

The Sapta Chiranjivi Stotram is a mantra that is featured in Hindu literature:

अश्वत्थामा बलरिर्व्यासो हनुमांश्च वभीीषण:।
कृप: परशुरामश्च सप्ततैं चरिजीवनि:॥
सप्ततैतान् संस्मरेन्नतिय मार्कण्डेयमथाष्टमम्।
जीवेद्वर्षशत सोपा सर्वव्याधविविर्जति:॥

aśvatthāmā balirvyāsō hanumāṁśca vibhīṣaṇaḥ |
kṛpaḥ paraśurāmaśca saptaitē cirañjīvinaḥ ||
saptaitān saṁsmarennityaṁ mārkaṇḍēyamathāṣṭamam |
jīvēdvarṣaśataṁ prājñaḥ apamṛtyuvivarjitaḥ ||
— Sapta Chiranjivi Stotram

The mantra states that the remembrance of the eight immortals (Ashwatthama, Mahabali, Vyasa, Hanuman, Vibhishana, Kripa, Parashurama, and Markandeya) offers one freedom from ailments and longevity.

THE NINE CHIRANJIVIS

VYASA: The sage who composed the Mahabharata. He represents erudition and wisdom. He is the son of sage Parashara and Satyavati, a fisherwoman. He is also the great-grandson of the sage Vashishtha. He was born towards the end of Dvapara Yuga, and saw the initial phase of Kali Yuga.

JAMBAVAN: The bear king, who made Hanuman realise his power. Jambavan, together with Parashurama and Hanuman, is considered to be one of the few to have been present for both the Rama and the Krishna avatars. His daughter Jambavati was married to Krishna.

HANUMAN: One of the greatest brahmachari, he served Raja Rama. He is the most ardent vanara devotee of Rama. He stands for selflessness, courage, devotion, intelligence, strength, celibacy and righteous conduct.

PARASHURAMA: The sixth avatar of Vishnu. He is knowledgeable in all astras, shastras, and divine weapons. The Kalki Purana writes that he will reemerge at the end of time to be the martial guru of Kalki. He will then instruct the final avatar to undertake penance to receive celestial weaponry, required to save mankind during the end times.

VIBHISHANA: The brother of Ravana. Vibhishana defected to Rama before his battle with Ravana. He was later crowned the King of Lanka after Ravana was killed by Rama. He stands for righteousness. Vibhishana is not a true Chiranjeevi, as his boon of longevity is to remain on the earth only until the end of the Maha Yuga.

ASHWATTHAMA: The son of Drona. Drona performed many years of severe penance to please Shiva in order to obtain a son who possessed the same valor as the deity. Ashwatthama is the avatar of one of the eleven Rudras. Kripa and he are believed to be the lone survivors still living that had fought in the Kurukshetra War. He is immortal, but Krishna bestowed upon him a curse that "he would live forever but with his body covered with painful sores and ulcers that would never be cured".

MAHABALI: The ruler of the Asuras, he is still revered in present-day Kerala. His son was Banasura. He was the virtuous emperor of the three worlds and son of Virochana, and grandson of Prahlada, who were also of Asura descent. He was exiled to the Patalaloka (the underworld) by the Vamana avatar of Vishnu to restore cosmic order. Every year, on the day of Onam (a major festival of Kerala), he is held in popular tradition to descend upon the earth from the heavens to visit his people

KRIPA: The royal guru of the princes in the Mahabharata. He was adopted by King Shantanu. His sister was Kripi, who married Dronacharya. He was blessed with long life because of impartiality among his students, and because he treated them as his own children. He, along with his nephew Ashwatthama, are the lone survivors of all warriors who actually fought in the Kurukshetra War.

MARKANDEYA: Markandeya is an ancient Rishi born in the clan of Bhrigu. The eponymous Markandeya Purana comprises a dialogue between Markandeya and a sage called Jaimini, and a number of chapters in the Bhagavata Purana are dedicated to his conversations and prayers. He is also mentioned in the Mahabharata.

CHAPTER THIRTY-SEVEN

DISCIPLES

AKRTAVRANA

Akrtavrana was a great sage of erudition and was a disciple of Parasurama. He is ex-tolled in the Puranas and it is said that Suta who recited first the story of Mahabharata to an assembly of sages in the forest of Naimisa was a disciple of Akrtavrana.**(Skandha 12 of Bhagavata).**

He became a disciple of Parasurama when Parasurama was returning after obtaining arrows from Lord Siva after pleasing him by fierce penance-He was walking briskly through the dense forests anxious to be at the side of his preceptors to get their blessings. As he passed a big cave, he heard a moan and on getting to the site of the sound found a Brahmin boy being attacked by a tiger. Parasurama challenged the tiger. The tiger immediately fell dead by an arrow from Parasurama. Then the tiger turned into a gandharvas freed now from a curse because he was for years living as a tiger. The gandharvas bowed down respectfully and thanked the sage for giving him relief and left the place. The Brahmin boy fell down at the foot of Parasurama and said, "Great Lord, because of you I have now become Akrtavrana meaning one who has not received any wound. (Akrta = not having secured. Vrana= wound). I shall, therefore, be your disciple forever hereafter". From that day onwards he never left Parasurama but followed him as his disciple

In Mahabharata, Akrtavrana in several different contexts appearing on behalf of Parasurama. It was Akrtavrana who told Dharmaputra the life and exploits of Parasurama during the exile of the Pandavas in the forests. **(Chapters 1 15 to 117, Vana Parva,' M.B.).**

In **Chapter 83 of Udyoga Parva**, Akrtavrana meeting Sri Krishna while the latter was going to Hastinapur. In **Chapter 173 of Udyoga Parva**, Akrtavrana detailing the history of the Kauravas dynasty to Duryodhana. Akrtavrana has played a very important role in the story of Amba, daughter of the King of Kail. Amba along with her two sisters, Ambika and Ambalika, were brought down to Hastinapur by Bhisma for his brother Vicitravlrya to marry. But on knowing that Amba had mentally chosen Salwa as her husband, Bhisma allowed her to go back to Salva. But on her return to Salva he refused to accept her and she came back to Hastinapur. Bhisma then requested Vicitravlrya to accept her as his wife which, unfortunately, Vicitravlrya also refused to do. Amba then turned to Bhisma and be sought him to marry her which, much to his regret, he could not do because of his vow of celibacy. Thus, forsaken by all, all her sweetness turned into bitter hatred towards Bhisma and she remained alive thereafter only to kill Bhisma, but even the foremost of warriors were not willing to antagonise Bhisma and so her appeal to help was not heeded by any. It was then that Hotravahana her grandfather on the maternal side met her and directed her to Parasurama. When she went to Parasurama it was Akrtavrana who received her and on hearing her sorrowful tale encouraged her to seek vengeance on Bhisma. Again, it was he who persuaded Parasurama to champion her cause and go for a fight against Bhisma. During the fight Akrtavrana acted as charioteer to Parasurama. **(Sloka 9, Chapter 179, Udyoga Parva, M.B.).**

MUCUKUNDA

Once Parasurama gave dharmopade, an Instruction on morality, piety etc to Mucukunda. **(Sloka 7,Chapter 143, Sand Parva)**

Mucukunda, one of the three sons of the king Māndhātā, the other two being Purukutsa and Ambarīṣa, was a rājarṣi of this type. After fighting with the Raksasas on behalf of the devas at their request and helping them to win, he got the boon of a long and deep sleep as rest. He was also assured that anyone disturbing his sleep would be reduced to ashes by his very look. When the demon Kālayavana attacked Mathura, Śrī Kṛiṣhṇa manoeuvred to lead him into the dark cave where Mucukunda was sleeping. Kālayavana kicked Mucukunda thinking that he was Krishna. When Mucukunda opened his eyes in anger and looked at him, he was immediately reduced to ashes. As Sri Kṛiṣhṇa appeared and revealed his divine form, Mucukunda praised him with a beautiful hymn. There is a hillock near Dholpur in Rajasthan. A cave in this hillock is said to be the place where Mucukunda slept. Mucukunda, son of King Mandhata, and brother of equally illustrious Ambarisa, was an Ikshavaku (Suryavanshi) king.

CHAPTER THIRTY-EIGHT

RIGVEDA

JAMADAGNI RAMA was there as author of Mandal 10 Sutak 110 having 11 Mantras. This is especially surprising that Parashurama has Vedic roots. His name was Rama Jamadagni and he was the composer of a Sukta of Rigveda Samhita. According to Rig-Veda Sarvānukramaṇi, Rāma Jāmadagnya (Rāma the son of Jamadagni) was composer of Rig-Veda Sukta.

<u>ऋषिः - जमदग्नी रामो वादेवता - आपरयिःछन्दः - नचित्ततरषिटपुसवरः - धैवतः</u>

समिद्धो अद्य मनुषो दुरोणे देवो देवान्यजसि जातवेदः । आ च वह
मतिरमहश्चकितिवान्तव दूतः कुविरसि प्रचेताः ॥ १०.११०.१ ।

तनूनपात्पथ ऋतस्य यानान्मध्वा समञ्जन्त्स्वदया सृजिह्व । मन्मानि धीभिरित
यज्ञमुन्धन्देवत्रा च कृणुह्यध्वरं नः ॥ १०.११०.२ ।

आजुह्वान ईड्यो वन्द्यश्चा याह्यग्ने वसुभिः सजोषाः । त्वं देवानामसियह्व होता स
एनान्यक्षीषितो यजीयान् ॥ १०.११०.३ ।

प्राचीनं बर्हिः प्रदिशा पृथिव्या वस्तोरस्या वृज्यत्र अग्रे अह्नाम् । व्यु प्रथते वतिर
वरीयो देवेभ्यो अदितिय स्योनम् ॥ १०.११०.४ ।

व्यचस्वतीरुरुवया वि श्रयन्तां पतिभ्यो न जनयः शुम्भमानाः । देवीर्द्वारो
बृहतीर्विश्वमिन्वा देवेभ्यो भवत सुप्रायणाः ॥ १०.११०.५ ।

आ सुष्वयन्ती यजते उपाके उषासानक्ता सदता नियोनौ । दिव्ये योषणे बृहती सुरुक्मे अधि
श्रियं शुक्रपिशि दधाने ॥ १०.११०.६ ।

दैव्या होतारा प्रथमा सुवाचा ममाना यज्ञं मनुषो यजध्यै । प्रचोदयन्ता विदथेषु कारू
प्राचीनं ज्योतिः प्रदिशा दिशन्ता ॥ १०.११०.७ ।

आ नो यज्ञं भारती तूयमेत्वळिा मनुष्वदिह चेतयन्ती । तिस्रो देवीर्बर्हिरिदं स्योनं
सरस्वती स्वपसः सदन्तु ॥ १०.११०.८ ।

य इमे द्यावापृथिवी जनित्री रूपैरपिशिद्भुवनानि विश्वा । तमद्य होतरिषितो यजीयान्देवं
त्वष्टारमिह यक्षि विद्वान् ॥ १०.११०.९ ।

उपावसृज तमन्या समञ्जन्देवानां पाथ ऋतुथा हवींषि । वनस्पतिः शमिता देवो अग्निः
स्वदन्तु हव्यं मध्ना घृतेन ॥ १०.११०.१० ।

सद्यो जातो व्यममीत यज्ञमग्निर्देवानामभवत्पुरोगाः । अस्य होतुः प्रदिशि्यृतस्य
वाचि स्वाहाकृतं हविरिदन्तु देवाः ॥१०.११०.११ ।

<u>**ऋषिः - जमदग्नी रामो वादेवता - आप्रयिः छन्दः - नचितुत्तरिष्टपुस्वरः - धैवतः**</u>

हे मेधावी अग्ने ! तुम मनुष्यों के घर में प्रवबुद्ध होकर सब देवताओं का पूजन करो । तुम्हारा
मतिर उपासक तुम्हारा यज्ञ करता है यह जान कर सब देवताओं को यहाँ लाओ । तुम श्रेष्ठ
बुद्धि वाले, दौत्य कर्म में चतुर हो । १०.११०.१ ।

अग्ने ! यज्ञ के साधन रूप जो पदार्थ हैं, उन्हें मधयुक्त करके अपनी श्रेष्ठ ज्वालाओं से
आस्वादन करो । श्रेष्ठ भावना के सहित हमारी स्तुति और यज्ञ को समृद्ध करो । हमारे
यज्ञ को देवताओं के लिए ग्रहणीय करो । १०.११०.२ ।

हे अग्ने ! तुम स्तुत्य, नमस्कार योग्य और देवताओं का आह्वान करने वाले हो । हे देवहोता
महान देव ! तुम वसुगण के सहित आगमन करो । तुम्हारे समान यज्ञकर्त्ता अन्य कोई नहीं हैं,
इसलिए हम तुम्हें प्रेरित करते हैं । तुम समस्त देवताओं के निमित्त यज्ञ करो । १०.११०.३

।

प्रारम्भ में कुश वस्तित्त कर वेदी को आच्छादित किया जाता है। उनके लिए श्रेष्ठ कुश को वस्तित्त करते हैं। उस कुश पर सब देवताओं सहित वे अदिति सुख-पूर्वक विराजमान होती हैं। १०.११०.४।

सुन्दर वेष-भूषा से सज्जित हुई नारियाँ जैसे पति के समीप जाती हैं, वैसे ही इन सब द्वारों की अभिमानिनी देवियाँ वस्तित्त हो। हे द्वार देवियों, तुम इस प्रकार खुल जाओ जिससे देवगण उसमें सरलता पूर्वक प्रविष्ट हो सकें। १०.११०.५।

रात्रि में नन्दिा का जो सुख है, उसे रात्रि और उषा प्रकट करें वे यज्ञ- भाग पाने में समर्थ हैं। अतः परस्पर युक्त होकर विराजें। वे दोनों दिव्यलोक में निवास करने वाली नारी के समान शोभावती और धारण करने वाली हों। १०.११०.६।

देवताओं द्वारा नियुक्त दो होता ही श्रेष्ठ स्तोत्र उच्चारित करते हैं वही यज्ञ- कर्म का सम्पादन करते हैं। वही ऋत्विजों को कर्म की प्रेरणा देते हैं। वे प्रकाश को प्रकट करने वाले और कर्म में चतुर हैं।१०.११०.७।

भारती हमारे यज्ञ में शीघ्र आगमन करें। इला भी इस यज्ञ को जानकर यहाँ आवें। यह दोनों और तीसरी सरस्वती अद्भुत कर्म वाली है यह तीनों देवता हमारे अभिमुख श्रेष्ठ आसन पर प्रतिष्ठित हों। १०.११०.८।

देवताओं की मातृ-रूपिणी आकाश पृथ्वी हैं उन दोनों को जिन देवता ने प्रकट किया और सम्पूर्ण विश्व के प्राणियों की रचना की है, उन त्वष्टादेव का, हे होता ! पूजन करो तुम अन्नवान् एवं मेधावी हो, अतः यज्ञ-कर्म में कोई अन्य तुम्हारी समानता करने में समर्थ नहीं हैं।१०.११०.९।

हे यूप! देवताओं के लिए यथा समय तुम स्वयं यज्ञीय द्रव्य लाकर अर्पित करो । वनस्पति, शमिता और अग्नि इस मधु-घृत-सम्पन्न यज्ञीय पदार्थ का सेवन करें ।१०.११०.१०।

अग्नि ने उत्पन्न होते ही यज्ञ की रचना की। वही देवताओं के लिए अग्रगण्य दूत हुए। अग्निरूप होता मन्त्र का उच्चारण करें जो यज्ञीय द्रव्य स्वाहा के साथ प्रदान किया जाता है, उसे देवगण स्वीकार करें।१०.११०.११।

Rishi- Jamadagni Bhargavo Ramo voDevta – Aprisukta , Chand- Trishtup

Oh ! Brilliant Fire , Grow up in the house of men and worship all the Gods. Bring all the deities here knowing that your friend worshiper is performing your yagya. You are intelligent and clever in your mission. ।१०.११०.१।

Oh Fire ! Taste the substancesthat are the means of yagya with your superior flames after mixing them with honey. Enrich your praise and sacrifice with the best spirit.Make your yajna acceptable to the Gods,

।१०.११०.२।

O Fire ! you are worthy of praise ,salutations and the one who invokes the Gods. Oh God , great God ! you come with vasugan. There is no one else who performsYagya like you, thats why we inspire you. You perform yagya for all the dieties. । १०.११०.३।

In the begining, the altar is covered by spreading the Kush. Lets expand the best kush for them . On that Kush , that aditi sits happily along with all the dieties. । १०.११०.४ ।

Like women dress in beautiful dresses approach their husbands, so may all these doors be wide open , Oh ladies , so that the dieties can easily enter them. ।१०.११०.५ ।

The pleasure of condemnation in the night, let the night and dawn reveal it, they are able to get part of the yagya. That's why sit united with each other. May both of them be graceful and wearable like a woman who resides in the divine world? । १०.११०.६।

As soon as two are appointed by the gods, they recite the best hymns, they perform the yagya-karma. He alone inspires the Ritvijas to do their work. He is the revealer of light and clever in action. । १०.११०.७ ।

May Bharti come soon to our Yagya. Ila should also come here after knowing about this Yagya. Both this and the third Saraswati are of wonderful deeds, may these three deities be established on the best seat facing us. ।१०.११०.८ ।

The sky is the mother-form of the gods. The deity who manifested both of them and created the creatures of the whole world, O Tvashtadev! Worship, you are foodless and meritorious, so no one else is capable of equalizing you in Yajna-karma. ।१०.११०.९।

hey yup! You yourself bring the sacrificial material and offer it to the deities at the appropriate time. Vanaspati, Shamita and Agni should consume this honey-ghrita-enriched sacrificial substance. ।१०.११०.१० ।

Agni created the Yagya as soon as it was born. He became the leading messenger for the gods. Chant the Agni Rup Hota mantra which is offered with the sacrificial liquid Swaha, the gods accept it. ।१०.११०.११।

CHAPTER THIRTY-NINE

NAGARJUNA BESHA

During the war with Sahasrarjun, , lord Parasurama was in 'Naga besha'. Lord Jagannath is the symbol of whole universe. To satisfy his devotees, he is dressed as many avatars by sebayata & pandas for whole 365 days in the year. Among them, one of the rarest besha is nagarjuna besha with weapons

In odisha , from kartika shukla ekadashi to purnami , everyone follow the ritual 'panchuka'. For these 5 days, even the all time carnivorous bird 'white crane' also adopts veg food habit. These 5 days are most sacred days of whole kartika month.The year where panchuka is more than 5 days, lord Jagannath is dressed in as Nagarjuna.

Nagarjuna is a warrior form Lord Jagannath is adorned with 16 types of weapons. The legend follows two tales (one from satya/treta yug, another one from dwapar yug).On ekadashi, Sri Krishna came to rescue Rukmani on warrior form and defeated sishupal and captured him. This Nagarjuna besha represent the undefeated form of lord Krishna. According to other Puranas, Arjuna, the son of King Kartavirya was also known as 'Kartavirya arjuna'. His father was king of Haihaya kingdom near the Shore of Narmada River. He served & pleased rishi Dattatreya & by the grace of him, he got the title and power of 'Sahasra bahu' (thousand hands). Once Sahasarbahu Arjuna went to the ashrama of Maharshi Jamadagni. Jamadagni had Kamadhenu cow who is believed to be one of the supreme powerful cow of heaven. To provide food for the whole army of Sahasarbahu, Jamadagni asked Kamadhenu to produce food. The food created by Kamadhenu fulfilled the stomach of whole army. Then Kartavirya tried to abduct Kamadhenu, but defeated by the army created by Kamadhenu. Later he came to ashrama of Jamadagni again and killed him. To avenge his father death, Parasurama defeated and killed Sahasra-bahu Arjuna and freed the world from the cruel king.

During the war, lord Parshuram was in 'Naga besha'. That's why lord Jagannath is dressed in as Nagarjuna besha to help the weak and victims in his warrior form.

CHAPTER FORTY

WEAPONARY- SHASTRAS

All our ancient weapons were divided into two categories. According to the Ramayana, Bala kanda, sarga 27:

1. Shastra- It is a weapon that is handheld or you can say a weapon that is used for cutting or wounding like a sword, lance or mace, etc.

2. Astra- a projectile weapon invoked by reciting hymns like Agneyastra, Pashupatastra etc.

• Astra Vidyas were only taught to strict discipline & deserving students, & passed only to the right person. The vidya was never written down to prevent the misuse of it as they were really very powerful.

• Among these astra, Brahmastra is considered to be the most powerful astra that has been ever used by anyone. It is the weapon of Bhagavan Brahma, the creator and like other astras, it is invoked with a special mantra, and then one can use it to destroy anything that is created by Brahma.

• The Brahmastra does refer to a special arrow, but an ordinary arrow can also be given the same power using the mantra, and as mentioned in Ramayana, Shree Rama had even used the mantra on blades of grass. The following description of the Brahmastra is mentioned in the Ahirbudhnya

Samhita of Pancharatra Agama: "It contains air, fire and cosmic poison, two goat-like fangs, full of poison, heavy, emits air, contains mercury, fiery, sparkling, enemy- killing, greatly radiant and it is projected with three hymns, Gayatri at its center, it is known as Brahmastra".

• Based on the principle of Brahmastra, further weopons were developed such as Brahmsirastra and Brahmandastra which are considered to be more powerful than the Brahmastra. They can also be regarded as the modified versions of Brahmastra.

Once Vishvakarma made two mighty bows, one of them was taken by Siva to burn the Tripura. That bow is known as "Saivacapa". The other bow was given to Vishnu. It is called "Vaisnavacapa". The Devas wished to see a trial of strength between Siva and Vishnu. They prompted Brahma to bring about such a conflict. Brahma succeeded in causing a quarrel between Siva and Vishnu. A fight began between Siva and Vishnu. Both the Saivacapa and Vaisnavacapa went into action. But Siva was defeated. After that, Siva gave his bow to Devarata, king of Videhas. By inheritance it came into the hands of king Janaka, the father of Sita.

It was this bow which was broken by Sri Rama at the time of Sita's Svayamvara (Marriage) . After the battle with Siva, Vishnu gave his bow to Rucheeka who, in turn gave it to Jamadagni. Jamadagni presented it to his son Parasurama. It was with this Vaisnavacapa that Parasurama confronted Sri Rama who was returning after Sita's Svayamvara. **(Ramayana, Balakanda, 75th Sarga)** .

SHIVA GAVE PARASHU (AXE)

The foremost of men, that son mastered the sciences, including the science of arms. Like unto a blazing fire, that son was Rama, the exterminator of the Kshatriyas. Having gratified Mahadeva on the mountains of Gandhamadana, he obtained weapons of that great god, especially the axe of fierce energy in his hands. In consequence of that unrivalled axe of fiery splendor and irresistible sharpness, he became unrivalled on earth.

~Mahabharata: Santi Parva: Section L

Brahmanda Mahapurana gave detailed description of the weapons obtained by him which included Narayanastra, Pashupatastra, Mahadeva's Trishul, Brahmastra, Shiva Kavacha named Trailokyavijaya.

After saying this, Śaṅkara taught him the Mantra (esoteric formula) that is extremely difficult to obtain and the following weapons etc.

viz.—extremely miraculous coat of mail named Trailokyavijaya; the Nāgapāśa (Serpentine noose), (missiles like) the Pāśupata, the Brahmāstra which is very much inaccessible, Nārāyaṇāstra, the trident.

It also included Agneyastra, Vayavyastra, Garudastra, Varunastra, Gandharvastra, Jrimbhanastra, Shakti spear, Mahadeva's mace, Brahmadanda baton, etc.

The Āgneya (Arrow with the firegod as deity), the Vāyavya (of the wind god), the Vāruṇa (of Varuṇa the ocean-god), the Gāndharva, the Gāruḍa, the extremely wonderful weapon Jṛmbhaṇāstra, the mace, the Śakti, the Paraśu (Axe) and the excellentDaṇḍa (baton).

~Brahmanda Mahapurana: Upodghata Pada: Chapter 32

On lifting up the bow that is already fitted with an arrow on bowstring, then Rama started to take aim with it, but being indecisive about the target, then Rama of Dasharatha irefully said this to Rama of Jamagadni. "This Vishnu's divine arrow is the conqueror of opponents' citadels, and a vanquisher of their vigour and vainglory, and it will not fall through wastefully... isn't it!"

Valmiki Ramayana Bala Kanda Sarga 76

Mahadeva's own pinaka bow,With the Pināka bowin his hand resembling the flame of a blazing fire, the scion of the family of Bhrigu discharged the excellent arrow Nāgapāśa (noose of the Serpents) after invoking the Mantra thereof. With the missile charged with Garuḍa Mantra, Somadatta of great strength.

~Brahmanda Mahapurana: Upodghata Pada: Chapter 39

Maheshwarastra missile of parameshwara mahadeva.Parasurama the son of Bhrgu then used the Mahesvara weapon which was neutralized by the king, by using the Vaisnava weapon. O Narada, thereafter Parasurama used Brahmastra for the destruction of the king. The king at that point of time shot the trident bestowed to him by Dattatreya for killing his enemy which was always successful in its mission.

~BrahmaVaivarta Purana Ganpati Khanda chapter 40

Guhyakastra , I wished to perform the superior deeds. In every direction, a great roar could be heard in the firmament. I used the vayavya weapon against Jamadagni's son. O descendant of the Bharata lineage! Rama countered this with his guhyaka weapon.

~BORI CE Mahabharata section 844(181), Udyoga Parva, Ambopakhyana Parva

Vijaya bow, indestructible chariot, 2 inexhaustible quivers, a divine armor and many other celestial weapons,after saying "So be it", Śambhu who was delighted gave Rāma missiles and weapons in their entirety in due order along with their Mantras. Saṅkara who stood in front of him with satisfaction made Rāma take up the four types of miraculous weapons along with the modes of their discharge as well as their withdrawal. Śaṅkara gave Rāma an excellent chariot of unobstructed speed and velocity,with white horses and beautiful banner. He gave him two inexhaustible quivers of arrows. He gave him an unaging (ever-new) unbreakable divine bow (named) Vijaya, with firm bowstring. He gave him a costly wonderful coat of mail that can withstand all types of weapons. ~**Brahmanda Mahapurana: Upodghata Pada: Chapter 25**

PARSHURAM JI KA FARSA (TANGI) OF JHARKHAND

There is a place in Jharkhand, whose name is Tanginath. It is said for Tanginath Dham that Parshuram ji's axe is buried here and till date there has been no war on this axe.

It is considered to be a weapon of and from this farse he had killed the wicked. It is said that this axe of Parashurama is buried in a village near Ranchi in Jharkhand. It is said that the axe of Parashurama is still buried in the dense forests 150 km away from Ranchi city of Jharkhand. The name of this place is Gumla and it is known as Tanginath Dham. This place is considered to be the penance place of Parashurama. People say that this furrow has been buried under the open sky for thousands of years, but this furrow has not been rusted. Because of this, there is a lot of recognition of this farsa.

Non-rusting is considered a miracle : The furrow in Tanginath, which is called that of Parashuram ji, is of iron. It is said that it has been buried in the ground here for thousands of years and is under the open sky. That is, no shelter etc. has been put on this furrow and it remains like this in rain and sun. The special thing about this furrow kept in the open for so many years is that it has not rusted yet and it is considered a miracle of Parashurama. People believe that it is quite common for iron to rust due to contact with water and air, but this is not the case with this ax and it has not rusted yet. However, many experts say that even certain types of iron do not cause rust.

Parashurama did penance: Along with the folk tale of Parshuram being buried, it is said that Parashurama did penance for many years at this place. According to reports, people believe that Parashurama beheaded his mother Renuka at the behest of his father Jamadagni. After this, he got him alive again in a boon from his father, but to get rid of the guilt of killing the mother, he pleased Lord Shiva by doing austerity in Tanginath and was freed from guilt. At the same time, many people associate this penance with getting angry on Lord Rama.

CHAPTER FORTY-ONE

PEER INCARNITATIONS

Owing to the curse of Bhrigu, Mahavishnu had to undertake so many incarnations, complete as well as partial. Complete incarnations are ten in number. They are called Dasavataras.

THE DASAVATARAS OF MAHA LORD VISHNU (TEN INCARNATIONS)

Mahavishnu is among the most important deities of Hinduism. Together with with Brahma and Shiva, Vishnu forms the principal trinity of Hindu religious practice. In his many forms, Vishnu is regarded as the preserver and protector. Hinduism teaches that when humanity is threatened by chaos or evil, Vishnu will descend into the world in one of his incarnations to restore righteousness. The incarnations that Vishnu takes are called avatars. The Hindu scriptures speak of ten avatars. They are thought to have been present in the *Satya Yuga* (the Golden Age or Age of Truth), when mankind was ruled by gods.

Collectively, the avatars of Vishnu are called *Dasavataras* (10 avatars). Each has a different form and purpose. When an individual is faced with a challenge, a particular avatar descends to address the issue. There is a belief associated with each avatar reference a specific period of time when they were most needed. Some people refer to this as the cosmic cycle or the Time-Spirit. For instance, the first avatar, Matsya, descended long before the ninth avatar, Balrama. More recent mythology states that Balrama may have been the Lord Buddha. No matter the specific intent or place in time, the avatars are meant to re-establish the *Dharma* the path of righteousness or universal laws taught in the Hindu scriptures. The legends, myths, and stories that include the avatars remain important allegories within Hinduism.

FIRST AVATAR- MATSYA AVATAR (FISH INCARNATION).

As per Aranya Parva Chapter 187, Agni Purana Chapter 2 and Bhagavata 8th Skandha Chapter 24, Kashyapa, the son of Marici, and the grandson of Brahma blessed with a son by his wife Aditi. He was called Vivasvanand the Manu. It was during the time of Manu that Lord Vishnu incarnated as a Matsya (fish). Vaivasvata Manu, the first and foremost of the God fearing, was once doing penance in a place known as Badari. He got down into the river Krtamala to take a bath. Then a small fish said to the Manu: "Oh King, I am afraid of large fishes. So please don't forsake me". Hearing this, Kind Manu took the fish in his hand and put it in an earthenware pot and brought it up. In a few days the fish began to grow. When the pot became insufficient the King put it in a larger pot. When that also became too small, the King put the fish in a pond. When the pond could not hold the fish any longer the King put it in the Ganges at its request. After a few days the Ganges also became too small for the fish. Finally, the fish told the King: "Oh, King, within seven days there will be a great flood in the world. You should make a boat and take the seven hermit-sages with you in the boat and escape. I will help you."Hearing this he got an immensely large boat ready and obeyed the instructions of the fish. Within seven days rain started in torrents. Everything in the world, the moving and the not moving, were under the flood. A horn began to sprout from the head of the fish. Manu tied his boat on that horn. The fish reached the summit of the Himalayas with the boat, which was tied to the highest peak. Since the peak came to be called 'Naubandhana Srnga' (The peak to which boat is tied).The rain ceased to pour. It was seen that everything in the world had been destroyed except the Manu and the seven hermit-sages saved in the boat.

SECOND AVTARA- KURMDVATDRA (INCARNATION AS A TORTOISE)- KURMA (TURTLE)

As per Bhagavata Skandha 8 Chapter 7, Agni Purana Chapter 3 & Valmlki Ramayana, Balakanda Sarga 45, Long ago when Durvasas visited the realm of Gods he presented Devendra with a garland made of flowers of exquisite fragrance. Indra tied it on to the tusk of Airavata (the elephant of Indra). When the beetles which gathered on the garland for honey became a nuisance, Airavata destroyed that garland. Durvasas who got angry at this cursed the gods as a whole that they would get wrinkles and grey hair.

The gods were advised by Maha Lord Vishnu that if they got Ambrosia (Amnacelestial honey) from the sea of Milk by churning it they could escape from this. Accordingly, the Gods called the Asuras for help, and they approached the sea of Milk. They made use of the Mountain of Mandara as churn drill and the huge snake Vasuki as churning rope and the churning commenced. The gods took hold of the tail of the snake and as the churning was preceding the churn-drill, the mountain of Mandara, having no fixation at the bottom sank down. Then Maha Lord Vishnu took the form of a turtle, and got under the Mandara Mountain and lifted it up on his back. By the force of lifting, it went higher and higher up. Then Maha Lord Vishnu took the form of an eagle and sat on the top of the mountain and it came down a little and placed itself in the right position.

There is a lake in the Himalayas called Indradyumna. Akupara is a tortoise living in it. There is also a statement that this is the Adi-Kurma. A description of Akupara is found in Chapter 199 of Vana Parva in Mahabharata.Chiranjivi (one who has no death}. When the Pandavas were in exile in the forests sage Markandeya tells many stories to Dharmaputra to console him in his sad plight. The Pandavas asked Markandeya whether he knew of anybody living before him. Then the sage said, "In times of old Indradyumna an ascetic King (Rajarsi) fell down from heaven when he fell short of his accumulated 'Punya'.

Sorrowfully he came to me and asked me whether I knew him. I replied in the negative adding that perhaps Pravlrakarna an owl living on the top of the Himalayas might know him since he was older than me- At once Indradyumna became a horse and taking me on its back approached the owl living in the Himalayas. The owl also could not remember Indradyumna but directed him to a stork named Nadljarhgha who was older than the owl. The Ascetic king took me then to the Indradyumna lake where the stork lived.

The stork also could not find the identity of Indradyumna. Perhaps he said that a tortoise of name Akupara living in that same lake might know him. We then approached the tortoise and enquired whether he knew Indradyumna. The tortoise sat in meditation for some time and then weeping profusely and shaking like a leaf stood bowing respectfully and said, "How can I remain without knowing him? There are several monuments of the useful work done by him here. This very lake is of his making.

This came into existence by the march of the cows he gave away to the people". The moment the tortoise finished speaking a chariot appeared from heaven to take the King away. The King after leaving me and the owl in their proper places ascended to heaven in the chariot.

THIRD AVTARA- VARDHAVATARA. (INCARNATION AS A PIG)

As per, Bhagavata, Skandha 3 Chapter 18, Bhagavata Skandha 2 Chapter 7 and Agni Purana, Chapter 4, Jaya and Vijaya were the two watchers who stood at the gate of Maha Lord Vishnu. Once the great hermit-sages Sanaka and others reached Vaikuntha to visit Maha Lord Vishnu. Then Jaya and Vijaya treated the hermits without respect.

The hermits cursed them that they would become Danavas (Asuras or giants). They also said that when they were slain thrice by Maha Lord Vishnu they would reach heaven. At that period when hermit Kashyapa was carrying on his evening prayer and devotional rites, his wife Aditi approached him with heartfelt bodily desire. Kashyapa told her that as he was engaged in prayer and meditation it was not proper on her part to select that particular moment for her heart felt bodily desire. But she persisted and the sage yielded and out of that union two sons were born.

They are the two Asuras Hiranyaksa and Hiranyakasipu. Of these Hiranyaksa was the incarnation of Jaya and Hiranyakasipu that of Vijaya. With the birth of these two the whole world began to tremble. These two Asura brothers began to terrorize the world. They wandered about causing destruction and devastation wherever they went.

As Hiranyaksa grew up he began to quarrel with the Devtas. When the fight grew fierce, he got down into the ocean and began to beat the waves in the ocean with his cudgel. The ocean began to sway and surge. Varuna (the Lord of water) was terrified and he ran to Maha Lord Vishnu and sought protection.

Maha Lord Vishnu took the form of a Pig and came to the ocean. When Hiranyaksa saw Maha Lord Vishnu he took the earth in his hand and ran to Patala (the nether world) .The Devtas went to Maha Lord Vishnu and prayed to him in order to get the earth back. At this time Manu Svayambhuva, the son of Brahma, was living with his father looking after his welfare.

The father, who was pleased with the services of his son said. "My dear son, you should worship Devi, who will be pleased with your devotion and will bless you. If she is pleased with you, you will become a famous Prajapati." Hearing the words of Brahma, Svayambhuva worshipped Devi with ardent devotion, deep meditation and severe vows and penance, at which Jagadamba was pleased. She appeared before him and asked him what boon he wanted.

Manu requested that he should be permitted to carry on creation without any obstruction. Devi gave him permission. Manu returned to his father Brahma and said. "Father, point out to me a solitary place. I will sit there and create subjects by the blessings of Devi." Only when he heard the request of his son, did Brahma begin to think about the exigency of providing his son with such a place. For, the earth was completely under water. For a long time even Brahma was being subjected too much inconveniences to carry on creation. Only Bhagvan Adi Narayana (Lord Vishnu) could do anything in this matter. So Brahma with the Manus, hermits and others began to meditate on Maha Lord Vishnu.

Instantly the young one of a Boar jumped out of the nose of Brahma through his breath. That divine figure of Boar stood in the air and began to grow. Within a few moments, it became a colossal Being. It grew up as big as an elephant. Soon it became as large as a mountain. Seeing this, Brahma and the others stood in amazement.

The Boar made a grunt in a loud roaring sound. The people of Janaloka, Satyaloka etc. understood that it was the sound of Maha Lord Vishnu. They raised glory and praise to Bhagavan, who heard all these praises, but without condescending to tell anything, looked at all of them with grace and love, and with a mighty force jumped into the sea. It was immensely troubled by the manes of God Almighty. Bhagvan folded his mane and went down to the deep water and made a search for the earth. The Boar walked smelling and snorting and found out the earth.

He slowly lifted it on his tusks and started from there. On the way, the fierce and wicked Hiranyaksa hindered him. Bhagavan Lord Vishnu used his club Nandaka and killed Hiranyaksa. It was besmeared with his blood; Maha Lord Vishnu came up to the surface of water with the earth. He set the earth firm over the water. Thus Brahma gave Manu a place in the earth which floated on the water like a lotus-leaf, and empowered him to perform creation.

As per Bhagavata Skandha 3, Devi Bhagavata Skandha 8 and 9, Agni Purana Chapter 5 and Padma Purana Bhumikhanda Chapter 91, there is also another Incarnation of Boar again. The goddess Earth, the deity of earth which was raised to the surface of water, fell in love with Maha Lord Vishnu and embraced him.

He embraced her in return. These mutual embraces continued for one complete Devavarsa (year of God) and consequently the goddess Earth became tired and weak and unconscious. So, the earth slid down a little underwater. Bhagvan took the form of a Boar again and lifted the earth to its original place and returned to Vaikuntha.

FORTH AVTARA- NARASIMHDVATARA. (INCARNATION AS LION-MAN)

As per Bhagavata Skandha 7 Chapter 8 Stanzas 20-22, with the death of Hiranyaksa, his brother Hiranyakasipu became furious more than ever. He wanted to avenge the death of his brother. His fury was turned towards Maha Lord Vishnu. So he got on the top of the Mountain of Mandara and did penance before Brahma and Brahma appeared and granted him boons, one of which was that nobody but Lord Vishnu should be able to kill him.

He returned with gladness and began to roam about torturing devotees of Lord Vishnu everywhere. A son named Prahlada was born to him. He was a god fearing child and from birth an ardent believer in Lord Vishnu. Hiranyakasipu tried his utmost to change his son to a hater of Lord Vishnu. He got a special teacher for the purpose and Prahlada was taken to the house of the teacher to live with him until he changed his mind. The result was that the teacher and all others who advised him ultimately became believers in Lord Vishnu.

Prahlada was thrown before mad elephants. But the tusks of the elephant missed the aim and were driven into the earth and broken. Venomous snakes were employed and those which bit him had their fangs broken. Finally, the child was put in blazing fire. But the child felt the fire to be cool and soothing. From that fire a ghost arose and tried to kill Prahlada. Instantly the Sudarshana, the wheel-weapon of Lord Vishnu came down and cut off the head of the ghost.

Hiranyakasipu jumped with anger and called out. "Where is your Lord Vishnu?" His son replied that his Lord Vishnu dwelt in every movable and immovable thing. Hiranyakasipu kicked at a stone pillar close by and asked him, "Is your Lord Vishnu in this pillar?" Prahlada replied, "My Lord Vishnu is in Pillar and in fibre". Before he had finished, the Pillar broke open and a monster as horrible as the Destroyer Siva, in the shape of a lion-man made its appearance.

The horrid monster Narasirmha (Lion with human head) caught hold of Hiranyakasipu pushed him to the ground and opened his heart with its fierce claws. Blood sprouted like a spring. With great ferocity he pulled out the intestines of Hiranyakasipu and wore them round his neck as a garland and roared loudly. Prahlada, with songs of praise and chanting of hymns of adoration pacified the stormy Narasirmha and bowed low down before him. The Narasirmha was pleased with the devotion of Prahlada. He blessed the child and then disappeared.

FIFTH AVTARA- VDMANDVATDRA. (INCARNATION AS A DWARF)

As per Bhagavata Skandha 8 Chapter 19, It was to expel the Emperor Mahabali, that Maha Lord Vishnu incarnated as a dwarf. To Kashyapa, the son of Marici and the grandson of Brahma, was born of Dili, Hiranyakasipu And from Prahlada the son of Hiranyakasipuwas born Virochana and Bali was the son of Virochana.

Bali got the name Mahabali because of his prowess. He was the emperor of the Asuras. A fierce battle began over the Ambrosia got from churning the sea of Milk, between the Asuras and the gods. In the battle Indra cut Mahabali down with his Vajrayudha. The Asuras took the body of Mahabali to Patala (the nether world) where their teacher Sukra brought him to life again. Then Mahabali worshipped the Bhargavas and became more powerful than before and went to heaven again and renewed the battle.

This time he defeated the Gods altogether and subjugated the realm of the Gods who were scattered to all sides. The Devtas or gods are the sons of Kashyapa born by his wife, Aditi. She felt very sorry at the defeat of the gods. Seeing that she was silent and sad Kashyapa asked her the reason. She replied that she was thinking of ways to enable the gods to recover their lost power and position. Kashyapa advised her to please Maha Lord Vishnu by observing Dvadall vrata (fast of the twelfth lunar night).

Aditi did so and Lord Vishnu appeared before her and asked her what she desired. Her request was that Lord Vishnu should take birth in her womb and recover Indra to his lost power and position. Thus Lord Vishnu took birth as the younger brother of Indra in the shape of Vamana (dwarf.)At this time Emperor Mahabali was celebrating a sacrifice on the bank of the River Narmada after having subjugated the whole of the world. A large number of hermits gathered there.

Vamana also was among them. He requested Mahabali to grant him three feet of ground as alms. The teacher Sukra warned Mahabali against granting the request. But the emperor granted the request and asked Vamana to measure the ground. Vamana immediately enlarged his body and measured the heaven, the earth and the Patala (the upper realm the earth and the lower realm) in two steps and asked for place for the third step. The honest Mahabali showed his head and requested to complete the three steps. Vamana put his step on the head of Mahabali and pushed him down to Patala. Thus the gods regained their lost places.

A description that by the toe of Vamanas' raised foot (raised for measuring the third step) the testicle of Brahma was cut open where from the Ganges originated, is seen in the Bhagavata, Skandha 5.When Visvamitra took Rama and Laksmana to the forest they entered a holy hermitage and Visvamitra told the boys that it was the hermitage where Aditi long ago had observed dvadall fast.

It was in that same place that Vamana incarnated and placed his step on the head of Mahabali."The bright Madhava took birth in Aditi as Vamanaand went to Mahabali, requested for three feet of ground and brought under control the three worlds for the good of all. By binding Bali by might, he gave to Indra the three worlds and this hermitage is the place where He once placed his steps. I am a devotee of that Vamana."This is in Valmlki Ramayana, Bala Kanda Sarga 29.

SIXTII AVTARA- PARASURDMDVATDRA. (INCARNATION AS PARASURAMA)

As per Harivarhsa Chapter 40, once god Agni went to Kartaviryarjuna and begged for food. The king allowed him to takes from his vast territory as much food as he wanted from anywhere he liked. Agni started burning forests and mountains and consuming them.

Deep inside one of the forests a sage named Apava was performing penance and the fire burnt the ashrama of Apava also. Enraged at this the sage cursed thus: "Kartaviryarjuna is at the root of this havoc. The arrogance of Ksatriyas has increased beyond limits. Maha Lord Vishnu would therefore be born on earth as Parasurama to destroy this arrogance of the Ksatriyas." Accordingly, Maha Lord Vishnu was born as Parasurama in the Bhargava race.

As per Bhagavata Skandha 9 Chapter 16, Maha Lord Vishnu took his sixth incarnation as Parasurama and fulfilled his duty of destroying the wicked Kshatriya Kings. Lord Parasurama is considered as the 'Avesha Avatar' of Lord Vishnu. His father, Jamadagni, a great Saint Bhargava was a direct descendant of Lord Brahma Ji. Renuka the wife of Jamadagni and mother of Lord Parasurama gave birth to four sons before Parasurama.

They were Vasu, Vishwu Vasu , Brihudyanu and Parasurama. Lord Parasurama was the fifth son. Before the birth of their fifth son, Rishi Jamadagni meditated with his wife Renuka at Tap Ka Tiba near Renuka Lake for divine providence. Lord Shiva blessed both and at the request of Lord Shiva, Lord Vishnu assured them that he would be their 5th son. Renuka and Muni Jamadagni named Rambhadra as their fifth and youngest son. The purpose of this avatar was to "end the dominance of the Ksatriyas, the warrior caste, who had 'taken to unrighteous ways' and have become a burden on the earth", once again completing Vishnu's duty to preserve and protect the earth from unrighteousness.

Parasurama incarnation is at Sixth place in Dasavataras and 20th incarnation among twenty-six incantations. Brahmanda Purana gives another version: Lord Vishnu promised Bhumidevi (mother earth) that he would be born on earth as Parasurama when Bhumidevi went to him in the form of a cow and complained to him about the atrocities of the wicked Ksatriyas kings. Brahmanda Purana, Chapter 59 also suggests that the birth of Parasurama was because of the wickedness of the Ksatriyas Kings, the goddess Earth became miserable.

She made a representation to Brahma who took her to the sea of Milk and told Mahavishnu every-thing. Mahavishnu promised to take an incarnation as the son of Jamadagni and destroy all the wicked Kings. Accordingly, Renuka gave birth to Parasurama. These texts also state that Parasurama lost the essence of Vishnu while he was alive, and Vishnu then appeared as a complete avatar in Rama; later, in Krishna. The story of Parasurama belongs to the Tretayug. The word Parasurama means Lord Ram with an axe.

SEVENTH AVTARA-RAGHUPATI RAMA - (INCARNATION AS SRI RAMA)

Maha Lord Vishnu took the incarnation of Sri Rama to kill Ravana. Rama, Ram, Sri Ram or Raja Ram also known as Ramachandra is the seventh and one of the most popular avatars of Vishnu. Rama has been born to Kausalya and Dashratha, the descendent of Ikshavaku Dynasty in Ayodhya. Kamba Ramayana, Purva Kanda narrates the reason Ravana terror to the world for his incarnation.

It was then, when Ravana was ruling over Lanka, evils and cruelties like matricide, patricide, fratricide, hatred for good people, children's death, abduction of women, killing of munis, thefts etc. became rampant. When the world became grief-stricken Bhumidevi (Goddess of earth) assumed the form of a cow and took refuge with Indra in Svarga. She told him about the atrocities committed by Ravana and the other Raksasas. Then Indra took Bhumidevi (cow) to Brahma, who took them to Siva at Kailasa as killing Ravana was beyond his (Brahma's) power.

Siva thought it improper on his part to kill Ravana and so he took Brahma and others to Lord Vishnu and submitted their grievance to him. Lord Vishnu consoled them by saying as follows: "I have decided to incarnate myself as the son of Dashratha, king of Ayodhya. Devtas should also take birth on earth to help me to kill Ravana and other evil Raksasas to protect Bhumidevi and the good people on the earth." His siblings included Laksmana, Bharata, and Shatrughna.

He married Sita. Though born in a royal family, their life is described in the Hindu texts as one challenged by unexpected changes such as an exile into impoverished and difficult circumstances, ethical questions and moral dilemmas. Of all their travails, the most notable is the kidnapping of Sita by demon-king Ravana, followed by the determined and epic efforts of Rama and Laksmana to gain her freedom and destroy the evil Ravana against great odds.

The royal birth of the god Rama in the kingdom of Ayodhya (Oudh), He took the formal training as Kshatriya under the sage Vishwamitra and became a warrior from his childhood days. He fulfilled the condition of bending Shiva's mighty bow to get married to bridegroom Sita, the daughter of King Janaka.

When the preparations were in full swing to handover the rule of Ayodhya, he was banished from his position as heir to the kingdom through a palace intrigue by his step mother Kaikeyi and her maid Mantra; he retreats to the forest with his wife and his favourite half brother, Laksmana, to spend 14 years in exile. There Ravana, the demon-king of Lanka, kidnapped Sita to his capital while Rama & Laksmana were busy pursuing a golden deer which was sent to the forest by Ravana to mislead them.

Sita resolutely rejects Ravana's attentions, and Rama and his brother set out to rescue her. After numerous adventures, they enter into alliance with Sugriva, king of the monkeys, and, with the assistance of the monkey-general Hanuman and Ravana's own brother, Vibhishana, they attack Lanka. Rama slays Ravana and rescues Sita, who undergoes an ordeal by fire in order to clear herself of suspicions of infidelity.

When they return to Ayodhya, however, Rama learns that the people still question the queen's chastity, and he banishes her to the forest. There she meets the sage Valmlki and at his hermitage gives birth to Rama's two sons. The family is reunited when the sons come of age, but Sita, after again protesting her innocence, plunges into the earth, her mother, who receives her and swallows her up.

EIGHTH AND NINTH AVTARA- BALABHADRARDMDVATDRA AND SRI KRSNDVATDRA (THE INCARNATION OF BALRAMA AND KRISHAN)

As per Dasama Skandha, Bhagavata. When the number of wicked kings increased Bhumidevi (goddess of Earth) turned herself into a cow and took refuge in Maha Lord Vishnu. Maha Lord Vishnu then promised to be born as the sons of Vasudeva named Balabhadrarama and Sri Krsna to destroy the wicked. Ugrasena was the king of Mathura.

His son Kansa was a cruel king. His sibling Devki marriage was fixed to Vasudeva. The marriage of Devaki with Vasudeva was celebrated but on the same day an Asashwani (a heavenly voice from above) said that the eighth child of Devaki would kill Kansa. Instantly Kansa put both Vasudeva and Devaki in jail. The first six sons born to Devaki were killed the moment they were born by striking them against the ground.

Devaki became pregnant for the seventh time. Devaki and Vasudeva were very frustrated with Kamsa's ways. The babe in the womb was Ananta incarnate by Lord Vishnu 's directive to be of help to him when he would also be born soon as ninth incarnation as Krsna. Therefore it was necessary to save the child from the cruel hands of Kansa as it was certain he would kill the babe the same way he had killed all the others before.

The subjects in the kingdom were very fearful of Kansa. Over time, they also got frustrated with the absolutely cruel ways of the king, constantly at battle with someone and then, killing these children. Slowly, dissension was beginning to happen within the palace. So when the seventh child came, he ordered Mayadevi to take the child from the womb of Devaki and place it in that of Rohini, another wife of Vasudeva.

Mayadevi did so and the boy got the name Samgharsana, also because of this. The news spread that Devaki aborted. Rohini delivered a boy and was named Samgharsana alias Balabhadrarama alias Balrama. He is also known as Haladhara, Halayudha, Baladeva, Balabhadra and Sankarshana. Balrama is sometimes described as incarnation of Shesha, the serpent associated with the god Vishnu.

Balrama increases the bliss of others, his name is Rama and because of his extraordinary strength, he is called Bala deva. As he grew up, he became like a giant and there are any number of stories about his strength and the feats that he performed.

When Krishna was born and a miracle happened. The doors of the prison opened up by themselves – all the guards fell asleep – the shackles broke. Immediately, Vasudeva saw that this was a divine intervention. He picked up the child and as if by intuitive guidance, he walked to the river Yamuna. Though the whole place was flooding, he found to his surprise that the ford which crossed the river was sticking out and he could clearly walk.

He walked across and went to the house of Nanda and his wife Yashodha. Yashodha had just delivered a girl child. She had a difficult labor and was unconscious. Vasudeva replaced the girl child with Krishna, took the girl child and came back to the prison. When Kamsa tries to kill the newborn, the exchanged baby appears as the Hindu goddess yogmaya, warning him that his death has arrived in his kingdom, and then disappears, according to the legends in the Puranas. Krishna grows up with Nanda and his wife, Yashoda. Two of Krishna's siblings also survived, namely Balrama and Subhadra.

The legends of Krishna's childhood and youth describe him as a cow herder, a mischievous boy whose pranks earn him the nickname *Makhan Chor* (butter thief), and a protector who steals the hearts of the people in both Gokul and Vrindavana. Krishna lifts the Goverdhan Hill to protect the inhabitants of Vrindavana from devastating rains and floods.

TENTH AVTARA KALKYAVATDRA (THE INCARNATION AS KALKI)

As per Agni Purana, Chapter 16, At the end of Kaliyuga (the Age of Kali) all the people would become atheists and sceptics. Rewards will be received from the depraved. The classes will be mixed. People would become degenerate having no good qualities. A religion called 'Vajasaneyam' with its fifteen doctrines only will be acceptable.

People would become irresponsible wearing the garment of duty. Lawless people would take the form of Kings and will begin to eatmen. In those days Lord Vishnu will incarnate as Kalki, the son of Lord Vishnuyasas and the priest of Yajnavalkya and learn the arts of wielding weapon and handling missiles and destroy all lawless ones. The subjects will be brought back to the four classes and the four agramasor stages of life and the doctrines and directions of the long established religion and peace and order will be restored.

Then the Lord will cast away the form of Kalki and go to heaven. After that, as of old, Krtayuga (the first age) will begin class distinctions and the four stages of life and such other establishments will once more prevail. Parashurama will again come as the preceptor of Lord Kalki, the final avatar of Lord Vishnu.

THE TWENTY-SIX INCARNATIONS OF MAHAVISHNU

The above are the usually recognised Avatars, but the number is sometimes extended. The Bhagavata Purana is the fifth place in the order of Puranas, but it is the most famous across the globe. Vaishnava consider this Purana of 12 wings, 335 chapters, and 18 thousand shlokas as Mahapurana. Bhagavata Purana enumerates twenty-two incarnations :—(1) Purusha, the male, the progenitor (2) Varaha, the boar (3) Narada, the great sage (4) Nara and Narayana (5) Kapila, the great sage; (6) Dattatreya, a sage (7) Yajna, sacrifice (8)

Dushyanta, a righteous king, father of Bharata (9.) Prathu, a king (10) Matsya, the fish; (11) Kurma, the tortoise (12) and (13) Dhanwantari, the physician of the gods (14) -Narasimha, the man-lion; (15) Yamana, the dwarf (16) Parasurama; (17) Yeda-Vyasa (18) Rama (19) Bala-rama; (20.) Knshraa; (21.)Buddha; (22) Kalki

But after this it adds—"The incarnations of Vishnu are innumerable, like the rivulets flowing from-an inexhaustible lake, Manus, gods, sons of Manus,Prajapatis, are all portions of him."

Sri Mahadevi Bhagavata, Skandha 1, Chapter 3 mentioned that Mahavishnu had taken the twenty-six incarnations. The ten avatars are common, the rest of the sixteen incarnations are:

(1) Sanaka (2) Sananda (3) Sanatana (4) Sanatkumara (5) Varaha (pig) (6) Narada (7) Nara Narayanas (8)Kapila (9) Dattatreya (10) Yajna (11) Rsabha (12) Prthu (13) Matsya (fish) (14)Mohini (15)'Kurma (turtle) (16) Garuda (eagle) (17) Dhanvantari (18) Narasimha (Lion-man) (19) Vaniana (dwarf) (20) Parasurama (21) Vyasa (22) Sri Rama (23) Balabhadrarama (24) Sri Krsna (25) Buddha(26) Kalki.

1) SANAKA 2) SANANDA 3) SANATANA 4) SANATKUMARA

As per Devi Bhagavata, Skandha 1 Skandha 7 & Bhagavata, Skandha 7, Bhavisya Purana, Sanaka, Sananda, Sanatana and Sanatkumara, the four Sages are known as Sanakadis. The Sanakadis are the mental sons of Brahma. When they stood in the form of infants, they were asked to create subjects. But they were the incarnation of 'Sattva'(the attribute of purity), and so were not prepared to undertake creation. Even at the age of four or five the four of them learned the Vedas, and travelled together. They were celibates forever. While the Sanakadis were travelling thus one day they reached Vaikuntha, and cursed Jaya and Vijaya who showed disrespect towards them. It is mentioned in that the Sanakadis were the incarnations of portions of Maha Lord Vishnu. Once Brahma praised the incarnations of Lord Vishnu. It is clear that the Kumaras (Sanakadis) had taken incarnation before the present Brahma began the work of creation.

As per **Bhagavata, Skandha 7,** it is mentioned that Jayavijaya were gate-keepers of Vaikuntha. As these two sons of Devtas were engaged in the service of Maha Lord Vishnu guarding the gate, the hermits Sanaka and others came to see Maha Lord Vishnu to pay him homage. Jaya and Vijaya stopped them at the gate. Sanaka got angry and cursed them to take three births on the earth as Asuras (demons). The sorrowful Jaya and Vijaya requested for absolution from the curse.

The hermit said that they had to take three births as Asuras and those they would be redeemed by the weapon of Maha Lord Vishnu. Accordingly, Jaya and Vijaya were born in the earth as Hiranyaksa and Hiranyakasipu. They were killed by Maha Lord Vishnu. In the second birth they were Ravana and Kumbhakarna. Maha Lord Vishnu incarnated as Sri Rama killed them. In the third birth they were Sishupal and Dantavaktra. They were killed by Sri Krsna, an incarnation of Bhagavan Lord Vishnu. So, Jaya and Vijaya, gate-keepers at Vaikuntha were born thrice in Asura womb as a result of the curse by munis like Sanaka. They were first born as Hiranyaksa and Hiranyakasipu, next as Ravana and Kumbhakarna and the third time as Sishupal and Dantavaktra. After this, Jaya and Vijaya returned to Vaikuntha.

5) NARADA

Narada was the son of Brahma, born from his lap. The Puranas refer to more than seven prominent births of Narada. He was first born as the son of Brahma, and after that, on account of Brahma's curse he was born as the Gandharvas called Upabarhana. Following that he was born as the son of emperor Drumila and was named Narada. Again born as the son of Brahma under the name Narada, he married Malati and ended his life as a monkey. He was again born as the son of Brahma and was cursed by Daksa. Afterwards he was born as the son of Daksa and also as a worm. All these births did not occur in one and the same Manvantara. Narada may be noticed doing something or other in connection with the various characters in the Puranas. There is no other character in the Puranas occupying so popular a place in them as Narada.

6) NARA NARAYANAS

As per **Devi Bhagavata, Skandha 4,** two hermits Nara and Narayana were having divine powers. These two hermits had spent many thousands of years in Badaryasrama doing penance. Arjuna was the rebirth of Nara and Sri Krsna was the rebirth of Narayana Brahma created Dharmadeva from his breast. Truthful and righteous Dharma married ten daughters of Daksa. Several sons were born to Dharma of his ten wives. But foremost among them were Hari, Krsna, Nara and Narayana. Hari and Krsna became great yogins and Nara and Narayana became great hermits of penance. The Nara-Narayana lived in the holy Asylum of Badaryasrama in the vicinity of the Himalayas for a thousand years performing penance to Brahma. Once, Prahlada saw near the tree two hermits, with matted hair, clad in the hide of black antelope, performing penance. Near them were two perfectly made divine bows named Sarnga and Ajagava and two quivers which would never become empty? Prahlada questioned them without knowing that they were Nara and Narayana. The questioning ended in a contest. The hermit Nara stood up and taking the bow Ajagava began sending showers of arrows at Prahlada. Prahlada checked every one of them. The hermit made his fight more severe. Prahlada also withstood it. At last pushing Nara back Narayana came to the front. The fight between Prahlada and Narayana was fierce. In the end Prahlada fell down, his breast being pierced by the arrow of

Narayana. Prahlada realized that the hermit Narayana was none but Lord Vishnu. He praised Narayana **(Vamana Purana, Chapter'8).**

On the occasion of the stripping of Panchli of her clothes at the palace of the Kauravas, Panchali cried, calling Nara and Narayana. Arjuna and Sri Krishna were the rebirths of Nara and Narayana. It is stated in Mahabharata, Santi Parva, Chapter334, Stanza 9, that the hermit Nara was one of the four incarnations taken by Maha Lord Vishnu in the Manusyayuga (age of man) of the Svayambhuva Manvantara. It is mentioned in Padma Purana, Uttara Khanda, Chapter 2, that, of the two viz. Nara and Narayana, Nara was of fair complexion and Narayana of dark complexion. This was because of the curse of the hermit Bhrguthat Nara-Narayana took birth as Arjuna and Krsna in the Dvapara Yuga. **(Devi Bhagavata, Skandha 4).** The meaning of the word 'Nara' is he who is not damaged. The universal soul named Nara has created water and so water got the name 'Naram'. Because he lives in that water which has the name Naram, the universal soul got the name Narayana. **(Manusmrti, Chapter1, Stanza 10).** Narayana descended on earth and chose Nara to be his associate in achieving the purpose of his incarnation. He admitted himself thus. Narayana himself told Narada **as per Santi Parva.**

7) KAPILA

The Brahmanda Purana states that Kapila was the incarnation of Lord Vishnu.In Chapter 93 there is a statement: "Bhagavan Narayana will protect us all. The Lord of the universehas now been born in the world as Kapila Acharya."Kapila imparts spiritual knowledge to his mother. Kapila started a severe penance. At that time Kardama Prajapati died and Devahuti wife of Kardama and mother of Kapila approached Kapila and asked him to instruct her on the path of Bhakti Yoga. Kapila imparted to her spiritual knowledge and gave her instructions to follow the path of Bhakti Yoga for Salvation. She entered into a life of austerities and attained Samadhi. **(3rd Skandha,Bhagavata) .**

Once there was a king called Sagara in the Solar dynasty. He had two wives named Kesini and Sumati. Kesini got a son named Asamanjas and Sumati got sixty thousand sons. Once Sagara conducted an Ashvamedha Yaga at a place where the rivers Sindhu and Ganga meet. Arhsuman, son of Asamanjasa led the sacrificial horse. Indra disguised as a demon stole the horse when it came to a mountain side and hid it in the nether worlds.

Sagara sent his sixty thousand sons in search of the horse. They dug the whole continent of Jambudvipa surrounded by mountains. Devtas, gandharvas and bhujahgas complained to Brahma. Then Brahma said: "The whole of this world belongs to Lord Vishnu. He has incarnated himself as sage Kapila to kill the sons of Sagara and is now in the nether-world bearing this world. In the fire of his anger the Sagara putras will be burnt to death". On hearing this all of them came back. The Sagaraputras returned to their father when they could not find the horse. But Sagara ordered "Go and dig again till you find it". They went to the netherworld. After circling the eight elephants that carry the world they dropped down to the nether world through the north-east corner of the earth. There they saw sage Kapila engaged in penance and the sacrificial horse grazing by his side. The sons of Sagara made a great hubbub there and Kapila produced a big sound of rebuke and stared at them. All the sixty thousand sons of Sagara were reduced to ashes. **(Sargas 39 and 40. Balakanda-Valmlki Ramayana)** .Kapila made the renowned Kapila shastras sitting in his Asrama and taught it to his mother Devahuti. Kapila was a great yogin. The yoga Sastrais based on the Sarikhya philosophy of Kapila. His Sarikhya Shastras, known as Kapila Shastras also, contains the distinctive yoga of meditation and it creates in you spiritual knowledge removing your ignorance totally. After teaching his mother his 'Kapila' he went to the Asrama of Pulaha and lived there. **(8th Skandha, Devi Bhagavata) .**

8) DATTATREYA

Anusuya, the wife of hermit Atri gave birth to Dattatreya. But Dattatreya was the incarnation of Maha Lord Vishnu. There is a story in Brahmanda Purana how Maha Lord Vishnu came to incarnate as Dattatreya. Once there was a hermit called Animandavya (Mandavya).While the hermit was engaged in silent meditation, some robbers passed by that way. The King's men, who were chasing the robbers, came to the hermit and asked him about the robbers. The hermit did not break the silence. The King's men, thinking the hermit to be the thief bound his hands and legs and took him to the palace. The King ordered Mandavya to be killed by piercing his body with a trident. Accordingly a trident was posted on a hill far away and Mandavya was seated

Dattatreya is known by the name 'Datta' also in the Puranas on the tip of it. Mandavya lay there in agony. It was at this time that Sllavati, famous for her conjugal fidelity, went to the house of a harlot, carrying her husband Ugrasravas on her shoulder. When they passed by that way Ugrasravas scolded Animandavya; getting angry at this Animandavya cursed Ugrasravas that he would get his head broken and die before the sun-rise. Sllavati became very sorry when she heard the curse and she also cursed. "Let the sun not rise tomorrow". The sun did not rise next day. Everything in the world was in chaos. The Devtas were flurried. They went to Brahma. Brahma took them to Siva. They could not find a solution. So, all of them approached Maha Lord Vishnu. The Trimurtis (three gods) told the Devtas that the problem would be solved, and the Devtas returned. Brahma, Lord Vishnu and Mahewara went to Sllavati. Before seeing Sllavati, they went to Anusuya the wife of Atri and sought her help to persuade Sllavati to recall her curse. Thus Anasuya and the Trimurtis approached Sllavati and spoke compassionate and consolatory words. At last, Sllavati recalled the curse. The Trimurtis convinced Sllavati, that Ugrasravas would not die. The pleased Trimurtis asked Anusuya to ask for any boon. She replied that she did not want any boon except that the Trimurtis should take birth as her sons. Accordingly Maha Lord Vishnu took birth as Dattatreya, Siva as Durvasas and Brahma as Candra, in the womb of Anusuya. This is how Dattatreya was born. Dattatreya did penance from his childhood and became a hermit. **(Brahmanda Purana, Chapters 39 to 44).**

When Kartaviryarjuna became King Dattatreya had become very famous. Kartaviryarjuna wanted to obtain supernatural powers. So he called the hermit Garga and asked for his advice. Garga advised him that Dattatreya was the incarnation of Lord Vishnu and that he would grant his wishes. So Kartaviryarjuna and his wife came to the river Narmada, and taking bath in the river, began to worship Dattatreya, who was doing penance close by. Dattatreyawas pleased and went to Kartaviryarjuna and asked him what his desire was. He requested for thousand hands and to be a youth forever, and such other things. Dattatreya granted his wishes. After that Kartaviryarjuna would very often go to the hermit Dattatreya for his advice. **(Brahma Purana, (Chapter 44).**

Once Ravana went to the hermitage of Dattatreya. The hermit had placed a water pot purified by reciting spells and incantations. Ravana stole that water pot. When the hermit came to knew this, he cursed Ravana saying, "Since the water, which was evoked by spells and incantations, has fallen on your head, Monkeys will pollute your head by treading omit." **(Valmlki Ramayana, Yuddha Kanda).**

9) YAJNA

An incarnation of Maha Lord Vishnu. Svayambhuva Manu had two sons, Priyavrata and Uttanapada and three daughters, Akuti, Devahuti and Prasuti. Ruci Prajapati married Akuti. Yajna was their son. **Devi Bhagavata, 8th Skandha** mentions that this Yajna wasan incarnation of Adi Narayana. Yajna got married to Daksina. The twelve sons who were born to them were the Devtas known as Yama's, during the Svayambhuva Manvantara. **(Lord Vishnu Purana, Part 1, Chapter 7).**Yajna's twelve sons were: Tosa, Pratosa, Santosa, Bhadra, Santi, Idaspati, Iddhma, Kavi, Vibhu, Sraghna,Sudeva and Virochana. Their father Yajna was the Indra of Svayambhuva Manvantara. **(Bhagavata, 4th Skandha).**

10) RSABHA

A muni (sage) who was the grandson of King Agnidhra and son of King Nabhi by his wife Merudevi.One. Hundred sons were born to Rsabha by his wife Jayanti. After entrusting his kingdom to Bharata, the eldest of his sons, Rsabha went to the forest and did tapas in Pulaha's ashrama. Pisabha and Rsabha did tapas in the forest for many years. The mountain peak on which he performed his tapas got the name "Rsabhakuta".The sage who wished to observe strict silence did not like the presence of strangers and visitors in the vicinity. So he pronounced a curse that the mountain should drop boulders on any one who ventured to come there. Once he ordered the wind to blow without noise as it passed by the side of the mountain. He declared that anyone who made noise in Rsabhakuta would be struck with thunder. A place of holy waters came into existence there. **(M.B. Aranya Parva, Chapter 11).**

Rsabha became a devotee of Siva by worshipping him. Once a Brahman named Mandara had an illicit alliance with Piiigala, a prostitute. Both of them died together. Mandara was re-born as Bhadrayu, the grandson of Nala and Pingala as Sumati, the wife of King Vajrabahu (Arhsuman, son) .Sumati became pregnant. Her co-wives who were jealous of her poisoned her. As a result of it, she and the child born to her fell victims to diseases. Dasharna abandoned them in the forest. Sumati lived in the house of a Vaisya with her child. While living there, the child died of disease. Rsabha went to the grief-stricken Sumati and comforted her. **(Siva Purana).** Rsabha performed tapas according to the rules of Vanaprastha ashrama and conducted yagasas ordained by Shastras. .On account of his austerity he became so lean and thin that all the veins in the body could be seen. Putting a pebble in his mouth, he went about in the forest, determined to renounce his body.**(Lord Vishnu Purana, Chapter 1, Section).**In the course of his wanderings in the forest a wild fire broke out in which his body was burnt up. Siva Purana says that the soul of Rsabha, who died in the wild fire, attained Siva Loka.

11) PRTHU

When Vena grandson of Yama was crowned king by the maharishis and he became the supreme lord of the world he announced to the world thus: "Yaga should not be performed; gifts should not be given; no kind of homa should be done. There is nobody but me to accept as Yajna purusa the share of yajna. I am the sole lord and consumer of yajna." The sages were dumbfounded. They all approached Vena and impressed upon him the necessity of performing a Yaga to propitiate Maha Lord Vishnu. Vena who got angry at this request of the sages told them thus:"There is nobody greater than I and I have none to be worshipped. Who is Hari, your Yajnesvara? (Lord of the yaga) .

All such great powers who can bless and curse alike and such eminent deities and entities like Brahma, -Lord Vishnu, Siva, Indra, Vayu, Yama, Varuna, Siirya, Agni, Dhata, Pusa, Bhumi and Candra are merged in me, the king. Do understand this fact and obey my orders."Despite repeated requests Vena did not give permission to conduct a Vaishnava yajna. The sages got angry and cried aloud "Kill this wicked man", "Kill this wicked man". Saying thus the sages killed Vena by Kusa grass .made sacred and powerful by mantras Vena, who was spiritually dead because of his contempt of the gods even before. Then the sages saw dust rising in columns from all sides and asked the people the cause of the same. The people said "When they knew that there was no king poor people have turned themselves into rogues and are plundering the wealth of the rich. The swift movements of these running in haste are raising dust from the ground below."

The rishis conferred together and to get a son from the dead Vena they churned the thigh of the wicked king. Then, from the thigh came out a short and black (as black as a burnt pillar) man with a compressed face, who stood before the sages in distress and asked "What am I to do?" The sages said

'Nisida' meaning 'sit down'. He thus became Nisadas (a forest dweller) . He went to the mountain of Vindhya and along with him went all the sins of Vena. Nisadas thereafter are said to be those who have destroyed the sins of Vena. Then the sages churned the right hand of Vena and from it came out a brilliant boy of great strength and power and he was named Prthu. At the time of his birth there dropped from heaven the divine bow Ajagava and many powerful arrows and divine armour. All animate objects of the world were happy at his birth. Vena attained Svarga for having delivered such a brilliant son. For the coronation of Prthu the oceans brought very many precious diamonds and the rivers holy water. Brahma along with Aiigirases came and crowned Prthu as the emperor. Brahma saw the line of Candra in his right hand and was, therefore, pleased to know that he was part of Maha Lord Vishnu. Thus Prthu, valiant and brilliant, was crowned their emperor by the virtuous people of Bharata. He united his people by his love for them. When he travelled through the ocean the water stood still and when he travelled on land the mountains gave way and his flag-pole was never obstructed anywhere.

After several years of benign rule Prthu became old. He then entrusted the affairs of the state to his son Vijitasva and left for penance with his wife Arccis. After doing severe penance for a long time he merged with Parabrahman. Arccis, who was all along serving her husband with devotion, ended her life by jumping into the funeral pyre of her husband following her husband like Lakshmi following Lord Vishnu.

12) MOHINI

Churning of the Milk Sea. After Lord Vishnu had vanished, the Devtas made a treaty with the Asuras and began to work for getting Amrtam. All of them joined together in bringing various kinds of medicinal herbs and after putting them in the Milk sea which was as clear as the cloudless sky, began to churn it, using Manthara Mountain as the churning staff and snake Vasuki as the rope. The party of Devtas was posted at the tail-end of Vasuki while the Asuras took their stand at the head. The Asuras became enervated by the fiery breath coming out of Vasuki's mouth. The clouds which were blown by that breath invigorated the Devtas.

Maha Lord Vishnu transformed himself into a tortoise, and sitting in the middle of the Milk Sea served as the foundation for the Manthara Mountain, the churning staff. Assuming another form, invisible both to Devtas and

Asuras, Maha Lord Vishnu pressed down the Manthara Mountain from above. While churning the Milk Sea like this, the first object that rose to the surface was Kamadhenu. Both Devtas and Asuras were strongly attracted towards Kamadhenu While all were standing spellbound, Varumdevi with her enchanting dreamy eyes next appeared on the surface. Parijatam was the third to appear.

Fourth, a group of Apsara women of marvellous beauty floated up. The Moon appeared as the fifth. Siva received the Moon. The venom which came out of the Milk Sea as the sixth item, was absorbed by Nagas. After that, arose Bhagavan Dhanwantari, dressed in pure white robes and carrying a Kamandala in his hand filled with Amrtam. All were delighted at this sight.

Next Maha Lakshmi made her appearance in all her glory with a lotus in her hand and seated in an open lotus flower. Gandharvas sang celestial songs in her presence ;Apsara women danced. For her bath, the Gariga River arrived there with her tributaries. The Milk Sea itself took on physical form and offered her a garland of ever fresh lotus flowers. Brahma bedecked her with ornaments. After that Laksmldevi, fully adorned in all her magnificent jewels, in the presence of all Devtas, joined the bosom of Maha Lord Vishnu.

The Asuras were displeased at it. They snatched the pot of Amrtam from Dhanwantari and fled away. With the loss of Amrtam, the Devtas were in a fix. They began to consider how the pot of Amrtam could be recovered. Accordingly, Maha Lord Vishnu transformed himself into a celestial virgin, Mohini, of extraordinary beauty.

She approached the Asuras as a shy girl. The Asuras were enchanted by her surpassing beauty. They asked her, "Who are you?" Looking down on the ground, Mohini replied:"I am the younger sister of Dhanwantari. By the time, I came out of the Milk Sea, the Devtas and Asuras had already gone. Being lonely I am going about in search of a suitable mate."On hearing her words, the Asuras began to make friends with her one by one, determined not to waste this opportunity.

They told her that she should distribute Amrtam to all of them and in the end; she should marry one of them. Mohini agreed, but added: "All of you should close your eyes. I shall serve Amrtam to all. He who opens his eyes last, must serve Amrtam to me and he will marry me". All of them accepted this condition. They sat in front of Mohini with closed eyes. In a moment Mohini left the place with the pot of Amrtam and went to Devaloka.

When the Asuras opened their eyes, Mohini was not to be seen. Finding that they were betrayed, they were in great perplexity. All of them pursued Mohini to Devaloka. Devtas had put the Sun and Moon gods on guard duty at the gates of Devaloka. At the instance of the Asuras, Rahu in disguise entered the divine assembly chamber. The, Sun and Moon gods detected him and Lord Vishnu with his weapon, Sudarshana cut open his neck. Swearing that he would wreak vengeance on the Sun and Moon, Rahu returned. In the 8th Skandha of Bhagavata it is said that even now from time-to-time Rahu swallows the Sun and Moon, but they escape through the open gash in his neck and this is known as solar eclipse and lunar eclipse. Indra and all other gods took Amrtam.

The enraged Asuras attacked the gods, who had gained strength and vigour by taking Amrtam. The Asuras were driven away in all directions. All the three worlds began to enjoy glory and prosperity again.

13) GARUDA (EAGLE)

Garuda is an avatar of Sankarshana, a form of Vishnu, and is endowed with extraordinary powers through the grace and penance of his father Sage Kashyapa. It is held that Garuda earned the privilege of eternal service to the Lord through his devotion, humility and his prowess. Kashyapa had two wives, Vinata and Kadru. Garuda's mother Vinata had lost a bet with Kadru, and had to become her slave.

Garuda was irked by this slavery and he was promised freedom by Kadru and her serpent sons if he got them the celestial nectar. Garuda braved all dangers and hurdles and secured the nectar while Indra and his celestial coevals were mere helpless spectators. Even the Vajrayudha was powerless against Garuda. Indra hit with the Vajra (his special weapon) the wings of Garuda who was returning from Lord Vishnu. It did not wound his body, but a feather of his fell in the atmosphere. Everybody who saw the feather acclaimed Garuda as Suparna (he with the good wings) .

Indra was wonder-struck, and he approached Garuda and requested that they should be friends in future and the pot of nectar be returned. Garuda replied that the nectar would be returned if he was granted the power to make Nagas his food, and Indra blessed him that he would live by consuming Nagas.

And then Garuda told Indra thus: "I took this pot of amrita not for my own use. The Nagas cheated my mother and made her a slave, and she will be freed if only this pot of nectar is given to them (Nagas). You may snatch off the pot from the nagas; I shall not object to it." Indra and Garuda thus became friends and the former followed Garuda on his way back home. Garuda handed over the pot of amrita to- the Nagas and Indra cheated them of it. Garuda handed over the pot of nectar to the Nagas, who on the suggestion of the former placed the pot on durbha grass spread on the ground.

Also, in accordance with Garuda's advice that they should take a purificatory bath before tasting the amrita the nagas went out to have the bath, and in their absence, Indra carried off the pot of nectar back to Devaloka. Failing to find the pot of nectar on their return from bath the aggrieved Nagas licked the durbha on which the pot was placed with the result that their tongues were cloven into two. It was from that day onwards that the Nagas became double-tongued (dvijihvas). And, thus Garuda redeemed his mother from slavery. **(Adi Parva, Chapter 34).** Commending Garuda for his extraordinary act, Vishnu offered him a boon. Garuda sought surrender at His feet as well as the honour of being the emblem of the Lord's flag. Granting this wish, Vishnu conferred immortality on him and in addition requested him to be his vahana to which Garuda willingly agreed.

14) DHANWANTARI

The Devtas and Asuras together churned the ocean, *ksheerabdi,* to salvage Amrta (Nectar) from it. After thousand years there arose from the ocean a deva with a Kamandala (water-pot of ascetics) in one hand and a danda in the other. That deva was Dhanwantari, **(Sloka 31, Sarga 45, Bala Kanda, and Valmlki Ramayana).** Further, the birth of Dhanwantari from the ocean of Milk is described in **Chapter 29 of Harivamsathus:** Prosperous-looking Dhanwantari rising above the water level of Kslrabdhi stood worshipping Maha Lord Vishnu. Lord Vishnu gave him the name of Abja. Dhanwantari is thus known by the name of Abja also. Dhanwantari bowing to Lord Vishnu said "Prabhu, I am your son. Allot to me yajna bhaga".

Vishnu replied thus: "Portions of yajna have already been allotted. Because you were born after the Devtas you cannot be considered as one among them. You will be born again in the world for a second time and then you will be a celebrity. In your second life even from while in the womb you will have knowledge of Anima and Garima. Therefore, you will be born as a deva incarnate. You will write in eight divisions a book on Ayurveda; your second life will be in Dvapara Yuga."After having said so much Lord Vishnu disappeared.

Suhotra, King of Kasi, in the second Dvapara Yuga had two sons, Sala and Grtsamada.

Sunaka was the son of Grtsamada. Sala got a son, Arstisena. Kasa was born to Arstisena. To Kasa was born Dirgha tapas (Dhanva). For a long time, Dhanva did not have any children and so he went and did penance to propitiate Abja deva. Abja deva (Dhanwantari) was pleased and was born as a son to Dhanva. Dhanva named the boy as Dhanwantari and the latter taught his disciples Ayurveda, by parts, eight in number. From Dhanwantari in order were born Ketuman Bhlmaratha Divodasa. **(Chapter 29, Harivarsha)** .

He appears in the Vedas and Puranas as the physician of the Devtas. Lord Dhanwantari is believed as the God of Ayurveda. It is common practice in Hinduism to worship Lord Dhanwantari and seeking his blessings for sound health. Dhanwantari was one of the ancient medical advisers in India. It's believed that the first surgery was made by him. His treatments were perfectly natural. He used herbs and natural medicines for curing diseases.

He could even find out the medicinal purposes of turmeric, salt and such many commonly used things. He used turmeric as an antiseptic, salt as a preservative. He is also believed to be the pioneer of modern medical practices. Dhanwantari is depicted as Vishnu with four hands, holding medical herbs in one hand and a pot containing of 'amrita' in another. Birth day of Lord Dhanwantari is celebrated every year which is two days before Diwali popularly known as Dhanteras.

15) VYASA

Vyasa was born to hermit Parashara by a fisher woman named Kali. His name when he was a child was Krsna. As his birth took place in an island (Dvlpa) he got the name Krsnadvaipayana. After dividing the Vedas he got the name Vedavyasa. He is the composer of Mahabharata, one of the greatest books in world literature. The births of great men, generally will be wonderful. Behind the birth of Vyasa also there is a wonderful story.

When king Vasu of Cedi went to the forest for hunting, he saw the coition of animals and he had seminal discharge. The king sent that semen to his queen. But on the way it fell in the river Kalindi and was eaten by a fish. This fish was a celestial maid named Adrika transformed to fish by a curse.

The fish conceived and got into the net of a fisherman, who lived on the banks of Kalindi. When this fish was cut open a male and a female infant were seen inside. The male child was given to the kin? Himself. The fisher man brought up the girl naming her Kali. As the girl had the gandha (smell) of Matsya (fish) , she got the name 'Matsya-gandha', also. This fisherman was also a ferry man. Kali used to help her father in ferrying people across the river Kalindi. She grew up and became a young woman.

Once, the hermit Parashara came by that way to go to the other side of the river. At that time, the fisher man who has been taking people across the river, was sitting on the bank of the river and having his meals. As soon as Parashara came, the innocent fisherman the foster father of Matsyagandha called her, who was standing close by and asked her to take the hermit across the river.

The hermit got into the boat. Matsyagandha began to row the boat. The beauty of the damsel sitting in front of him and the little waves of the river, combined together had the effect of arousing passion in the hermit. He became sexually excited and sat close to her. Discerning his intention she moved away from him and prayed to him humbly not to violate her chastity. She repeated her prayer.

The hermit Parashara created an artificial fog around the boat. The smell of fish was gone from her and the fragrance of Musk took its place. The hermit created an artificial island in the middle of the river. They got down on the island arid acted a love drama. She became pregnant. Parashara said to her."Beautiful girl! Even after your confinement you shall remain a virgin. A son, who will be a portion of Lord Vishnu, a man of purity, famous throughout the three worlds, highly learned, the teacher-priest of the whole world, shall be born to you.

He will divide the Vedas and will be exalted by the people of the world."After this the great hermit took his bath in Yamuna and went away. The pregnancy of Kali was completed instantly and she gave birth to a very handsome boy in that island of Yamuna. As soon as he was born, he grew up and became a hermit radiant with devotion and as suminga vow of purity and abstinence he said to his mother. "Mother! You can go anywhere, as you please. You need have no worry on my account. I am about tog o for penance. When anything unpleasant happens to you, just think of me. The moment you wish to see me, I will be there by you. I wish you a happy life. I am going." Saying thus the brave boy walked away. **(Devi Bhagavata, Skandha 2; Mahabharata, Adi Parva, Chapters 60 to 63)**

16) BUDDHA

The founder of Buddhism was also an incarnation of Lord Vishnu. In days of old in a battle the Devtas were defeated by the Asuras and the gods approached Lord Vishnu with their grievance. Maha Lord Vishnu incarnated as the son of Suddhodana with the name Gautama Buddha (Siddhartha). Then lay went to the Asuras and made them reject the Vedas and the laws thereof. All the Daityas (Asuras) became Buddhists. There is a story in Agni Purana, Chapter 16, that thus it was the purpose of Buddha to convert every Asura to Buddhism and send him to hell.

The story given above is in accordance with the Puranas. The following are the facts gained by historic investigations. Gautama Buddha was born in B.C. 560, in Kapilavastu near the Himalayas. His father was Suddhodana. He was born in the family of the Sakyas. The word 'Sakyas' is another form of the word Ksatriyas.

The real name of Buddha was Siddhartha. Suddhodana brought up his son in such a way that he should not be subjected to any sort of mental pain or worry. So he kept Buddha aloof from the outer world. Thus he spent his childhood in comfort and pleasure. Once by chance he happened to see a sick man, an old man and a dead body. The sight made him thoughtful. He began to think upon a way to remove sorrow and pain from the world and to bring about peace and comfort. The change that appeared in the son worried the father. So at the age of sixteen he made Siddhartha marry Yasodhara.

A son was born to them. But the mind of Siddhartha was restless, distressed and agitated. One day Siddhartha discarded everything and went out of the palace alone. Siddhartha wandered from place to place learning from various teachers. But he did not find peace. Once on a full-moon day while he was sitting in meditation under a banian tree he got 'Buddha'. (Insight or conviction). From that day onwards he began to be known by the name 'Buddha'. After that he came to Kasi, and told his disciples how he got Buddha or conviction. The number of his followers increased day by day.

Thus Buddhism came into being. Buddha said that the reason for pain and sorrow in the world was desire and that sorrow could be exterminated only by controlling and overcoming all desire. To attain Eternal Bliss one should be true and righteous in thought, deed and word and that 'Not Killing' was the foundation of righteousness. Buddhism spread everywhere in Bharata. Gautama Buddha died at the age of eighty.

INCARNIATION SUMMARILY

In the first Skandha of "Bhagavata Kilippattu" the incarnations are summarily dealt in a manner ''And after that to make it possible for the Lord with four faces to rule his subjects justly and well. He took various incarnations with his portions, the first four of which are four persons, Sanaka, Sananda, Sanatana and Sanatkumara, in the order given, four or five-year old children, well-versed in the four Vedas, the four always inseparable wandered everywhere come to the world to show the merits of Bramhcharya (the vow of celibacy). To kill Hiranyaksa and to lift up the earth He took the form of Sukra (Pig). To show the world the tattva (essence) of Sat (good) and tama (darkness). He took the form of hermit Narada. To show the merits of penance He became Nara and Narayana. To impart to the world the meaning of Sarikhya Yoga (Indian Philosophy dealing with evolution and union with the

Supreme Spirit) He came as Kapila the learned. To teach the world the laws of chastisement, he was born as Datta of the wife of Atri. Then He came as Yajna to become Indra. The next incarnation He took was Rsabha, the noble King. To shorten and flatten the earth He came as Prthu. To recover the Vedas he took the form of Matsya (fish). To remove wrinkles and grey hair the gods had churned the sea of Milk and then to lift the mount Mandara He went under it and as a bird He got up on it. To give the world Ayurveda (the scripture of medicine) He came as Dhanwantari. To entice Asuras and to recover Ambrosia from them He took the form of Mohini. To save the devoted Prahlada and to slay his father He came in the form of Narasirmha. Then as Vamana the younger brother of Indra to deceive Mahabali and to recover the lost worlds for thc gods he came. To destroy the Kings who were haters of Brahmins He came as the son of Jamadagni. Then he took the incarnation of Veda Vyasa. And to slay the giant Ravana He became Sri Rama. Next, we see Him as Balabhadrarama. Then He came as Devaklsuta [son of Devaki (Krsna)]. Next, He came in the Kaliyuga as Sri Buddha and at the end of Kali-yuga He will come as Kalki.

CHAPTER FORTY-TWO

KUND & LAKES

There is a Parashurama Kund in Lohit district of Arunachal Pradesh which is dedicated to the sage Parashurama. Thousands of pilgrims visit the place in winter every year, especially on the Makar Sankranti day for a holy dip in the sacred kund which is believed to wash away one's sins.

This Kund dedicated to Parashurama is situated on the Brahmaputra plateau in the lower reaches of the Lohit River and 21 km north of Tezu in Lohit district of Arunachal Pradesh, India. This popular site attracts pilgrims from Nepal, from across India, and from nearby states of Manipur and Assam.

It is a shrine of all-India importance located in the lower reaches of the Lohit River. Lacs of devotees and sadhus take a holy dip in its water each year on the occasion of Makar Sankranti, in the month of January especially on the Makar Sankranti day for a holy dip in the sacred kund which is believed to wash away one's sins. There is a mythological story behind this beautiful place as told by the local people. It is believed that Lord Parashurama on the orders of his father Rishi Jamadagni beheaded his mother Renuka with his axe. Since he had committed one of the worst crimes of killing one's mother, the axe got stuck to his hand. His father pleased with his obedience decided to give him a boon to which he asked for his mother to be restored back to life. Even after his mother was brought back to life the axe could not be removed from his hand.

This was a reminder of the heinous crime he had committed. He repented for his crime and on taking the advice of eminent rishis of that time; he arrived at the banks of Lohit River to wash his hands in its pure waters. It was a way to cleanse him of all the sins. As soon as he dipped his hands into the waters the axe immediately got detached and since then the site where he washed his hands became a place of worship and came to be known by sadhus as Parashurama Kund. Also there are many stories varying from region to region in India that describe the above incident and there are numerous temples dedicated to Lord Parashurama most of which are in Kerala. But this place attracts many pilgrims from near and far and quite a few sanyasis reside here and take care of the temple that is dedicated to Lord Parashurama. The site of the Parashurama Kund as established by the sadhus was in existence until the 1950 Assam earthquake that shook the whole of the North-East and the kund was completely covered. A very strong current is now flowing over the original site of the kund but massive boulders have in a mysterious way embedded themselves in a circular formation in the river bed thus forming another kund in place of the old.

BHRIGU LAKE

Bhrigu Lake: located in Kullu district of Himachal Pradesh, it is named after Maharishi Bhrigu. It is said that a saint named Maharishi Bhrigu used to meditate here and be made this water sacred as the water in the lake never fully freezes even in freezing temperatures.

RENUKA LAKE AND PARASHURAMA TAL

Renuka Lake and Parashurama Tal are Located in Sirmour district of Himachal Pradesh, Renuka Lake is the largest lake in Himachal Pradesh. This lake is named after the goddess Renuka. It is said that Renuka jumped in this lake to protect herself from the lusty eye of a king named Sahasrarjun, who killed her husband Maharishi Jamadagni to get her. When her son Parashurama learnt about this incident, he marched towards the king's Kingdom and destroyed the whole race of Kshatriyas. It is considered a sacred place, people from around the country come here and pay their respects to Goddess Renuka and her Son Lord Parashurama (the sixth incarnation of Lord Vishnu).

Another story behind this beautiful lake is the reason this lake is named after Renuka Mata. Locals say that Bhagwati Renuka and her husband, Maharishi Jamadagni used to sit and meditate at a hilltop called Tape Ka Tibba. Lord Vishnu after being impressed by their dedication fulfilled a divine promise to take birth as their son, by the blessings of Lord Shiva. Their child was named Parshuram after the divine weapon Parshu. It is said that a Kshatriya king named Sahasrarjun killed Maharishi Jamadagni to kidnap Renuka; she jumped in the lake to protect herself from the lusty eyes of the King. As soon as she jumped inside the lake it took the shape of a lady, and since then the lake got its name Renuka Lake. Many Gods and Goddesses tried to bring her back, but she refused to come out. After hearing this news Parshuram exterminated the King in war and destroyed his whole race of Kshatriyas. It is also believed that after the war Parshuram gave his father Maharishi Jamadagni a new life with the divine powers vested in him. He went to the banks of the lake and prayed for his mother to come out of the lake but she denied. After many requests of Lord Parshuram, she promised that she would only come out on the occasion of Devprabodhini Ekadashi every year to meet her son. It is said that Parshuram did a "mahayagya" at a spot near Renuka Lake to save the masses from king Sahasrarjun. After the Yagya, the place was filled with the water from Renuka lake. Since then, the place is called Parshuram Tal. Till today on Dashmi, Lord Parshuram is brought to Renuka Ji on a Palki; from an ancient temple in Jamu Koti village in a traditional manner known as 'Shobha Yatra' to meet his mother Mata Renuka

EIGHT KSHETRA

Eight Kshetra are popularly known as Parashurama Kshetras or Parashurama Srishti:
1. Gokarna
2. Kollur
3. Konkan Maharashtra
4. Koteshwara
5. Mangalore
6. Shankaranarayana
7. Subramanya
8. Udupi

Let us pray to Parasurama, the incarnation of Maha Vishnu so that our enemities will ward off and have peaceful life through out.

KSHETRAS

Puranas write that the western coast of India was threatened by tumultuous waves and tempests, causing the land to be overcome by the sea. Parashurama fought back the advancing waters, demanding Varuna release the land of Konkan and Malabar. During their fight, Parashurama threw his axe into the sea. A mass of land rose up, but Varuna told him that because it was filled with salt, the land would be barren.

Parashurama then did tapas for Nagaraja, the King of Snakes. Parashurama asked him to spread serpents throughout the land so their venom would neutralize the salt filled earth. Nagaraja agreed, and a lush and fertile land grew. Thus, Parashurama pushed back the coastline between the foothills of the Western Ghats and the Arabian Sea, creating modern day Kerala.

The coastal area of Kerala, Konkan, Karnataka, Goa and Maharashtra, are today also known as Parashurama Ksetra or Land of Parashurama in homage. Puranas record that Parashurama placed statues of Shiva at 108 different locations throughout the reclaimed land, which still exist today Shiva, is the source of Kundalini, and it around his neck that Nagaraja is coiled, and so the statues were in gratitude for their baneful cleansing of the land

Then he took a winnowing basket, or Surpa, and threw it at the sea. The water retreated, and from the place the basket fell at Gokarna, land rose again Gokarna. This land is called Kerala, or 'Siirparaka' **(bramhandapurana , Chapters 98 and 99).** It is also said that while beating back the sea, Parashurama fired an arrow from his mythical bow that landed in Goa at Benaulim, creating Salkache Tollem, or 'Lotus Lake'

The ancient **Saptakonkana** is a slightly larger region described in the Sahyadrikhanda which refers to it as Parashurama Ksetra (Sanskrit for "the area of Parashurama"), Vapi to Tapi is an area of South Gujarat. The area blessed by Lord Parshuram and called "Parshuram nibhoomi". The region of Konkani is also considered as Parashurama Kshetra.

MAHURGAD

Mahurgadis one of the Shaktipeeth in Maharashtra's Nanded district, where a famous temple of Goddess Renuka exists. This temple at Mahurgad is always full of pilgrims. People also come to visit Lord Parashurama temple on the same Mahurgad.

In Karnataka, there are a group of 7 temples in the stretch of Tulunadu (coastal Karnataka), known as Parashurama Kshetras, namely, **Kollur, Koteshwara, KukkeSubrahmanya, Udupi, Gokarna, Anegudde (Kumbhasi) and Shankaranarayana.**

JAMNI IN JIND HARYANA

Jamni is a village in Safidon Tehsil of Jind district in Haryana. It is said to get name from Jamadagni who was Parashurama's father. It is believed that Jamni Safidon name has been originated from the name of Rishi Jamadagni and now is called Jamni. Rishi Jamadagni was Parashurama's father. Rishi Jamadagni is also one of the "Sapta Rishis" that we have. He lived and meditated in Jamni village for long time. Rishi Jamadagni received Kamadhenu as a gift in response to his penances.

RAMRAI IN JIND HARYANA

Ramraiis an ancient village in Jind tahsil and district in Haryana. Its ancient name was Ramahrada mentioned by Panini and in Mahabharata **(3.81.22)**, **(III.81.178)**. Panini mentions a village in category ending Harda **(IV.2.142)** - Ramahrada. The Mahabharata knows Ramahrada in Kurukshetra **(Aranyakaparva, 81.22)**. Ramrai or Ramahrada is a traditional south-west Yaksha of the Kurukshetra region. It is connected with the mythological story of Parasurama who after the annihilation of Kshatriyas, filled five pools with their blood and propitiated his forefathers there. It is believed that a bath at Ramahrada tirtha and Sanet tirtha is very holy. There is an old temple of Parsuram where he is worshipped. The Vamana Purana, a product of medieval period **(900-1700 AD)** dedicated to Thaneshwar, associated the ancient pilgrimage of **Ramahrada (3.81.22)**, identified with Village Ramray near Jind, with Parasurama who according to Mahabharata **(III,81,26f,117,9ff)**, filled the five tanks (Samantapanchaka) with the blood of Kshatriyas, annihilated 21 times by him. He is said to have performed the *tarpana* with their blood **(Adi Parva, 1,2,5)** in the lakes made by him **(Vana Parva, 81,22)**. These lakes made by him are said to have been full of blood like water.

SOPARA IN MAHARASHTRA

The Mahabharata and the Puranas state that the Śūrpāraka was reclaimed from the sea for the dwelling place of Parashurama and it became a tirtha for this reason. The finding of the relics in a stupa and the rock edicts of Ashoka in 1882 proves the importance of this port town from the 3rd century BCE to the 9th century CE.

Vana Parva, Mahabharata/Book III Chapter 83 mentions Surparaka in verse Mahabharata **(III.83.40)** one should proceed to Shurparaka, where Jamadagni son had formerly dwelt. Bathing in that tirtha of Rama, one acquires the merit of giving away gold in abundance. Yudhishthira plunged his body in all the holy spots, and then came again to Shurparaka (3:118).

Bathing in the Narmada as also in the tirtha known by the name of Shurparaka, observing a fast for a full fortnight, one is sure to become in one's next birth a prince of the royal line. (13:25).

The Ocean created for Jamadagni's son (Bhargava Rama), a region called Shurparaka (12:49). Having made the earth destitute of Kshatriyas for thrice seven times, the puissant Bhargava, at the completion of a horse-sacrifice, gave away the earth as sacrificial present unto Kashyapa. Kashyapa having accepted the earth in gift, and made a present of it unto the Brahmanas, entered the great forest. There is a different opinion on the subject which says that this gave rise to the myth of Parashurama, reclaiming the land from the sea. The people of Shurparaka brought this myth to Kerala where this myth still exists.

CHAPTER FORTY-FOUR

PARASURAMA TEMPLES

It is believed that Lord Shree Ram brought the North and South India together and Lord Shri Krishna connected the East and West India. However, thousands of years before them, Lord Parshuram brought the entire Indian subcontinent culturally together through his massive travels and enterprise. It was a phenomenal contribution towards national integration and nation building. His endeavors connected Himachal to

Kanyakumari and Arunachal and to Kashmir. The following is the record of the significant geographical locations found related to Lord Parashurama's life and work.

1. NIRMUND: A very important place from the interiors of Himachal. It is known by this name because it at this very place that Parshuram beheaded his mother Mata Renuka on the orders of his father. It is 200 km away from Shimla. The place is adorned by several temples. Even the ancient village of Nirmand – with the temples of Parsuram, Ambika

Devi, and Dakhani Mahadeva – is situated in the Satlej valley.In a village near the last mountain there is a Parashurama temple, located centrally. The temple is built with carved wood and follows the Kangra architecture style. The temple boasts of several sections like Sabha Mandap (Outer pandal), Antaral (Inner sanctum) and Garbhagriha (Innermost sanctum). The temple has a surrounding wall as well. The idol is made of platinum. It is believed to have been adorned by diamonds and other precious stones. However, it was stolen but found again. But now it was without the jewellery. The temple also has idols of Uma-Maheshwar and Shri Vishnu-Lakshmi.

A short distance away from the village is Lord Parashurama's palace. The structure is made of stone with a heavily carved wooden door. There is a separate space for Havan. Nearly 15000-20000 devotees arrive here for Parashurama Jayanti every year. The descendants of Parashurama's family stay on a hillock behind the temple. There is rope way to be used to cross the valley between. The Discovery Channel had made a documentary on the phenomenon in 2005.

There is annual fest every year at the time of Parshuram Jayanti on the third day in Vaishakh. (March-April) The month-long festival is visited by millions of devotees from Tibet, Bhutan, Nepal, China and India. People believe that if the funeral rites and rituals are performed in the place, the dead get immediate salvation.

2. RENUKA: This place is situated in the Sirmour District of Himachal Pradesh. There is a direct bus from Ambala and Chandigarh. Before we reach this place, there is a small village Kaurik which has a small temple of Lord Parashurama. On entering the Renukagiri Gram we can see a huge statue of Lord Parashurama welcoming everyone.

Renukagiri gram is situated on a saucer-like land, with Himalaya mountain range on all the sides. The Pradakshina route is approximately 6 km and goes through deep forests. On the way we can see Parashurama Taal (Lake), Renuka Mata idol, Renuka Taal, Dashavtar temple, Tapeka Teela(Lord Parashurama is believed to have meditated here), Sahastradhara and a sanctuary. There is a lake at the foot of the mountain where Renuka Mata gave up her life. The Dashavtar Garden has ten statues made.

3. PARSHURAM KUND: This pond is situated to the South western region in Arunachal Pradesh near the borders of Burma and China, in the basin of river Lohit. It is 20 km away from Tinsukhiya in north Asaam. It is said that after beheading Renuka Mata, the Parshu (the axe) of Parashurama stuck to his hand. Then he heard the divine orders to wash the Parshu in the waters of river Lohit to wash away the sins. Therefore Parashurama travelled to this place from Nirmund. Parashurama put the blood-stained Parshu in the river but still he could not get rid of it. So he struck it forcefully in the river basin. Then it got detached. But the force created the pond. It is further believed that there was an earthquake at that moment and it created a mountain of the shape of the axe near the pond.

The pond is huge with a diameter of 150 ft. The water of the pond became red because of the blood on the Parshu. The water is very deep. The original Parshuram temple near the pond is believed to have been destroyed by earthquakes and other natural events. Another temple is recently built in 1972. The temple celebrates a festival on the auspicious occasion of Makar Sankranti (in January) every year.

4. KURUKSHETRA: Kurukshetra in Haryana is a known as the battle field mentioned in Mahabharata where Kauravas fought the battle with Pandavas. There are five lakes in the region out of which Brahmasarovar has links with Lord Parshuram's life. It is properly built and is 2km long and 1km wide.

There is a huge, south facing statue of Parshuram in front of the lake. The idol has aggressive stance. There is a Parshuram Dharmashala (a place to stay for the devotees). On the east of the place there is another lake Sannihat lake with a recently built Parshuram temple.

5. JAMMU: Lord Parshuram is believed to have travelled in the region between Karakoram Pass and Arunachal. Therefore, there are several temples of Parshuram found in the region. On entering Jammu we see a huge Parshuram temple situated on a mountain.

6. JANAPAVA: This is the birthplace of Lord Parshuram in the Jamadagni's house situated in the river valley of Chambal. It is on a mountain. Janapava is 10 km from Mahu in Madhya Pradesh. It is known by the Jamadagni Ashram there. There is an ancient temple with an idol of Rishi Jamadagni. There is also another temple of Shri Parshuram. The idol is made in black stone. In spite of the five Jatras every year, the place was neglected so far by the tourists. However, the government of Madhya Pradesh gave it a status of a tourist place. And it has become a place of pilgrimage. There is a tourist lodge, ample parking space and a community hall.

The Parshuram temple is huge and has ivory idols of Rishi Jamadagni and Renuka Mata as well. The Janakeshwar Temple, Panchmukhi Maruti temple and Bhairavnath temple founded by Rishi Jamadagni are also situated in the premises. A pond by the name Brahma Kund is flocked by devotees attending the festivals on Maha Shivaratri, Parshuram Jayanti, Shravan Somvar , Sarvapitri Amavasya and Kartik Paurnima. This place is especially visited by tribals in the region.

7. UDAWAD GUFA MANDIR (UDAWAD CAVE TEMPLE): Udawad Temple is situated on a hillock in a cave near Sadadi village in Rajasthan. The cave is 20X20ft in size, so only 15-20 people can enter it at one time. This temple has an exceptional feature, i.e. it has Lord Parshuram as one god of the Panchayatan along with Ganesh, Kartikeya, Shiv and Parvati. Lord Parshuram here is in a meditative stance. The temple shows one demon killed by the gods.

The cave temple is 2000 ft. above sea level. It has all the amenities of lodging and boarding. People believe that a bath in the nearby Parshuram Kund cures skin dideases. The place can be reached by a direct bus from Udaypaur or by train up to Falana and by bus to Sadadi.

8. TRYAMBAKESHWAR: This well known pilgrim place near Nashik is one of the 12 Jyotirlingas. This place is also known as a place chosen by Lord Parshuram for meditation. There was an ancient temple of Parshuram. Presently, there is a temple 125 years old. The idol is made in Vaishnava style with four hands. There is an idol of Lord Narayana. The Stone tablets found at the place speak of the glory of the Emperor Satvahan. The temple is believed to be constructed at the time of Yagna performed by the Kings.

9. SHOORPARAK KSHETRA: The place known as Nalasopara, a port in Mumbai was known in ancient times as Shurparaka. Vimalasur, a demon was creating obstacles in the religious Yagna. So Lord Parshuram killed him and re-established the people there. Therefore it is known as Parshuram Kshetra as well. The idol is flanked by Kaal and Kama on both sides. There are separate temples of rishi Jamadagni and Renuka Mata in the premises. It is on the Mumbai-Surat railway route.

10. TIRUVANTANTPURAM: Near this capital city of Kerala, the two rivers Kalamanayar and Parvatipu meet making it a holy place. There is a Parshuram temple with a 6ft tall idol of Lord Parshuram. The temple is situated in deep forest. The wood crafted temple is in Keralaput style of architecture. The temple was renovated 300 years back. The inner sanctum is a hexagon. The temple has small temples of Shiva and Brahmadev. There are celebrations on Parshuram jayanti, Vaikunth Chaturdashi, all the Ekadashi days (11th Day of every fortnight) and Kartik Krishna Navami.

11. GUNJ- KATI GUNJ, MAHARASHTRA is one of the rare temples of Shree Parashurama where he is depicted as teenage boy as he was born here built by Pandavas on mountain.

12. GUDIMALLAM LINGAM, is an ancient temple from 2nd Century in the garbhagriha of the in the Parasurameswara Swamy Temple of Gudimallam, a small village near Tirupati city in the Yerpedu mandal of the Tirupati district of Andhra Pradesh, It is situated about 13 kilometers south-east of Tirupati city. Though Gudimallam is a small village, it is well known because it has a very early lingam that is unmistakably phallic in shape, with a full-length standing relief figure of Shiva carved on the front. This is, Hindu temple dedicated to Shiva. This is perhaps the second earliest lingam associated with Shiva discovered so far, and it has been dated to the 2nd/1st century BC, or the 3rd century BC, or much later, to the 2nd century AD, 3-4th century AD, or even, according to one source, as late as the 7th century AD.

13. KUMBHALGARH of Rajasthan is located in the Pali district of the state. This famous temple is dedicated to Lord Shiva or Mahadev. There is an ancient cave here which has to be reached down through the 500 stairs leading to the cave. The temple also offers an amazing view from the top of the Aravalli hills and gives you a small trekking experience while reaching the temple gates. This place is considered one of the best in Kumbhalgarh forest which is not only a religious spot but also has beautiful surroundings to offer to the visitors. You will also get to know many stories of the past related to this place from the priests of the temple including the various formations known as the Kamadhenu. In the temple you will also notice the Idol of Lord Ganesha and nine kund which never dry out and are considered pious and holy. You can also visit the Kumbhalgarh fort from here which is located near to the temple.It is believed that saint Parshuram who is said to be the sixth avatar of Lord Vishnu had built a cave with his axe and worshipped Lord Shiva in the foothills of the Aravalli Mountain. After this, the Parshuram temple was built on the top of the hills which we see even today.

14. KOLAR , It is the district head quarter in Karnataka State. Parashurama swamy temple is on M.B.Road. Kolar is 71kms from Bangalore and 185kms from Tirupati.

15. KUNJARUGIRI, It is a small village in Udupi district, Karnataka. Parashurama Temple is here. Kunjarugiri is just 11kms from Udipi.

16. ATTIRALA , It is a tourist place in Kadapa district, Andhra Pradesh State. Pagoda of Parashurama Temple is here. It was constructed in 6th century. Attirala is just 10kms from Rajampet, 65kms from Kadapa and 98 kms from Tirupati.

18. MUNDAJE, It is a small town at Belthagadi taluk in Uttara kannada district, Karnataka. Kere Parashurama Temple is here. Mundaje is 15 kms from Belthagadi, 75kms from Mangalore and 49kms from Mudigere.

19. NANJANGUD, It is the taluk town in Mysore district, Karnataka State. It is on the bank of river Kabini. Parasurama Temple is here. Nanjangud is 24kms from Mysore.

20. IRINJALKUDA , It is a town in Trissur district, Kerala. Ramapurath Parasurama Temple is here. Irinjalkuda is 25kms from Trichur (Trissur)

21. THIRUVALLAM, It is a temple village in Thiruvanthapuram district,

Kerala State. It is on the bank of river Karamana. Parasurama Temple is here. Thiruvallam is just 6kms from Thrivendrum and 6kms from Kovalam beach on Thiruvananthapuram road.

22. SOMANATH, It is a temple town in Junagadh district, Gujarat State. It is on the bank of Arabian Sea. It is also one of the 12 Jyothirlinga Kshetras. Parasuramji Temple is here near Triveni Ghat. Somanath is 410 kms from Ahemdabad and 235kms from Dwarka.

23. PADUBELLE , It is a small village in Udupi district, Karnataka. State. Parashu Kshetra Temple is here. Padubelle is just 12kms away from Udupi.

24. JALALABAD, It is a small town in Shajahanpur district of Uttar Pradesh State. According to Indian Mythothology this is the birth place of Lord Parasurama. Parasurama Temple is here. It was constructed in early ages. Jalalabad is 35kms from Shahjahanpur.

25. GHAZIPUR UP, Parashurama Temple is located at Yamdagnipuri Harpur Zamania . This is an Octagonal Temple: Jamaniya famous as the birthplace of Lord Parashurama. Jamaniya is famous as the Tapasthali of Maharishi Jamadagni and the birthplace of Lord Parshuram. The temple of Lord Parashurama is situated on the NH 24 side in Harpur of the municipality. It is believed that 250 years ago, the then king of Sakaldiha Kot, Vats Singh had consecrated the idol of Lord Parashurama with full religious rituals. Since then, people from rural areas including cities and other states including UP, Bihar, MP reach here for worship. It is a legend that King Vats used to come to his place due to being in the princely state of Zamaniya. One day Lord Parashurama came in a dream and told him that there is my idol in the middle of the Ganges in front of my father Jamadagni 's ashram, get it removed and install it at a distance of 360 bows, so that the area can be well-being. In the morning, the king immediately got the fishermen's statue removed. After this, the king measured the distance of 360 bows, then Harpur fell in the municipality area, where the king established the idol of Lord Parashurama with rituals and built a temple. The temple is unique in many respects as it is octagonal and Panchayat. It was King Vats who consecrated the idol of Lord Ganesha in the east corner of the temple, Lord Surya Narayana in the west corner, Lord Shankar in the north-east corner along with Maa Bhagwati in the north. The idol of

Lord Parashurama is seated in the midst of these four deities. Further , The temple of Yamdagni Rishi, the father of Lord Parshuram, is situated on the Balua Ghat of the municipality, where regular people worship. It is believed that Mother Ganga became Uttar Vahini for the darshan of Jamadagni Rishi; even today Mother Ganga flows from the side of Jamadagni Rishi's ashram. When the vow is fulfilled, people perform rituals and worship by reciting Ramayana and Kirtan

26. GOKARNA AND KANYAKUMARI , Lord Parshuram also created the land connecting Gokarna and Kanyakumari. Lord Parshuram the sixth avatar of Lord Vishnu was the son of Sage Jamadagni and Renuka. As a mark of remorse for Kshatriya Nigraha sin, Parshuram meditated at Gokarna and invoked Lord Varuna (the Lord of the Oceans). Parshuram asked him for a boon. To pardon himself of the sins he had did, he wanted to contribute some land to the Brahmins. There was no land available because he already donated the whole land he obtained by the 21 round Kshatriya Nigraha to Sage Kashyapa. Lord Varuna told Bhagvan Parashurama that he would give him as much land as he wish. He told him to toss his Parasu (axe) from where he stood at Gokarna. The land from Gokarna till the point where the axe land would be given to him was the benefit that Lord Varuna promised him. The throw of the `axe' from Gokarna to Kanyakumari created Kerala. Parashurama contributed this land to the Brahmins and established Brahmins there in 64 gramams or villages. 32 out of the 64 gramams are in the Tulu speaking district (in between Gokarnam and Perumpuzha) and the remaining 32 grammas are in the Malayalam speaking region (in between Perumpuzha and Kanyakumari) in Kerala. Those in Kerala scheduled in the Keralopatti, the tale of Kerala history are

1. Payyannoor
2. Perumchelloor (Talipparambu)
3. Alatthiyoor
4. Karanthol
5. Chokiram (Shukapuram)
6. Panniyoor
7. Karikkau
8. Isaanamangalam
9. Thrussivaperoor
10. Pcruvanam.

11. Chamunda (Chemmanta)
12. Irungatikkootal (Iringalakkuda)
13. Avattiputhur (Avittathoor)
14. Paravoor
15. Airanikkulam
16. Muzhikkalam
17. Kuzhavur
18. Atavur
19. Chenganatu(Chengamanadu)
20. Ilibhyam
21. Uliyannoor
22. Kalutanatu.
23. Ettumanoor
24. Kumaranalloor
25. Kadamuri
26. Aranmula
27. Tiruvalla
28. Kidangoor
29. Chengannoor
30. Kaviyoor
31. Venmani and
32. Neermanna (Niranam)

After the formation of these gramams, Parshuram had sanctified 108 Shiva temples and 108 Durga temples for the happiness and affluence of the people in Kerala. Among these 216 temples, the Lord Shiva of Gokarnam Mahabaleswara Temple in the north and Goddess Kumari of Kanyakumari temple in the south were measured as the protectors of Kerala. The first Shivalaya created by Parshuram was the Thrissivaperoor Vadakkunnathan Temple and the last one was the Thrikkariyoor Mahadeva Temple.

The names of these temples were given in the eminent 108 Shivalaya Nama Stothra. This stothra is written in Malayalam and is unidentified. There are many temples with the same place names. Also some old names do not exist as their names have changed. So in this list you can find more than 110 Shiva temples in Kerala. It is clear that this stothra was written in Thrissur area of Kerala because 64 temples were located in this region(9 in Palakkad district, 43 in Thrissur district and 12 in Ernakulam district.

District wise distribution of rest of the temples are – 4 in Thiruvanathapuram, 5 in Kollam, 3 in Pathanamthitta, 6 in Alappuzha, 11 in Kottayam, 1 in Idukki, 7 in Malappuram, 4 in Kozhikkode, 1 in Vayanad and 5 in Kannur. Now 2 temples are in Karnataka and one is in Tamil Nadu.

It is believed that Sri Parasurama created the land referred Kerala which is between Gokarna and Kanyakumari. Parasurama had constructed 108 Siva temples and 108 Durga temples for the well-being and prosperity of the people in Kerala . Among these 216 temples, the Lord Shiva of Gokarnam Mahabaleswara Temple in the north and Goddess Kumari of Kanyakumari temple in the south were considered as the protectors of Kerala. The first Durgalaya created by Parasurama was the Kanyakumari Devi Temple and the last one was the Kumaranalloor Devi Temple. The names of these temples were given in the famous 108 Durgalaya Nama Stothra.

LIST OF 108 DURGA TEMPLES IN KERALA http://www.vaikhari.org)

- 1. Aattur Karthiayani,Thrissur
- 2. Ayroor Pisharikkal Durga,Ernakulam
- 3. Aykunnu Durga ,
- 4. Ayyanthole Karthiyani ,Thrissur
- 5. Anthikadu Karthyani,Thrissur
- 6. Avanamgattu Bhagavathy,-
- 7. Azhagam Devi,Thrissur
- 8. Azhiyur ,-
- 9. Bhakthisala ,-
- 10. Chathannur ,-
- 11. Chembukkavu Karthiayani,Thrissur
- 12. Chengalathukavu Devi,Kottayam
- 13. Chenganam Kunnu Bhagavathy,
- 14. Chengannur ,
- 15. Cheranallur Bhagavathy,Ernakulam
- 16. Cherpu Bhagavathy ,Thrissur
- 17. Cherthala Karthiayani,Ernakulam
- 18. Cherukunnu Anapoorneswari,Kannur
- 19. Chittanda Karthiyani ,Thrissur
- 20. Chottanikkara Rajarajeswari,Ernakulam
- 21. Choorakodu Bhagavathy, Thrissur
- 22. Edakkunni Durga, Thrissur

- 23. Edappaly,
- 24. Edanadu Durga ,
- 25. Edayannur,
- 26. Elampara,
- 27. Ingayur,
- 28. Iringolam,
- 29. Kadalayil,
- 30. Kadalundi,
- 31. Kadamberi Chuzhali Bhagavathy,
- 32. Kadampuzha Bhagavathy,Malappuram
- 33. Kadapuru,
- 34. Kamakshi,
- 35. Kannannur Bhagavathy,
- 36. Kanyakumari,
- 37. Karamukku Bhagavathy,
- 38. Karayil ,
- 39. Karumapuram ,
- 40. Karuvalayam ,
- 41. Kaveedu Bhagavathy,Thrissur
- 42. Katalum ,
- 43. Kattur Durga,
- 44. Kavidu Bhagavathy ,
- 45. Kidangethu ,
- 46. Kezhadoor Durga ,
- 47. Kizhakkanikadu ,
- 48. Korattikadu Bhuvaneswari ,
- 49. Kothakulangara Bhagavathy,Ernakulam
- 50. Kulambu ,
- 51. Kumaranalloor Devi,
- 52. Kuringarchira ,
- 53. Kurinjikavu Durga ,Kottayam
- 54. Kuttanelloor Bhagavathy ,
- 55. Maangatur ,
- 56. Maavattur ,
- 57. Madipetta Bhagavathy,
- 58. Mangala Devi,Idukki
- 59. Manikyamangalam Karthiayani,Ernakulam
- 60. Maravancheri ,

- 61. Maruthur Karthiyayani,Thrissur
- 62. Mezhakunnathu ,
- 63. Mookambika Saraswati ,
- 64. Mukkola Bhagavathy,
- 65. Nellur Bhagavathy,
- 66. Nelluvayil Bhagavathy,
- 67. Njangattiri Bhagavathy ,
- 68. Palarivattom Devi,Ernakulam
- 69. Panniyamkara Durga ,
- 70. Panthallur Bhagavathy ,
- 71. Pathiyoor Durga ,
- 72. Pechengannur ,
- 73. Perurkkavu Durga ,
- 74. Peradoor Durga,Ernakulam
- 75. Pisharikal ,
- 76. Pothannur Durga ,
- 77. Punnariyamma ,
- 78. Puthukodu Annapoorneswari,Thrissur
- 79. Puthur Durga, Thrissur
- 80. Poovathussery Durga ,
- 81. Runanarayanam ,
- 82. Saala Bhagavathy,
- 83. Sirasil Devi ,
- 84. Thaikkattusery Durga ,
- 85. Thathapalli Durga ,
- 86. Thechikkottukavu Durga ,
- 87. Thevalakode ,
- 88. Thirukkulam ,
- 89. Thiruvallathur ,
- 90. Thottappaly ,
- 91. Thozhuvannur Bhagavathy ,
- 92. Thrichambaram Bhagavathy ,
- 93. Thrikkanikadu Bhagavathy ,
- 94. Thrikkavu Durga,Malappuram
- 95. Thriplery Bhagavathy ,
- 96. Uliyannur Devi ,
- 97. Unnannur Devi ,
- 98. Urakathamma Thiruvadi,Thrissur

- 99. Uzhalur ,
- 100. Vallotikkunnu Durga ,
- 101. Vallur Durga,
- 102. Varakkal Durga,Calicut
- 103. Vayalpuram ,
- 104. Veliyamkode ,
- 105. Veliyennur Bhagavathy,Thrissur
- 106. Vellathattu Bhagavathy ,
- 107. Vellikunnu Bhagavathy ,
- 108. Vengoor Durga,Ernakulam
- 109. Vilakodi Devi ,
- 110. Vilappa Devi,
- 111. Virangattur Devi ,

108 SHIVA TEMPLES WORSHIPED BY PARSHURAM IN KERALA

SHIVALAYA NAMA STOTHRA (templepurohit.com)

- 1. Dakshina Kailasam Thrissivaperoor Vadakkunnathan Temple
- 2. Udayamperoor Ekadasi Perumthrikkovil Mahadeva Temple/ Peroor Kaipayil Shiva Temple
- 3. Raveeswarapuram Temple Kodungalloor/ Iraveeswaram Mahadeva Temple Kudamaloor
- 4. Sucheendram Sthanumalaya Perumal Temple
- 5. Chowara Chidmbareswara Temple
- 6. Mathoor Shiva Temples
- 7. Trippangott Shiva Temple
- 8. Mundayoor or Mundoor Shiva Temple
- 9. Thirumandhamkunnu Mahadeva Temple
- 10. Chowalloor Shiva Temple
- 11. Panancheri Mudikkode Shiva Temple
- 12.Koratty Annamanada Mahadeva Temple/ Thrukkoratty Mahadeva Temple
- 13. Puramundekkat Mahadeva Temple

- 14. Avanoor Sreekandeswaram Mahadeva Temple
- 15. Kolloor Mookambika Temple
- 16. Thirumangalam Mahadeva Temple
- 17. Thrikkariyoor Mahadeva Temple
- 18. Kunnathu Mahadeva Temple
- 19. Velloor Perunthatta Mahadeva Temple
- 20. Ashtamangalam Mahadeva Temple
- 21. Iranikkulam Mahadeva Temple
- 22. Kainoor Mahadeva Temple
- 23. Gokarnam Mahabaleswara Temple
- 24. Ernakulam Mahadeva Temple
- 25. Pazhoor Perumthrikkovil Mahadeva Temple
- 26. Adattu Mahadeva Temple
- 27. Parippu Mahadeva Temple
- 28. Sasthamangalam Mahadeva Temple
- 29. Perumparambu Mahadeva Temple
- 30. Trukkoor Mahadeva Temple
- 31. Panayoor Paloor Mahadeva Temple
- 32. Vytila Nettoor Mahadeva Temple
- 33. Vaikom Mahadeva Temple
- 34. Rameswaram Mahadeva Temple Kollam
- 35. Rameswaram Mahadeva Temple Amaravila
- 36. Ettumanoor Mahadeva Temple
- 37. Edakkolam Kanjilassery Mahadeva Temple
- 38. Chemmanthitta Mahadeva Temple
- 39. Aluva Mahadeva Temple
- 40. Thirumittakkod Anchumoorthy Temple
- 41. Cherthala Velorvattom Mahadeva Temple
- 42. Kallattupuzha Mahadeva Temple
- 43. Thrukkunnu Mahadeva Temple
- 44. Cheruvathoor Mahadeva Temple
- 45. Poonkunnam Mahadeva Temple
- 46. Trukkapaleeswaram Mahadeva Temple Nadapuram
- 47. Trukkapaleeswaram Mahadeva Temple Peralassery
- 48. Trukkapaleeswaram Mahadeva Temple Niranam
- 49. Avittathoor Mahadeva Temple
- 50. Kodumon Angadikkal Perumala Tali Maha Shiva Temple/ Parumala Valiya Panayannarkavu Temple

- 51. Kollam Anandavalleeswaram Mahadeva Temple
- 52. Kattakambala Mahadeva Temple
- 53. Pazhayannoor Kondazhi Trutham Tali
- 54. Perakom Mahadeva Temple
- 55. Chakkamkulangara Mahadeva Temple
- 56. Kumaranalloor Temple/ Enkakkad Veeranimangalam Mahadeva Temple
- 57. Cheranelloor Mahadeva Temple
- 58. Maniyoor Mahadeva Temple
- 59. Nediya Tali Mahadeva Temple
- 60. Kozhikkode Tali Mahadeva Temple
- 61. Thazhathangady Tali Mahadeva Temple
- 62. Kaduthuruthy Tali Mahadeva Temple
- 63. Kodungalloor Mahadeva Temple
- 64. Vanchiyoor Sreekandeswaram Mahadeva Temple
- 65. Thiruvanjikkulam Mahadeva Temple
- 66. Padanayarkulangara Mahadeva Temple
- 67. Truchattukulam Mahadeva Temple/ Kadungalloor Chittukulam Mahadeva Temple
- 68. Alathoor Pokkunni Mahadeva Temple
- 69. Kottiyoor Mahadeva Temple
- 70. Truppaloor Mahadeva Temple
- 71. Perunthatta Mahadeva Temple
- 72. Truthala Mahadeva Temple
- 73. Thiruvalla Thiruvatta Mahadeva Temple/ Thukalassery Mahadeva Temple
- 74. Vazhappally Mahadeva Temple
- 75. Puthuppally Changankulangara/ Puthuppally Thrukkovil Mahadeva Temple
- 76. Anchummoorthy Mangalam Mahadeva Temple
- 77. Thirunakkara Mahadeva Temple
- 78. Kodumbu Mahadeva Temple
- 79. Ashtamichira Mahadeva Temple
- 80. Pattanakkad Mahadeva Temple/ Mattannoor Mahadeva Temple
- 81. Uliyannoor Mahadeva Temple
- 82. Killikkurussimangalam Mahadeva Temple
- 83. Puthoor Mahadeva Temple
- 84. Chengannoor Mahadeva Temple

- 85. Someswaram Mahadeva Temple
- 86. Venganelloor Mahadeva Temple
- 87. Kottarakkara Mahadeva Temples
- 88. Kandiyoor Mahadeva Temple
- 89. Palayoor Mahadeva Temple
- 90. Taliparamba Rajarajeswara Temple
- 91. Nedumpura Kulasekharanelloor Mahadeva Temple
- 92. Mannoor Mahadeva Temple
- 93. Trussilery Temple
- 94. Sringapuram Mahadeva Temple
- 95. Kottoor Karivelloor Mahadeva Temple
- 96. Mammiyoor Mahadeva Temple
- 97. Parabumthali Mahadeva Temple
- 98. Thirunavaya Mahadeva Temple
- 99. Karikkode Kanjiramattam Mahadeva Temple
- 100. Cherthala Nalppathenneeswaram Mahadeva Temple
- 101. Kottappuram Mahadeva Temple
- 102. Muthuvara Mahadeva Temple
- 103. Velappaya Mahadeva Temple
- 104. Chendamangalam Kunnathoor Tali Mahadeva Temple
- 105. Thrukkandiyoor Mahadeva Temple
- 106. Peruvanam Mahadeva Temple
- 107. Thiruvaloor Mahadeva Temple
- 108. Chirakkal Mahadeva Temple

CHAPTER FORTY-FIVE

WHOSE WHO

DATTATREYA

Each Yuga or era has an Avatar, like Shri Krishna in Dvapara Yuga. Dattatreya was the Yuga Acharya or the Supreme Master of the era preceding the Dvapara Yuga, known as the Treta Yuga. When Dattatreya was born, he had three heads, Brahma, Vishnu, and Shiva. His mother said, in this way, it will be difficult for you to survive in society. People will easily see you and recognize you. So, they condensed into one head. Dattatreya temples today either worship him as Maha Vishnu or as Shiva, differently in various temples. This is because, ultimately, he represents everything – he represents the Supreme Consciousness.

While Dattatreya's historical origins are unclear and trace to inconsistent mythologies, His life stories are more consistent. He is described in the Mahabharata as an exceptional Rishi (sage) with extraordinary insights and knowledge, adored and raised to be a Guru and an Avatar of Vishnu status in the Puranas. These texts describe him as having renounced the world and left his home early to lead a nomad, ascetic life. After leaving home, Dattatreya wandered naked in search of the Absolute. He seems to have spent most of his life roaming the area between North Mysore, Maharashtra, and Gujarat as far as the Narmada River. He attained complete realization at a place not far from the town now known as Ganagapur near the peak at Mount Girnar. The original footprints of Datta are believed to be located at the top of this mountain.

Dattatreya is a unified form of the supreme Trinity, Brahma, Vishnu, and Shiva, and hence, is the repository of their combined divinity. He was born as the son of the great Sage Atri and his devout consort, Anusuya. Datta means 'to give' or 'given' and 'Atreya' stands for, 'Atri's son.' As the three supreme Gods merged and gave themselves to Atri in the form of his son, he is called Dattatreya. He is a simple monk, who looks unique, with three heads and six arms. He is seen holding a rosary and water pot, a conch and discus, and a trident and drum in his hands, thus representing all the three Gods. He is usually seen in the company of four dogs and a cow.

Nath tradition holds that Parashurama, after enacting his vengeance, sought out Dattatreya atop Mount Gandhamadana for spiritual guidance. Their conversations gave rise to Tripura-rahasya, a treatise on Advaita Vedanta. It was here the deity instructed the warrior-sage on knowledge of scripture, renunciation of worldly activities, and non-duality, thus freeing him from the karmic cycle of death and rebirth.

RAMBHOJA

Ksetra scripture has a legend in which a king named Ramabhoja worshipped Parasurama. He was the ruler of the lands between Gokarna and Kanyakumari and was proclaimed king of the entire Parasurama Ksetra. While performing Aswamedha Yajna, he was ploughing the land, but mistakenly killed a snake that was a raksha in disguise. In repentance, Ramabhoja was directed by Parasurama to build a rajathat peetha, or large silver pedestal, with the image of a serpent at its four corners in obeisance. Parasurama also ordered that he distribute gold to the needy equal to his own weight as Tulabhara. Ramabhoja performed the aswamedha yajna successfully and Parashurama appeared before him again, declaring that he was pleased. To this day, the silver pedestal remains a center of pilgrimage. The surrounding land is known as Thou lava, in remembrance of the Tulabhara of Ramabhoja.

KAILASH - KRATJNCHA

A pass situated somewhere in the Himalayas, said to have been opened by Parasurama with his arrows to make a passage from Kailash to the southwards. The Vayu Purana attributes the splitting of the mountain to Karttikeya. Indra and Karttikeya had a dispute about their respective powers, and agreed to decide it by running a race round the mountain. They disagreed as to the result, and therefore appealed to the mountain, who untruly decided in favour of Indra "Karttikeya hurled his lance at the mountain and pierced at once it and the demon Mahisha." There is also a tradition that Parasu-Rama with his axe cleft a passage through the Himalaya. This story is perhaps most expressively referred to in the well-known verse, **Meghaduta, 57** :

praleyddrerupatatamatikramya tarns tan visesdn
hamsadvdram Bhrgupatiyasovartmayat Krauncarandhram |
tenodlclmdisamanusarestiryagdydmasohhi
sydmahpddo Baliniyamandhhyudyatasyeva Visnoh

and is shortly alluded to in the **Raghuvarnsa XI, 4** :
hihhrato ' stram acale pyakunthitam, etc.

Later traditions have it that Parasurama with his axe opened a way for the Brahmaputra.

MAHENDRA

This mountain has great Puranic importance.After slaughtering the Ksatriyas to extinction sage Parasurama made Mahendra his place of abode. **(Sloka 53, Chapter 129, Adi Parva)** The presiding deity of this mountain sits in the court of Kubera worshipping him. **(Sloka 30, Chapter 10, Sabha Parva)**. If one bathes in the pond of Ramatirtha on the top of this mountain one would get the benefit of per- forming an Asvamedhayaga. **(Sloka 16, Chapter 85, Vana Parva)** . A holy spot on the top of the Mahendra mountain where Parasurama lived. A bath here brings the benefits of performing the asvamedha yajna. **(Vana Parva, Chapter 85 Verse 17)**.Brahma once went to this mountain and conducted a yaga there. **(Sloka 22, Chapter 87, Vana Parva)** . Yudhisthira during his pilgrimage visited this mountain. **(Sloka 30, Chapter 114, Vana Parva)**. Parasurama gave a darsana to Yudhisthira on a Caturdasi day on this mountain. **(Sloka 16, Chapter**

117, Vana Parva). Hanuman ji, when he was going in search of Sita maiya visited this mountain also along with the other monkeys. **(Sundara Kanda, Valmiki Ramayana)**

MUNJAVATA

A place on the Himalayas. Once Parasurama went to this place and calling the sages there instructed them to keep their tufts knotted together. **(Sloka 3, Chapter 112, Sand Parva).**

SUSKA

A Maharsi who lived in the Gokarna temple. When Bhagiratha brought Ganga from heaven to the earth, sea water began to rise and the temples situated near the sea were submerged. At that time Suska went along with other Maharishis to visit Parasurama at the Mahendra Mountain. In response to Suska's prayer, Parasurama raised the submerged temples including the Gokarna temple, above the water.

TALAJAS

Jayadhvaja, fifth son of Kartavirya, got a son named Talajamgha. The sons of this valiant man are called Talajarighas. There was once a great fight between Vitihotras, the eldest of these sons, and Parasurama. **(Chapter 88, Brahmanda Purana).**

VITIHOTRA J

The eldest of the hundred sons of Talajangha. When Talajangha was defeated by Parasurama, he and his men went to the Himalayas under the leadership of Vitihotra and hid themselves there They returned when Parasurama had gone to Mahendragiri for penance. **(Brahmanda Purana, Chapter 89)**

VITIHOTRA IV

A Kingdom' of ancient India. It is mentioned in **Mahabharata, Drona Parva, Chapter 70 Stanza 12,** that all the Ksatriyas of this country were exterminated by Parasurama